THE LOST SECRETS OF
MAYA TECHNOLOGY

By James A. O'Kon, PE

NEW PAGE BOOKS
A division of
The Career Press, Inc.
Pompton Plains, NJ

THE LOST SECRETS OF MAYA TECHNOLOGY
EDITED AND TYPESET BY DIANA GHAZZAWI
Cover design by Noir33
Printed in the U.S.A.

To order this title, please call toll-free 1-800-CAREER-1 (NJ and Canada: 201-848-0310) to order using VISA or MasterCard, or for further information on books from Career Press.

The Career Press, Inc.
220 West Parkway, Unit 12
Pompton Plains, NJ 07444
www.careerpress.com
www.newpagebooks.com

Library of Congress Cataloging-in-Publication Data

O'Kon, James A.
    The lost secrets of Maya technology / James A. O'Kon.
       p. cm.
    Includes bibliographical references and index.
       ISBN 978-1-60163-207-4 -- ISBN 978-1-60163-610-2 (ebook) 1. Mayas--Science. 2. Maya astronomy. 3. Mayas--Mathematics. 4. Mayas--Civilization. 5. Technological innovations--History--To 1500. 6. Discoveries in science--History--To 1500. I. Title.

F1435.3.S32O46 2012
972'.6--dc23

                                                                    2011045928

Acknowledgments

When the laborious research for this book was finally completed and my thoughts collected, I prepared an outline for the book with a summary of each chapter. I sent the summary to an archaeologist who is a longtime friend and asked him for his opinions. "Congratulations on your book," he responded. "Just realize that archeologists will roast, reject, or ignore any book that alters popular misconception." When I had completed the manuscript and Career Press had contracted to publish the book, I contacted a number of distinguished archaeologists and requested that they consider reviewing my manuscript. I was expecting the worst after the early warning from my friend.

However, I was pleasantly surprised and flattered by the gracious and positive responses I received from this venerable group. I cannot adequately express my gratitude for the fashion in which this book was received by some of the most highly acclaimed archaeologists in the world. I was honored to receive positive acceptance for review from George Stuart, Mark Van Stone, Ed Barnhart, and Tom Sever. I want to thank then all for making this into a much better book.

I owe a special debt of gratitude to George Stuart, a true legend. He carefully read the manuscript, annotating the pages with insightful and helpful comments. His frequent e-mails with recommendations for historical accuracy and helpful comments were an education for me not only for sharing his personal knowledge and wisdom but his humanity and sensitivity.

I also want to thank Ed Barnhart for his review of this book and his contributions relating to his work with the water resources at Palenque.

Mark Van Stone is Mayanist and a noted epigrapher. I want to thank him for using his expertise in the improvement of Maya glyphs in the cover design and making contributions to dates in the history of European mathematics. I also want to thank him for inspiring me to write the Epilogue in this book.

Tom Sever, working as an archaeologist for NASA, pioneered the application of remote sensing in archaeology. His work in detecting sacbeob and ruins that are hidden in the rainforest was truly an inspiration for this book, and I thank him for his insightful comments.

I am not a trained archaeologist but a crossover engineer with a life-long passion for the Maya civilization. My education in archaeology was on-the-job training. Nicholas Hellmuth was the first archaeologist that I ever met, in the 1980s, deep in the jungle of Guatemala. Nicholas guided me on expeditions deep into the rainforest and has traveled with me to sites verifying discoveries in Maya technology. He has a special knowledge of architecture and engineering technology learned at the knee of his father, George Hellmuth, the famous architect. These skills and his photographic artistry set him apart from others. I thank Nicholas for his belief in Maya technology, and his belief in me and my quest.

There are many individuals that I want to thank for my education in technology, history, and archaeology. These include my muses, teachers, mentors, and the veteran archaeologist Claude Baudez, who told me that I was "the only man in the world who could have written this book." This is the highest of praise for a crossover archaeo-engineer. Grady Randolph was a teacher dedicated to changing the lives of students from my blue-collar neighborhood. He counseled me throughout my life until his passing in 2005. He called me to his side and presented me with his complete set of the works of William H. Prescott. I treasure all 15 volumes. My thanks also go to writers, living and deceased, that enriched my knowledge of archaeology. These include John Lloyd Stephens, Alfred Maudslay, Sylvanus Morley, V. Gordon Child, Richardson Gill, Jared Diamond, and especially Michael Coe, who has guided me for a half century.

Dr. Lev Zetlin, my engineering mentor, was a landmark engineering thinker and a larger-than-life figure in the revolution of new engineering technology. He became my friend in addition to my mentor in the leadership of state-of-the-art engineering. He responsible for my ascendency in the engineering sciences.

I owe a huge debt to a lifelong friend, Cliff Graubart, my spirit guide to the world of publications. We met in New York during our salad days of the 1960s. He returned to Atlanta before me and became a successful rare-book dealer while nurturing some of America's most popular writers, including some on the current *New York Times* Bestsellers list. He is truly the Gertrude Stein of our times.

I fell in love with Yucatán and the Maya nearly a half century ago. Many of my expeditions were in the company of my lifelong friend, Vernon Harris. We vowed to travel to the Yucatán and find the answers to questions surrounding the Maya. It has become my task to complete the unveiling of the secrets of Maya technology.

I must also thank my muse, Bill Nash. His encyclopedic knowledge of everything enabled us to discuss abstract concepts of archaeology, technology, and mathematics. My relationship with Bill is similar to Mark Twain's with the great Rudyard Kipling. Twain said, "Between us we cover all knowledge; he knows all that can be known, and I know the rest."

Key elements of *The Lost Secrets of Maya Technology* would never have been uncovered without the talent and knowledge of Philippe Klinefelter. He is a kindred spirit that literally flew into my life while landing his aircraft on the airstrip at the ancient Maya city of Yaxchilan. I was stumbling in the dark relative to the secrets of the technology of Maya tools until I encountered Philippe. He is a fine arts sculptor of international note and the world's foremost expert on Maya stone tools. Together Philippe and I have explored Maya jadeite mines and Classic Period jadeite workshops. His work is the foundation for the chapter on Maya tool technology. I thank Miguel Alvarez for the photographs of the Maya stone tools.

The creation of illustrations for the book, especially the "how to" drawings of ancient technologies, required a special visionary artistic talent. I owe Alex Tuan Nguyen a great personal debt for transforming my complex, technical sketches into dynamic computer renderings that clearly translate my technical concepts.

I am the illustrator of the drawings of Maya construction workers, which hark back to my college days as a cartoonist for the Georgia Tech humor magazine. My thanks go to Kira Francklin for quality and coordination reviews of the illustrations.

The Internet introduced me to Dr. Horacio Ramirez de Alba, Dr. Ramiro Pérez Campos, and Dr. Heriberto Díaz Coutiño, all from the Universidad Autónoma del Estado de México. They authored an article in the Mexican scientific journal *Ciencia Ergo Sum,* which was intended to assess the infeasibility of the technology used in constructing the Maya bridge at Yaxchilan. At the conclusion of their studies they became believers in the Maya technology that I had postulated for the bridge. They carried out laboratory testing of ancient Maya cement that proved its reality and value to Maya engineering. I owe them profound thanks for their pioneering work and their support.

Through the Internet I also met Douglas Peck, a noted historian, naval architect, and expert on ancient Maya marine technology and celestial navigation. He has contributed his many talents to this book and enabled my work on Maya marine technology to become a reality.

My grateful thanks go to Ken Carper, expert in forensic architectural engineering and editor-in-chief of the *Journal of Performance of Constructed Facilities*, for reviewing and editing the manuscript. His comments were a great assistance to the overall quality of the work.

My agent, Gary Height, came on board and guided me through steps for attaining a publisher, including the preparation of a proposal that answered all the questions about my book. I am especially grateful for his speed in working with Career Press to set this book up for success.

Many thanks and intellectual compliments go to Diana Ghazzawi, my editor at Career Press. She constantly surprised me with insight into the cognitive mind of the Maya. Her interpretation of the Maya quadripartite cosmic philosophy as an analogy to the space-time continuum was truly an amazing bit of literary magic.

I wish to thank the individuals who braved the heat and insects and who joined me on my adventures in discovery deep in the rainforest. These include Carl "Killer" Stimmel, Tammy Ridehour, Greta Pasche, Jim Dion, and Max Wilson.

I would have been lost in this endeavor without the support of my wife, Carol. She has accompanied me on most of my expeditions into the jungle and has always managed to make rudimentary accommodations more livable. She was my assistant in measuring the dimensions of many of the Maya ruins and can manage both the dumb end and the smart end of the measuring tape. When it came to the actual writing of the book, she shepherded me through the dichotomy of pure science and archaeology, helping me keep one foot firmly planted in sound scientific precepts while the other foot was on the slippery slope of the mysteries and unknowns of Maya technology, until I finally became stabilized with both feet firmly planted on the truth.

Contents

Preface

It has long been an enigma how the Maya achieved elevated scientific and technological levels in the relative isolation of a tropical rainforest. The ancient Maya were avid sky-watchers, and after millennia of observations of the heavens, they gained an uncanny knowledge of the harmonious composition of the cosmos. Their study of the vast expanse of the universe and the mysterious movements of the astral bodies evolved into their quadripartite philosophy of the cosmos. This philosophy, combined with their fascination of the interlocking movements and cycles of the sun, moon, planets, and astral bodies, inspired them to develop scientific disciplines that enabled them to track heavenly bodies, predict astronomical events, and record them in accurate written records.

The mystery of the Maya and the origins of their advanced science and technology have always intrigued me and initiated my quest for answers to their riddles. My interest in archaeology began while playing in the Civil War battlefields covering the hills near my boyhood home in Atlanta. They were still littered with rusted military armament and wasted shot, fueling a young boy's imagination. My early reading included classic books dealing with the Spanish conquest and rediscovery of the lost Maya civilization. My interest in lost civilizations was accelerated by my brilliant high school history teacher, Mr. Grady Randolph, who did not teach typical history courses, but delighted his students with accounts of ancient civilizations, extinct languages, and occult religions. These history courses stimulated my interest in archaeology, and my reading evolved toward history and archaeology.

My student days at Georgia Tech were filled with the study of civil engineering and extracurricular activities that enhanced the capabilities of a future explorer. I was on the football team, and my ability to illustrate enabled me to become art editor on the school's newspaper and the humor magazine. The years at Georgia Tech made me a problem-solving engineer with writing and illustration skills, and the athletic training gave me the strength and stamina to endure future arduous jungle expeditions.

After several years of professional experience as a structural engineer, the siren song of the ancient Maya called out to me, and I decided to take a lengthy sabbatical to explore the pre-Columbian cultures of Mexico. My family and I headed south of the boarder in our new Volkswagen camper, driving down through Mexico and into British Honduras. I was excited by this opportunity to live among ancient Maya cities, to see them up close and study their engineering technology. For a person who grew up in the only American city completely destroyed by war, just the sight of a building constructed before 1865 was really a thrill; one that was more than 1,000 years old was awesome. It was on this adventure that I first felt a real affinity for the Maya engineers who had constructed these wondrous structures. I had many questions about Maya technology and construction practices that could not be answered by archaeologists. They could not answer these inquires because they did not possess the knowledge behind Maya technology that lay hidden in plain sight. This quest for the truth led me on the path of investigations and revelations of the brilliant Maya technology that is the basis for this book.

In New York City, I worked on designing landmark structures, like the Roosevelt Island Tramway, aviation projects, and aerospace structures. Returning to Atlanta to manage a branch office of the New York City engineering firm, I expanded the practice to include architecture in addition to engineering. I subsequently bought the firm and led it to a national reputation for designing award-winning projects and forensic engineering in the investigation of high-profile building failures. A civil engineering education at the Georgia Institute of Technology and an advanced degree from New York University provided me with an excellent background for my professional career, which has been devoted to bringing science to engineering, developing new computer techniques for engineering design, and advancing new methodologies for investigating distressed structures. This experience gave me the ability to "reverse engineer" complex, distressed buildings and identify the cause of the distress or failure. This experience as a forensic engineer also gave me unique insights used in the research and writing of this book. It enhanced my ability to discover, dissect, analyze, and reconstruct projects of lost Maya technology.

Investigation of Maya technology continued during my engineering career. As often as possible, I traveled to the Yucatán, driving across the domain of the ancient Maya, traveling by dugout canoe, and hacking my way through the jungle with a machete in order to explore remote sites. My breakthrough revelation in Maya technology was the discovery of a Maya suspension bridge over the Usumacinta River at the ancient Maya city of Yaxchilan. My research has unveiled the advanced technology that was used to construct monumental Maya engineering projects. Investigations and identification of Maya technology included field exploration, remote sensing, digital tools, virtual reconstruction, and forensic engineering skills. Further investigation and research efforts have revealed additional examples of lost Maya technology. My efforts were rewarded by identifying Maya engineering projects were that constructed with a technology that was 1,000 years in advance of similar European technology.

It became apparent to me that the technology of the Maya was a direct extrapolation of their scientific cosmology. My work has unveiled the technological secrets that enabled this great scientific civilization to thrive in a challenging natural environment. This book will detail the technology used by the Maya to fabricate cement, which was used to build innovative, cast-in-place concrete structures that included high-rise buildings towering above their great cities, water management systems that enabled dependable water supplies for potable and agriculture usage, paved all-weather highway networks, and structural systems for bridges that included the longest bridge in the ancient world. They utilized specialized stone tools that were harder than steel to carve their monuments and buildings, and developed a transport system using manpower that was more efficient than dray animals and carts.

Because of this brilliant technology, the Maya had an artificially high population. When disaster struck the Yucatán Peninsula in the form of a drought, the worst in 7,000 years, the same advanced technology that built amazing cities with large populations could not save the Maya. Technology failed and catastrophe befell the Maya; their scientific civilization was no more. Their beautiful cities were abandoned and enveloped by the encroaching jungle.

1

The Maya

More than 1,000 years before Europeans landed on the shores of the Americas, the Maya developed a science-based civilization in the almost total isolation of the tropical lands of the Yucatán Peninsula. The towering skylines of their magnificent high-rise cities loomed above the emerald rainforest. These architectural wonders, detailed with magnificently carved facades, were resplendent in artistic relief and hieroglyphic inscriptions. During the middle of the first millennium AD, these sophisticated urban centers were the largest cities on the planet (Figure 1-1). The sprawling Maya city-states were more than technologically dazzling examples of art and architecture conceived to overwhelm the observer with a sense of wonderment. These cities were centers of power, incubators of science and technology, seats of learning, and the hub of commercial operations that generated the wealth of the kingdom.

The embellished structures of these magnificent cities endured against all odds for more than a millennium after the demise of the Maya civilization (Figure 1-2). Resisting the degradation of the environment, the ravages of time, environmental disasters, and the prying roots of the encroaching jungle, the longevity of the structures is attributed to the innovative Maya technology employed in their construction. In addition to the advanced construction techniques preserving their cities, this brilliant society evolved scientific advances and technological methodologies that were a millennium in advance of similar discoveries by European sciences. Even more remarkable is that these advances in science and technology were created with little benefit of influence by outside cultures, unlike Europe.

Figure 1-1: Shining towers of Maya Classic Period cities rise high above the rainforest. Image by Peter Spier, National Geographic Archives.

Maya cities were planned and constructed on a grand scale with functional efficiency and artistic elegance. Each city, with its monumental palaces and temples, had a unique setting and was a triumph of grace and power. Maya architecture is unlike any other style in the world. Its inventive character of design is alien and bizarre, dissimilar to that of any other Mesoamerican culture and unlike any other world architectural style. What was the source of this unique Maya style? Like their advanced sciences and technology, their artistic style owes its inspiration to their veneration of the cosmos and its influence on the philosophy of the Maya civilization (Figure C-1). The Maya civilization, one of history's longest-lived cultures, included more cities and pyramids than ancient Egypt. The Maya were governed by more than 50 independent city-states dispersed across the 125,000-square-mile area of the Maya world (Figure 1-3). Maya cities were the base of power for the elite class of royalty, scribes, scientists, intellectuals, and merchants, who energized the civilization for more than a millennium.

This was not a society that existed in the annals of lost prehistory, for which historical dating had to be performed by scientific data testing methods. Rather, the chronology of historical events has been determined with some exactitude by deciphering the written inscriptions and the accurate calendar system of the Maya. Their unique form of writing, once considered an unsolvable riddle, was undecipherable for a century after the rediscovery of the lost civilization. It did not become readable until the code was broken by brilliant epigraphers. The unfolding of the chronological events of their history, their epic adventures, and their scientific messages reads like an exciting historical novel. The thoughts, history, and accomplishments of this civilization became known to the world. Archaeologists have studied the abandoned cities and the inscribed art that was integrated into the facades of the Classic Period buildings. These inscriptions have provided abundant evidence of the accomplishments of this brilliant culture. Additionally, accomplishments of the Maya have been revealed through translations of their surviving books and other written documentation.

Though their achievements continue to fascinate the academic world, scholarly research devoted to the Maya has largely overlooked the technological achievements of Maya engineers. These technological achievements enabled the survival, health, and favorable lifestyles of the inhabitants who populated the world's densest urban centers. Technology enabled the survival and growth of Maya society in spite of their precarious tropical environment, one that had an inconstant supply of rainwater, poor soil

Figure 1-2: The other-worldly art of the Maya looks down from pyramid at Ek Balam. Author's image.

conditions, and a lack of surface water. Maya engineers successfully developed efficient water-management systems and technologically advanced agriculture systems that overcame the shortfalls of their environment and enabled the prosperity of the society.

The Maya enjoyed the height of their golden age during the eighth and ninth centuries. Their Classic Period cities featured dramatic architecture, with high-rise pyramids smoothly coated in stucco and painted in brilliant colors laid out around grand plazas. The stepped pyramid structures topped by temples towered over art-adorned palaces, universities, ball courts, and public buildings. The grand Classic Period cities were purposely conceived to be awe-inspiring spectacles; the dazzling art and architecture was intended to impress all who viewed the array. These large city centers were planned urban spaces with nodes of artistically styled buildings connected by elevated paved roadways. Paved routes crossed the cityscape and extended out of the city into the hinterlands. This all-weather road system traversed the tangled and slippery jungle floor, smoothing the way for travelers. These roads served as the intercity transportation system required for trade and communication with other city-states. These Maya cities were centers of political, religious, educational, scientific, and business activities that managed the multi-faceted affairs of the city-state. For more than 1,000 years, the Maya intellectual hierarchy practiced an efficient management system that enhanced and maintained the wealth of the city-state and the quality of life in the sprawling urban centers.

Since the rediscovery of the Maya civilization in the 19th century, there has been great interest in the Maya culture. Their advanced levels of scientific disciplines, with achievements in astronomy, mathematics, calendrics and written languages have amazed the Western world. At the height of their civilization, their scientific and technological achievements were more advanced than any other culture on the planet. They have been compared to the Egyptians for their use of hieroglyphic characters in their writing, to the Greeks for their development of advanced sciences, to the Romans for construction of well-drained, paved highways, and to the Phoenicians for long-range trade in seagoing vessels. In astronomy, they computed the time of the earth's revolution around the sun to an accuracy that was more precise than that calculated by most modern scientific instruments. The Maya created written almanacs of solar and lunar cycles containing accurate predictions of eclipse cycles and charted cycles of Venus, Mars, Mercury, Jupiter, and Saturn with great precision.

The mathematical system of the Maya was unique and well-suited to calculate large array numbers. The Maya mathematical system used a base of 20, rather than a base of 10 (used in European mathematics), and enabled the calculation of massive numbers using only three symbols in addition to the basic functions. Their development of positional mathematics enabled the calculation of numbers in magnitudes of the hundreds of trillions.

Calculations using their mathematical system are flexible and exquisite for large-magnitude astronomical calculations, as well as minute calculations for practical applications such as bookkeeping, census-taking, record-keeping, and engineering calculations. The Maya mathematical system was vastly superior to the Roman, Greek, and Egyptian systems. These other mathematical systems were limited in their scope of functions and confined to numbers in the positive mathematical range. The Maya understood the concept of the number zero and computation of large array calculations in the negative range 1,100 years before European mathematicians.

The Maya writing system is a unique development of this brilliant civilization and is one of the world's five original written languages. Maya scripts are considered to be one of the most visually distinctive writing systems in the world. The intricate and artistic flow of the characters creates a brilliantly derived art form for their language, which enabled them to write anything they could speak. The Maya script was the thread that bound together the sciences of astronomy, mathematics, and calendrics. The content of the narratives was not just the jotting of scribes trained to record proceedings. Maya scribes were of royal lineage, and as part of the royal family, they were part of the decision-making process. These masters of the written word not only chronicled the history of the Maya and executed daily correspondence that managed the city-state, but they wrote thousands of books dealing with numerous and diverse subjects including history, royal lineage, matters of astronomy, mathematics, calendrics, technology, medicine, law, ritual, music, and the natural history of plants and animals, among other subjects. During the Classic Period, from AD 250 to AD 900, the sophistication of Maya arts and sciences soared while Europe stumbled through the Dark Ages. When the Maya were enjoying the good life in their grand cities with populations of 100,000, London was a swampy river trading town with 9,000 inhabitants.

While Maya scientists achieved heights of scientific knowledge in mathematics, astronomy, and written chronicles, Maya technicians, the

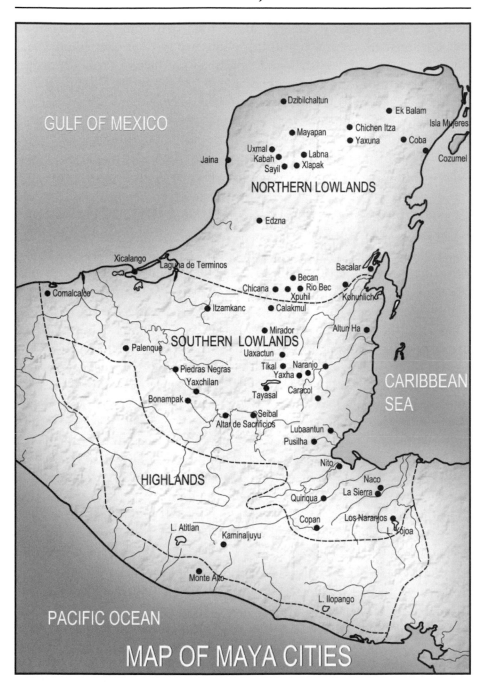

Figure 1-3: Map of Yucatán indicating major Maya cities. Author's image.

Americas' first engineers, created unique high-rise buildings, designed an efficient water-management and infrastructure system, devised land and water transportation systems, and developed productive agricultural systems that trumped the environment and enhanced the wealth and power of the city-state. How did the Maya achieve these lofty accomplishments? What motivated their thirst for knowledge? What were the influences that aided their formula for success? The answer is "home cooking," a cultural self-determinism motivated by the need to overcome their complex tropical environment while keeping their gaze turned to the heavens.

Mesoamerican Influence on Maya Sciences

Mesoamerica is the term applied to an amoeba-shaped geographical area located in the Central American Isthmus (Figure 1-4). This culturally defined area extends from the northern Mexican highlands southward to the rainforests of Honduras, and encompasses the Maya homeland located in the Yucatán Peninsula. The most complex and advanced pre-Columbian cultures of the Americas excelled in this area. Mesoamerica is one of the five cradles of civilization on the planet—the others being Mesopotamia, Egypt, India, and China. The Maya were influenced by Mesoamerican cultures predating or paralleling their ascendancy as the primary culture of the area. Mesoamerica was also was the domain of other developed civilizations, including the Olmec, Zapotec, Toltec, Teotihuacán, and Aztec cultures. The Maya shared common traits with other cultures due to the high degree of interaction that characterized cultures in the region. Cultural concepts and ideas were disseminated throughout the length of Mesoamerica through contact generated by long-range trading activities, rather than through conquest traditions. The Maya adopted these basic Mesoamerican concepts and enhanced them by creating advanced scientific and technological disciplines.

The Mesoamerican cultural tradition did not spring full-blown with the emergence of the Olmec in 1500 BC, but developed over millennia through the influence of numerous native cultures. The Olmec culture, which had a long-range influence across Mesoamerica, has been termed the "mother culture" by some scholars. Their unique art forms ranged from sculptures of giant stone heads to the intricate carving of jadeite figures and jewelry. Their influence on the Maya, including the notion of writing, lapidary skills, and the 260-day ceremonial calendar, is apparent.

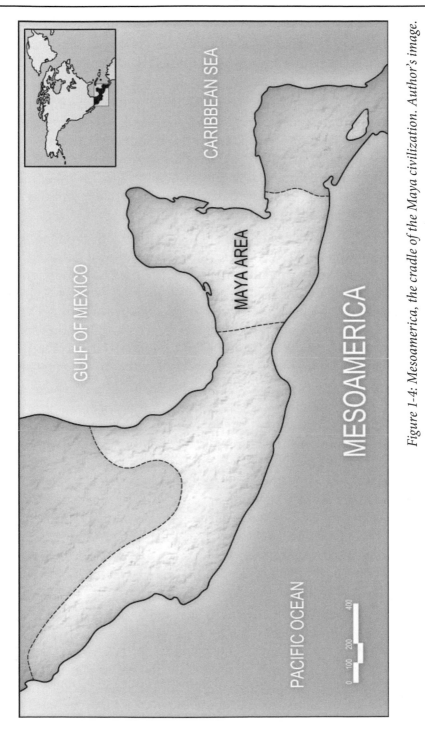

Figure 1-4: Mesoamerica, the cradle of the Maya civilization. Author's image.

Though the elements of commonality are apparent, the wide diversity of Mesoamericans can be found in their language, politics, economics, social organization, art, styles, and other facets of their lifestyle.

In political organization, the contrast between central Mexico in the north of Mesoamerica and the Maya world was quite divergent. Political organization in central Mexico was based on a single central city controlling a sprawling empire consisting of large political states. These metropolitan centers emerged as imperial capitals, holding sway over the vast area of their domain. Imperial political organizations included the Teotihuacán Empire that paralleled the Maya Classic Period, the Toltec, and the Aztec Empire that flourished centuries after the decline of the Maya.

By contrast, the Maya world did not follow the political philosophy of the empire builders. Their political organization was based on small, independent polities. The basic political unit of the Maya was a sovereign city-state, placing emphasis on individuality. The urban centers of their city-states were home to tens of thousands of inhabitants, including the elite ruling classes, scientists, merchants, engineers, artisans, and other specialists. The majority of the populace dwelled in the hinterlands, in outlying agricultural areas and villages dispersed throughout the sovereign territory.

The cultivation of domestic agriculture products and creative agronomy had begun in Mesoamerica by 8000 BC. A great variety of agriculture products and efficient agriculture methods were developed by Mesoamerican cultures and enhanced by the Maya. These agriculture innovations culminated in successful farming methods, producing the rich harvests of the Classic Period. The diverse and sophisticated Maya agriculture methodologies overcame the adverse environment and enabled enhanced food production. The innovative systems included permanent raised fields, terracing, aquaculture, canal irrigation systems, and wild harvesting. During the Classic Period, these systems became a critical part of supporting the large city populations in addition to a surplus of food for trading.

The major agriculture product of Mesoamerica was maize, which, to this day, remains Mesoamerica's major food staple. Maize was domesticated around 4000 BC through a process of selective cultivation by Mesoamericans. The propagation of maize, which is totally dependent on human agronomy, was derived from the native plant *teosinte*. A 7,000-year-old fossil maize pollen grain has been recovered in Tabasco, and a 5,000-year-old pollen has been encountered in the Maya domain. Maya agronomists enhanced the varieties of maize, creating a wide range of cultivars that expanded their agriculture capabilities.

The significance of an abundant agriculture has played a major role in the growth of successful civilizations. Efficient agriculture practices enabled by technology reduced the distance from points of cultivation to the marketplace and produced an abundant harvest enabling the feeding of a large population while producing a food surplus. This surplus enabled sufficient food for trade and subsequent economic enhancement.

A great variety of foodstuffs were part of the Mesoamerican way of life. They included agricultural products, domesticated animals, and wild game. Crops included maize, beans, tomatoes, chili peppers, squash, avocado, papaya, guava, yam, manioc, amaranth, vanilla, plums, achiote, zapote, annona, peanuts, pineapple, sweet potato, sunflower, cacao, and the fruit of the Ramon tree. The Mesoamericans optimized the available animals that could be domesticated, including the duck, turkey, dog, and the stingless bee. They hunted wild land and water species to complement their diet. These included the deer, peccary, armadillo, manatee, tapir, rabbit, monkey, fowl, fish, turtle, caiman, insects, and iguana. Dogs were a major source of protein in Mesoamerica.

The legacy of Maya agricultural genius changed the world's eating habits. The conquistadors brought the Maya agricultural products to Europe and Asia, and these foodstuffs changed the tastes of many countries. We still benefit from Maya agriculture today. Can one imagine the change in Thai, Indian, or Chinese food without chili peppers? Roaming the aisles of a modern supermarket, the agricultural legacy of our Maya antecedents becomes apparent. Observe the commercial offerings contributed by the Maya: tomatoes, squash, chili peppers, beans, avocado, sweet potato, papaya, chocolate, peanuts, vanilla, pineapple, jicama, sunflower seeds, and a wide variety of other foodstuffs.

Native American fauna did not include beasts of burden, such as cows, horses, and donkeys. The lack of work animals created a void in the animal power available for transportation and agriculture, resulting in the development of a special Maya technology using manpower for transportation, lifting, and cartage.

The Influence of the Natural Environment on Maya Sciences

Maya civilization and its technological developments were greatly influenced by the diversity and demands of their natural environment. The interaction of the lithosphere, biosphere, and hydrosphere of their remarkable environment presented unique and complex challenges to Maya engineers. The blossoming of the Maya civilization, the survival of their densely populated cities, and their agriculture bounty were dependent on technological solutions for resolving adverse environmental conditions.

Geographically, the Maya zone lies in some of the most diverse terrain of the tropics, the Yucatán Peninsula making up the principal geographic landform of their domain. Bordered by the Pacific Ocean on the southwest, it extends northward, jutting outward from the mid-America isthmus, forming a landmass that divides the Gulf of Mexico and the Caribbean Sea. Geologically, the Yucatán Peninsula is a broad flat shelf of karstic limestone that extends on a north-south axis from the base of massive volcanic mountains as they curve southeastward along the Pacific Coast. The climate of the Maya world is dependent partially on this geography. The hot tropical climate of the rainforests in the lowlands (Figure 1-5) contrasts with the temperate climate of the high volcanic mountains in the southern highlands (Figure 1-6).

The diversity of the climate is compounded by unique rainfall patterns. The Maya world has some of the heaviest yearly rainfall in the tropics. Approximately 75 percent of the total yearly rainfall occurs during the six-month rainy season. The lack of precipitation during the dry season creates drought-like conditions for the area, creating a seasonal desert. The Maya faced alternating conditions of deluge or drought each year. In order to survive, Maya cities and the civilization as a whole required a reliable year-round source of water. This need for water management presented a challenge for Maya technology.

The diversity of the range in climatology and the extremes of precipitation were complicated by the geology and hydrology of the Yucatán Peninsula. The geology of the Yucatán is composed of karstic limestone, a porous material that directly absorbs surface water, drawing it down into an aquifer and resulting in a lack of surface water on the Maya landscape. The near absence of natural bodies of water in the form of rivers or lakes

Figure 1-5: Maya rainforests feature dense forests and tropical environments. Author's image.

Figure 1-6: Maya highlands have an alpine environment. Author's image.

deprives the majority of the Maya population with a natural water supply during the dry season.

An anomaly to the paucity of surface water supply occurs in the northern Yucatán. A unique characteristic of the geologic substrate in the north is the source of plentiful water from surface wells at the northern end of the Yucatán platform. This is the site of the Chicxulub crater, formed by an extraterrestrial impact occurring during the Cretaceous Period some 65,000,000 years ago. A concentric ring of stress fractures from the impact formed natural wells, or cenotes, in the limestone. These natural wells provided the Maya in the northern lowlands with direct access to a water source on a year-round basis.

The Classic Maya cities were home to thousands of people. To survive, these cities required a dependable source of water for drinking and agriculture. In other parts of the world, civilizations usually located their cities near bodies of fresh water and could rely on a dependable water supply. However, in the Maya world, natural sources of free-flowing surface water were not available. The inconstant rainfall and the fickle environment compounded the paradox. These challenges stimulated the native ingenium of Maya engineers. In response, they developed innovative water management systems that insured a year-round supply of potable water for use in the cities and water for agricultural irrigation systems that made them independent of the fluctuating rainfall and the seasonal desert.

The limestone under the Maya world is a sedimentary rock that provided them with unlimited building materials for their cities. However, this sedimentary rock does not contain deposits of metal ore. Igneous rock deposits, likely to contain valuable minerals, are located in the southern volcanic regions and along tectonic plates that extend across the isthmus. Deprived of a source of metal ore, the Maya created tools from minerals mined in the volcanic region and along tectonic plates. The volcanic belts and the tectonic fault line produced deposits of jadeite and obsidian; these two minerals have hardness properties greater than steel. Their unique characteristics were recognized by Maya technicians as viable materials for fabricating specialized tools. In this case a negative factor—the lack of metal ores—was turned into a positive factor: the fabrication of specialized tools from jadeite and obsidian.

The Time Line of Maya Civilization

The rediscovery of the Maya civilization in the mid-19th century stunned the academic world and resulted in the rewriting of history. The Classic Period, representing the height of Maya power, intellectualism, art, and wealth did not happen overnight. The brilliance of the culture and its significant accomplishments were a millennia-long work in progress, beginning in 8000 BC with agronomist-farmers domesticating maize.

The Paleo-Indian Period: 20,000 BC to 8000 BC

It is generally theorized that hunters and gatherers of Siberian origin crossed the frozen Bering Sea and settled America during the last Ice Age. This was not a purposeful migration southward, but a natural expansion into new areas that attracted the migrants. During this period, animals such as the giant ground sloth, mammoths, and wild horses still roamed the North American continent. A band of nomadic hunters, whose descendants would form the basis of the Maya civilization, migrated to the southern sector of Mesoamerica, liked what they saw, and made camp. They began their evolution into a great civilization.

The Archaic Period: 8000 BC to 2500 BC

During the Archaic Period, the proto-Maya began to practice sophisticated agricultural techniques. Their greatest contribution to agriculture was the domestication of maize. Maya agronomists were able to alter tenocinte, a wild native grass, into the high-yielding grain that is now known as maize. Recent genetic evidence suggests that domestication of maize began nearly 8,000 years ago. The ecosystem of the Maya world was an excellent environment for the growth of maize, as well as a wealth of other agriculture products that complemented their diet.

The agriculture lifestyle of the Maya included the skillful domestication of plants and animals, which increased agriculture yields. This secure food supply allowed the Maya to slow their travels and settle down, adopt a sedentary lifestyle, advance their culture, and stabilize their population. The sedentary lifestyle and the abundance of agriculture led to the establishment of villages and towns. These settlements became the focus of their newly formed society.

It was the establishment of towns, with their increased population base, that enabled the emergence of industry and trading skills, which enhanced the development of their technical arts. The technical arts flourished and created a new class of artisans who developed techniques, including loom weaving, basketry, stylized pottery, and specialized tool-making. These new industrial products and the surplus of agriculture yields created a merchant class, as well as the opportunity for long-range trade routes to other parts of Mesoamerica.

The Pre-Classic Period: 1200 BC to AD 250

The burgeoning of the Maya accelerated throughout the Pre-Classic Period. Conversely, the Olmec civilization, with whom the Maya had close contact, decayed during this period. The Olmec influenced the emerging Maya in the fabrication and design of exquisite carved jadeite jewelry, the artwork on large stone monuments, and the building of massive earthen pyramids. The Olmec also shared the notion of written script and the 260-day calendar.

The Pre-Classic Period witnessed the ascent of the Maya civilization in the southern highlands and in the northern lowlands. The earliest Maya cities included Nakbe, El Mirador, and Cerros. These early cities initiated the trend toward life in urban places and monumental architecture, including platforms and pyramids with exotic artworks.

In the middle and late Pre-Classic Period, multiple Maya cities rose to prominence and later became archetypal of the Classic Period. As the cities expanded, the scale of their architectural structures and monumental art grew in size and sophistication. The vast El Mirador possessed all the characteristics of a Classic Period Maya city, including pyramids of more than 70 meters in height, whose stairways were flanked by gigantic carved masks of great Maya deities; groups of massive architectural wonders connected by paved roads (sacbeob); and monumental carved stele of historic figures. The construction was coated with stucco and painted a deep red. All of these features became the characteristics of a Classic Maya city. However, El Mirador did not survive into the Classic Period and was abandoned in AD 150, some 100 years prior to the start of the Classic Period.

Tikal, located in modern Guatemala, is considered to be the earliest of Maya Classic Period cities. Monuments deciphered in Tikal include the date of AD 292. Tikal has been established as the prototype for a Classic Maya city.

The Classic Period: AD *250 to* AD *900*

The Classic Period is considered to be the golden age of Mesoamerican culture, when the Maya reached the height of their scientific, technological, and artistic achievements. This time period encompasses both the flowering of the great city of Teotihuacán, which ruled a vast empire from their capital in the central Mexican plateau, as well as the peak of the Maya civilization. The ascendance of Teotihuacán was both parallel to and contemporary with the blossoming of the great Maya scientific civilization and the growth of powerful Maya city-states to the south. During its height, the sophisticated Teotihuacán culture influenced the style of art and architecture of the Maya, though it did not espouse scientific skills or a written script. However, Teotihuacán established colonies in the Maya heartland and practiced exchange, interaction, and dissemination of knowledge with the Maya. Archaeological research indicates that the great city was sacked and burned, and abandoned in the seventh century. The demise was sudden and could have been a victim of "barbarians at the gate" syndrome.

During the Classic Period, new technology emerged to implement the design and construction of public buildings and the efficient infrastructure for the burgeoning urban power centers. Fueled by the engine of "big business," the city-states grew rich and powerful. Long-range trading activities prospered, enhanced by the sacbeob system and the design and construction of large seagoing cargo vessels. The Maya roads led traders to distant cities, and the cargo vessels carried goods to trading partners in the Gulf of Mexico, Caribbean Sea, and the Pacific.

The Classic Period Maya organized their domain into individual city-states. A total of more than 50 city-states were located in the 125,000-square-mile Maya area. As one would expect, some cities were larger and more powerful and sophisticated, and thus more influential than others. The larger Classic Period cities had greater influence on the development of the cultural, scientific, and technical advances of the Classic Period Maya culture. The grand scale and influence of the leading cities reflected their great wealth, and led to enhanced commercial power and the establishment of large universities offering a wide range of learning. Dissemination of scientific knowledge was enhanced by more powerful cities, such as Tikal, Calakmul, Palenque, and Copan, through their larger trade networks, political influences, and dominance.

The Classic Period Maya cities were the epicenter of politics and social life within their own city-state and their relationships with other city-states. The cities served as foci for the government, as well as incubators of learning, scientific development, and technical capabilities. To support the activities required of a densely populated Classic Period power center, the process of urbanization required specialized buildings to satisfy specific functions. Large buildings unearthed in ruined Maya cities are simply referenced as palaces; some of the buildings were probably just that. However, many of these buildings had other vital functions: they served as royal residences, facilities for governmental bureaucracy, theological seminaries, observatories, and centers for technical and mercantile functionaries. The role of the Maya engineer was committed to the planning, design, construction, and operation of urban centers.

Archaeology defines that Classic Period cities should be characterized as grand-scale metropolitan centers with large populations, monumental art, and structures adorned by art and carved inscriptions that chronicled the history of the ruling elite, describing heroes and villains, victories and defeats. The Classic Period cities featured pyramids towering high above the plazas below. Many of these skyscrapers topped out at more than 250 feet or 25 stories in height. These jungle high-rise buildings surpassed the height of structures in cities around the world until the late 19th century, when skyscrapers were erected in large American cities.

The population of the inhabitants of large Classic Period cities is uncertain. Scholars have developed estimates of the population based on the remnants of dwellings in the urban area. For instance, it has been estimated that the city of Tikal had a population of 100,000 people. Based on the urban area of the city, a population density of 2,500 persons per square mile lived in the city. Maya cities were one of the most densely populated areas in the pre-industrial world. These high population densities required a major engineering effort to plan, design, and construct the structures, effective water-management systems, and efficient infrastructure to sustain a prosperous and viable lifestyle for the cities.

The powerful city-states, fueled by the wealth from bountiful agriculture, multi-faceted industries, and a long-range trading network, produced a wealthy political environment. This power and wealth enabled sophisticated science and technology to flourish during the Classic Period. The scientific and technical levels achieved by the Maya during the Classic Period pre-dated similar achievements of European scientists by 1,000 years.

The Decline of the Classic Period

Great and powerful empires have emerged throughout history. These civilizations rose to power and created elevated levels of philosophy, knowledge, and science; then, in turn, each all-powerful state declined. The elite and educated classes of these empires dissolved, and their great cities were abandoned and eventually decayed. This pattern of decline was true of Egypt, Greece, the Roman Empire, the Indus Valley, Persia, and most recently the Soviet Empire.

The ninth century saw the golden age of the Maya burning bright, and then mysteriously the brilliance dimmed. The Maya had enjoyed more than 3,000 years of civilization before their Classic Period and 600 years of unparalleled enlightenment and prosperity during the Classic Period. As the 10th century approached, the Classic Period civilization of the Maya mysteriously declined, and their magnificent cities were abandoned, surrendered to the encroaching rain forest.

An analysis of the chronology of the collapse of the Classic Period Maya cities indicates that these power centers were systematically abandoned during a 100-year period. The dates inscribed on the final monuments erected in Classic Period cities ranged from AD 822 to AD 910. These end dates inscribed on monuments are clues to the demise of the Classic Period cities.

Analysis of paleo-climatic and meteorological historical data concurrent with this period indicates that the root cause of the failure of the Maya society was an environmental catastrophe combined with the inability of Maya technology to overcome the natural crisis. The root cause of the demise of the Classic Period cities and the death of the Maya civilization was not due to the "barbarians at the gates" syndrome, the revolt of slaves, or invasion from outside forces as has been surmised by scholars, but by an apocalyptic environmental disaster and the inability of Maya technology to cope with the vagaries of Mother Nature.

The Post-Classic Period

The Post-Classic Period refers the resurrection of a number of Maya cities in the 11th century. The rebirth and dominance of cities in the northern lowlands, including Uxmal, Mayapán, and Chichen Itza, were the result of outside cultural influence from Central Mexico. This was a militaristic epoch operated under the rule of the Toltec culture, which originated from central Mexico. The Toltec and Maya cultures interacted to construct the new cities with a composite art and architectural style reflecting both Maya and Toltec stylistic modes. The brief fluorescence of these cities extended until about AD 1200. Then this last remnant of the Maya civilization followed suit and fell into ruin. In the 13th century, the mighty Aztec empire rose to power and eventually dominated all of Mesoamerica, including the Maya region.

The Maya scientific heritage and their universities did not survive into the Post-Classic Period. However, thousands of Classic Period Maya books containing the collective knowledge inscribed by the intellectual elite did survive and were preserved and copied by Maya scribes well beyond the Post-Classic Period.

The Spanish Conquest

The cultures of Mesoamerica, including the dominant Aztecs and the repressed Maya, were extinguished by the Spanish conquest. The Maya Classic Period and their scientific civilization had collapsed more than six centuries before conquistador Hernán Cortés landed on the Mexican coast, and their ancient cities were worn down by the passage of time and jealously hidden by a veil of rainforest tendrils. The conquistadores had no interest in these ruins and their resplendent artwork; they were seeking gold and treasure.

The knowledge of the Maya scientific civilization lived on through the thousands of books carefully protected by the Maya elite. These priceless treasures of scientific knowledge, which survived hundreds of years beyond the Classic Period, were destroyed by the Spanish colonial government and the Church during the period from 1563 to 1697. As the centuries passed, the colonial government suppressed all outside references to the lost cities of the Maya. The exploration of the ancient cities was forbidden by Spain until the Mexican Revolution in 1820.

The Maya Today

The Maya civilization of the Classic Period has faded into the dust of history, but the Maya people have not disappeared. The Maya people and their spirit live on today in the distinctive set of culture, traditions, language, and beliefs practiced by millions of contemporary Maya living in Mexico and Central America. These Maya cherish their heritage and are continually reminded of its past grandeur as archaeologists uncover the ruins of ancient cities constructed by their ancestors.

2

The Mystery of the Codices

The discovery of Maya codices spans 500 years and is complicated by the cruelty of the Spanish conquest, the severity of the Spanish Inquisition, the neglect of the Bourbon Kings, the xenophobia of colonial Spain, and the impenetrable jungle that housed Maya ruins. The grand cities of this scientific civilization lay buried beneath the luxuriant vegetation of the tropical jungle for six centuries before the conquistadors landed on the coast of Mexico, but a millennium would pass after the Maya collapse before the outside world knew of their existence. However, the riddle of Maya achievements would stay a mystery for an additional century after the discovery of the ruined civilization. When the Maya code was broken, it revealed the amazing truths of their philosophy, history, and scientific accomplishments.

The Conquest

It is a historic tragedy that the royal chronicles of Spain, carefully transcribed by the priests and the conquistadors, did not provide narrative or illustrative images of the magnificent pre-Columbian cities. The only accounts of the magnificent cities are off-hand references in letters to the Spanish royal court and to King Carlos V. The single reference from Cortés relating to pre-Columbian architecture compared the streets of the Aztec capital of Tenochtitlán to the streets of Madrid, and the high-rise Templo Mayor to the soaring cathedral of Seville. Letters from one of Cortés's captains, Bernal Díaz del Castillo, described the sacred precinct of

Tenochtitlán as a great enclosure of courts that are larger than the Plaza of Salamanca in Spain.

The remarks from Cortes and Del Castillo are the sole reports by the conquistadors relating to a description of pre-Colombian cities. These minimal firsthand accounts formed the total of European images, leading to misconceptions of the configuration of the destroyed Aztec city. Today, it is difficult to believe that sketches or detailed narratives were not prepared to describe images of the most magnificent living city in the New World. However, this lack of interest in art and architecture reflected the skewed mentality of the hard-bitten conquistadors and the overzealous priests who came to rule the Maya world. The correspondence of the conquistadors did not describe or report the existence of ruined Maya cities in the south of New Spain.

Francisco de Montejo, governor and captain general of the Yucatán, and his band of conquistadors had little interest in the ruins of the Maya civilization. The abandoned Maya cities did not contain booty for enriching the Spanish court. The Franciscan priests were well aware of the ancient Maya cities. However, the priests brought their own religion to the Yucatán and were devoted to destroying the religion of the indigenous Maya culture and converting them to Catholicism. The colonizers' sole interest in the fate of the ruined cities lay in destroying the pagan carvings, demolishing the monumental Maya structures, and using them as stone quarries for the construction of churches and municipal buildings for the cities of New Spain. This use of ancient Maya stones for new building construction was typified at the Maya city of Tho', now Mérida, the capital of the Yucatán state, and at Izamal, a major Maya religious destination converted by the Spanish to a Christian religious center. The massive Cathedral de San Ildefonso at Mérida and other important structures in these new cities were constructed by Maya masons using their tools of jadeite (Figure C-2).

The lack of interest in the art and architecture of the pre-Columbian cultures was a predictable failing of an uneducated band of soldiers of the king. The Franciscan priests were educated men of God, who should have had some curiosity in the artistic treasures. However, they not only consorted with the conquistadors in the demolition of Maya cities, but went even further in the wanton destruction of Maya books containing the scientific and intellectual legacy of a sophisticated society.

The Franciscan order was granted the spiritual monopoly for the Yucatán by the Spanish Crown. Their goal was to convert the Maya from their indigenous religion to Catholicism. However, the Spanish Inquisition was at its height, and its pitiless and brutal mandates were integrated into the process of converting souls. The Franciscan priests, led by the rabid religious fanatic Bishop Diego de Landa, were sometimes directed to carry out cruel methods to save the souls of the Maya in their care. De Landa would secure his place in history by two acts: the burning of the surviving Maya books at Maní and the writing of the ethnographic masterpiece *Relación de las cosas de Yucatán*.

The Maya books extant during the 16th century were mostly copies of works originally written during the Classic Period, almost a millennium before the conquest. The books were composed by the Maya literati and were permanent records of the learning, history, and science of the Maya civilization. Those that survived the centuries before the conquest had been protected, copied, and updated by generations of Maya scribes, who were still writing in 1534. The contents of the Maya manuscripts were verified as invaluable records of historical and scientific significance by contemporary Spanish reviewers, including de Landa. Alonso de Zorita wrote in 1540 that he reviewed numerous books that recorded Maya history more than 800 years back and were interpreted for him by elderly Maya, who wrote the script.

The Franciscans considered the Maya books the works of the devil. Untold numbers of books were seized and burned by zealous priests from 1562 to 1697, when the last Maya stronghold fell. The Maya world did not fall easily before the force of Spanish arms; it was a long and fierce fight. The last Maya city fell in 1697, in Tayasal, Guatemala, some 180 years after Hernán Cortés landed at Veracruz, Mexico, and at that time the scribes were still literate. However, after the Maya were defeated, all the Maya books in the defeated city were burned. The city was razed, and its stones used as a quarry to build the churches and buildings of Flores, Guatemala, situated on the site of Tayasal. There is no method of estimating the number of Maya books that were burned in the name of Christianity, but only four Maya books, now known as codices, are known to have survived the zealous priests.

In the summer of 1562, de Landa (Figure 2-1) oversaw the most notorious of incidents related to the burning of Maya books. In the month of May

Figure 2-1: Bishop Diego de Landa persecuted the Maya, but his writings as-sisted in breaking the Maya writing code. Image in public domain.

of that year, Franciscan priests at the Yucatán town of Maní discovered that certain Maya had reverted to their traditional religion. The friars instituted methods of the Inquisition that included interrogating suspected heretics using various means of torture. De Landa soon arrived in Maní and took charge of the proceedings, instituting an "episcopal" inquisition. In July, de Landa conducted an *auto da fe*, or act of faith, during which he burned all the Maya codices he could find as well as 5,000 works of art. He report-ed that 27 scrolls were burned, but other witnesses stated that 99 times as many were destroyed (Figure 2-2).

After the incident at Maní, de Landa continued his fanatical religious activities through the destruction of books, and the torture and execution of Maya by burning them alive, hanging, and drowning. Contemporary Spanish observers were troubled by de Landa's widespread use of torture. The Church also became concerned that de Landa had exceeded his authority by conducting an illegal inquisition. In 1563, Bishop Francisco de Toral sent de Landa back to Spain to stand trial and defend his actions before the Council of the Indies. The pace of the trial went slowly, and nine years passed. De Landa was strongly condemned by the Council of the Indies. Eventually, a committee of doctors was assembled by the Church to judge the actions of de Landa. The committee investigated de Landa's alleged crimes, determined that he was not guilty, and absolved him of the charges.

During the nine years he spent in Spain defending himself against the charges of his accusers, de Landa wrote the classic work *Relación de las cosas de Yucatán* (*Account of the Affairs of Yucatán*). Despite his overt acts of cruelty to his converts, de Landa had a great interest for the Maya culture. He developed intimate relationships with the Maya, and they were willing to teach him some of the secrets inscribed in their books. He gained their confidence and extensively interviewed learned Maya. He became familiar with the Maya hieroglyphic script, calendars, and other facets of their culture. He obviously kept notes from his interviews and collected other material that was used to write his manuscript. It has been conjectured that he had secreted a Maya codex in his file of source material, which he transported back to Spain on the sea voyage to answer his accusers.

The existing copies of de Landa's manuscript are considered to be the most important document written that deals with all the aspects of everyday Maya life in the Yucatán. He describes in narrative and hieroglyphic format the 260-day Maya calendar with the names of the days of the month, as well as the hieroglyphic names of the months of the solar year of 360 days. More importantly, this treatise included an explanation of the logic of the Maya writing system. After de Landa was declared innocent, he was elevated to the title of the fourth Bishop of the Yucatán, where he returned to live out his days.

The place of de Landa in history is both famous and infamous; his infamy stems from the destruction of Maya codices, and his fame was earned for *Relación de las cosas de Yucatán,* which would one day help revolutionize the study of the ancient Maya and assist in breaking the Maya hieroglyphic code. However, fate entered the attempt to solve the riddle of the Maya: De Landa's manuscript was filed away in the un-catalogued clutter of the Royal Academy in Madrid and was lost for three centuries.

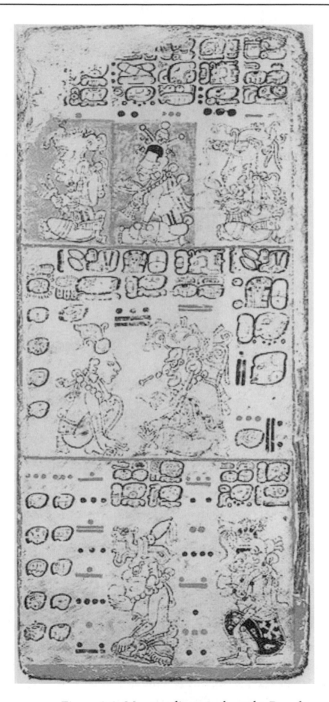

*Figure 2-2: Maya codices, such as the Dresden
Codex shown here, were written in artistic
Maya script. Image in public domain.*

The Xenophobia of New Spain and the Beginnings of Discovery

During the 16th, 17th, and 18th centuries, several volumes were published in Europe describing travel adventures in New Spain. The volumes contain erroneous narrative and fanciful depictions of pre-Columbian architecture. The artists who illustrated the works had not traveled to the New World and did not have firsthand experience. Their images reflected Greek, Roman, and French art and architectural influence in the carved details of pre-Columbian cities. Spain's xenophobia deterred exploration of the colonies, and travel by foreigners to the ports of New Spain was all but forbidden. Entrance to New Spain was totally forbidden to Protestants. The imagery of pre-Colombian art and architecture in European publications were reflections of the minimal descriptions of pre-Columbian cities derived from the letters and accounts of conquistadores. They pursued the concept that pre-Colombian civilizations had European roots.

The Bourbon Dynasty has ruled Spain from 1700 to the present day, with inconsistent results. However, nearly 250 years after the conquest, King Charles III (1759–1788) became ruler of Spain and set out on a policy of enlightenment with administrative reform that reversed the decline of Spain as a colonial power. He had a great interest in learning and science, and found scientific significance in the culture of indigenous peoples in the Spanish colonies. Furthermore, he encouraged exploration of his colonies and exploitation of their natural resources to increase the crown's revenue. This interest in the culture of New Spain led to the first exploration of ancient Maya cities.

Reports of a large abandoned city, near the village of Palenque, in the providence of Ciudad Real of Chiapas, resulted in the formation of an expedition to the site led by a local priest. Father Ramon Ordoñez de Agilar explored the site in 1773 and submitted a report on his findings to the Royal Audiencia of Guatemala. (Politically, Chiapas was part of Guatemala until it was ceded to Mexico in 1824.) Word of the discovery of a lost city in the rainforest traveled to the Royal Court in Madrid and reached the ears of King Charles III. This discovery attracted his interest and was just the type of scientific issue that held the possibility of treasures while fostering the enlightened atmosphere of seeking scientific truths during his reign. The royal court directed the colonial authorities to conduct an investigation of the ruined city.

In response to the king's wishes, Joseph Estachería, president of the Royal Audiencia, ordered detailed explorations to be carried out of the Maya classic city of Santo Domingo de Palenque. The initial report in 1784, prepared by José Antonio Calderón, was considered unsatisfactory. In 1785, Estachería dispatched the Royal Architect, Antonio Bernasconi, to Palenque for further investigation. The narratives and illustrations included in the report of the second expedition apparently were seriously flawed and were also considered unsatisfactory. In 1786, Estachería had a stroke of luck and commissioned a Captain of the Dragoons, Don Antonio del Rio, along with a capable Guatemalan artist named Ricardo Almendáriz, to explore the site and prepare a comprehensive report. Through his choice of this talented team, Estachería enhanced the chances of a successful effort. He used the classic combination of a talented writer and an insightful artist to prepare an accurate report of the investigations.

Commissioned by Royal Order of King Charles III, the expedition led by Captain del Rio reached the site on May 3, 1787. The negotiation of the site was difficult due to dense fog and the impenetrable rainforest that covered the ruined buildings. Del Rio commandeered 79 men from the nearby village of Tumbala to clear the site. The survey commenced as the team of workers used axes to fell the trees and uncover the buildings of the ruined city.

During his stay at the site, del Rio encountered a Franciscan priest, Father Thomas de Soza. During conversations, the priest described other ruined cities that he had observed during his travels in the Yucatán. Captain del Rio made note of these other lost cities in his report. Though his report was a clear narrative of his observations of the ruins, his imagination strayed when he compared some of the art figures to Greek prototypes. However, he made a leap of consciousness while describing specific symbology carved into the monuments. He surmised that these symbols were hieroglyphics that had significance in the language of the original natives. His observations correctly recognized the symbols as a written language and they were the work of indigenous peoples.

The result of this expedition to Palenque included a collection of artifacts from the site and an insightful report that contained accurate narrative descriptions of the city and its monuments written by del Rio, accompanied by the drawings prepared by Ricardo Almendáriz. The drawings, however, strayed from accuracy and reflected the classical education of Almendáriz by introducing classical European art and architecture into his illustrations.

The report and artifacts, dated June 24, 1787, were submitted to Estachería. Various copies were made and deposited in the appropriate places in the Madrid and Guatemala City archives. Once more, the xenophobic and isolationist policy of Spanish bureaucrats caused the report to be buried deep in the archives. Captain del Rio's erudite report represented the first attempt to accurately assess a Maya classic city. It was also the first to suggest that the symbology carved on the ruins represented a written script, to attribute the source of the art and architecture to an indigenous culture, and to report the existence of other lost cities of the Maya.

In 1807, King Charles IV commissioned the most extensive surveys of pre-Columbian cities to date and the last such effort by the Spanish crown. Three expeditions were carried out in response to the king's desire to know more about the colony of New Spain and its history and natural resources. These expeditions were led by Captain Guillermo Dupaix, who was accompanied by artist Jose Luciano Castañeda. They made an excellent team; Dupaix was a passionate aficionado of pre-Colombian architecture, and Castañeda was the artist for the National Museum in Mexico City.

The expeditions visited Palenque, Mitla, Tula, and Monte Alban. Though Dupaix's narratives were confined to visual evidence, he opined that the cities were the work of a culture previously unknown to European scholars. His report stated that the ancient cultures produced works endowed with their own genius, their own force of imagination, without the help of foreigners. Castañeda rendered the illustrations of the sites with an accuracy that surpassed that of previous artists. His efforts produced 150 drawings that constituted the most complete visualization of pre-Columbian art and architecture yet assembled. However, Castañeda was also a victim of his classical education, and his works were often distorted and inaccurate by reflecting classic European influence.

Dupaix did not credit the indigenous peoples living in the area of the sites with the construction of the ruined cities. He asserted that the monuments were built by a long-vanished people. As Dupaix completed the report, he lamented that he had ended his exploration with conjecture relative to the source of the ruins. However, his insistence that peoples of independent American origin constructed the ruined cities served as the entrée for the investigations of future explorers. The report was completed in 1808, and was sent to the archives in the National Museum of Mexico City. There it gathered dust until it was reported to have been lost in the chaos of the Mexican Revolution. Fortunately, the report was rediscovered in 1828.

The control of Spain over its colonies began to falter in 1810, and by September 1821, the Spanish crown admitted defeat and, with the signing of the Treaty of Cordoba, recognized Mexico as an independent nation. The collapse of the Spanish rule opened the way for exploration of the country, investigation of its ruins, and the publishing of pre-Colombian scholarship. In 1822, nearly 40 years after the completion of Captain del Rio's report, a copy of the report was secreted away from the royal archives in Guatemala City and found its way to British publisher Henry Berthoud. Berthoud claimed that the report was not stolen from Guatemala, but was rescued from the oblivion of the archives and had been legitimately secured. He published the report in 1822 under the title "Description of the Ruins of an Ancient City." Captain del Rio's report was translated into English and was largely re-written, the contents barely resembling the original document. The volume also included a fanciful essay by Doctor Paul Felix Cabrera, of Guatemala, who proposed that America's first colonists were either from Mount Hebron or Mount Olympus. The volume contained 17 engraved plates, which were taken from Almendáriz's illustrations in the original report. It is of note that nine of the engravings bear the initials "JFW" and were prepared by the flamboyant Jean Frederick Waldeck. This volume, with its narrative and engravings, constitutes the first published illustrations of Maya art and the inscriptions carved into their monumental buildings.

In 1830, fate took a hand in the final disposition of the Dupaix report. This report reached Europe by a route of devious means. The manuscript was spirited away from the archives of the National Museum of Mexico and found its way into the Parisian library of Frenchman Francois Latour-Allard. The manuscript then found its way into the collection of Englishman Edward King, Lord Kingsborough. Lord Kingsborough included all the then-known reports in his nine-volume work entitled *Antiquities of Mexico*. The series appeared between 1830 and 1848, and include works relating to ancient Mexico. This series published, among other matters, all known works relating to pre-Columbian art and architecture. The works included the Maya Dresden Codex, the Aztec Mendoza and Telleriano-Remensis codices, the Aztec Florentine Codex prepared under 16th-century Franciscan friar Bernardino de Sahagun, selections from Humboldt's *Picturesque Atlas*, and scholarly works by Kingsborough and other intellectuals. The scholarly chapters in Kingsborough's volumes supported his belief that ancient Mexican civilization had been founded by the lost tribes of Israel.

Jean Frederick Waldeck, the artist who engraved some of the plates in Berthoud's 1922 volume, traveled to Mexico in 1825. Waldeck, who claimed to be a count, spent nine years working in Mexico City as a hydraulic engineer before traveling south to the Yucatán, where he sketched and painted the ruins of Maya classic cities. He found his was to Palenque, where he lived in the ruined structures from May 1832 to July 1833. The building he used as his place of habitation is still known as the "Temple of the Count." He then traveled to the ancient city of Uxmal in 1834, producing architectural reconstructions of the site. He returned to Paris and began work on the production of lithographs developed from his renderings of the Maya sites. In 1838, he published *Voyage Pittoresque et Archéologique dans la Province d'Yucatan*. Illustrations in this book indicate the Eurocentric spin that Waldeck infused in his interpretations of Maya art. His paintings of Uxmal reflect a pronounced Egyptian style. The most skewed prejudices are in his renditions of hieroglyphics, which depicted elephants in his illustrations of Maya monuments. The illustrations in his book, though flawed, provided the first eye-witness accounts of classic Maya ruins since Mexico's independence.

The Mystery of the Maya Codices

The greatest compilation of Maya knowledge was set down in the thousands of Maya books destroyed by the zealous Spanish conquistadors. Only four examples of these marvelous works are known to survive today. These few examples of a once-voluminous library were the key to the decipherment of the Maya script and the unveiling of the secrets of the Maya (Figure 2-2).

A single Maya book, the Dresden Codex, was known to survive in European libraries during the mid-19th century. The origin of this singular artifact is clouded in the mist of time, though it may have been a part of the treasure sent back to Spain by conquistadors. In 1519, before his conquest of Mexico, Hernán Cortés and his bloodthirsty band were sacking the coast of the Gulf of Mexico near the present-day city of Vera Cruz. They were collecting loot from the cities of Gulf Coast Maya. While ransacking the houses of the local inhabitants, it was reported that the Spanish encountered innumerable books. Some samples were collected for their artistic value, along with other looted valuables and captives. Their trove included valuables collected from local raids plus bribes paid to Cortés by the Aztec emperor. Part of the booty, the "royal fifth," was the 20 percent to be paid to the Spanish royal court. Reports from Francisco López de Gómara, Cortés's private secretary, indicated that the royal fifth included some books, folded like cloth, which contained figures like the Mexicans (Aztecs) use for letters. These books were of little value to the cut-throat conquistadors, who did not value them because they did not understand them.

The ship transporting the royal fifth, including captives from the raids, treasure, and the books, reached Spain safely. In a letter, Giovanni Ruffo da Forli, Papal Nunico at the Spanish court who had inspected the treasure, described his memories of the books. He stated that there were some paintings, folded and joined in the form of a book, and that in these were figures and signs in the form of Arabic or Egyptian letters. Italian Peter Martyr d'Anghiera, present at the review, described the books as being made of the inner bark of a tree, the pages coated with plaster and the cover made of wooden boards. He described the writing as characters written in a line and that they greatly resembled Egyptian forms.

One of the passengers on the treasure ship with the royal fifth was Francisco de Montejo, the future governor of the Yucatán, who was quite knowledgeable about the Maya. He had gained his knowledge from Gerómino de Aguilar, a Spaniard held captive by a Maya chief for eight years. Through Aguilar, Montejo knew of the existence of Maya books and their writing capabilities. Peter Martyr interviewed Montejo and learned of the contents of Maya books. Martyr reported that the contents of the books included descriptions of laws, sacrifices, ceremonies, rites, astronomical notations, and mathematical computations. There can be no doubt that the "works of art" that fascinated the European men of learning were Maya codices.

The fate of the Maya books reaching Spain as part of the royal fifth is unknown. An exception could be the invaluable Dresden Codex. In 1739, the Royal Library of Saxony in Dresden purchased a unique book from a private collection in Vienna. This book was not catalogued and went unnoticed until 1796, when it surfaced in a most unlikely place. That year a treatise was published in Leipzig relating to the art of interior design. The five-volume work was entitled *Darstellung und Geschichte des Geschmacks der vorzüglichsten Völker* (*Depiction and History of the Taste of Superior Peoples*) by Joseph Friedrich, Baron von Racknitz. The volumes included a plate showing a room decorated with icons from the Dresden Codex. However, though this was the first publication of Maya script in print, the contents of this volume, no doubt, escaped the study of scholars.

Alexander von Humboldt, the famous German explorer, made significant studies in American geology, meteorology, and natural history, and published an atlas in 1810. The volume entitled *Vues de Cordillères et Monuments des Peuples Indigènes de L'Amérique* (*Views of the Mountain Ranges and Monuments of the Indigenous Peoples of the Americas*). This work includes a plate showing five pages from the Dresden Codex in intricate detail. This was the first publication of a portion of a Maya codex and the first accurate representation of a Maya hieroglyphic text.

At the mid-point of the 19th century, there were no researchers in the Americas attempting to decipher the Maya script. Extensive research into the Maya civilization was almost impossible due to the lack of access to the published works on the topic. All published works on the Maya were printed in Europe, in limited numbers with a costly price tag. They consisted of multiple volumes printed in elephant folio format, each weighing 20 to 40 pounds and measuring 30 inches × 24 inches (77 cm × 60 cm). Furthermore, they cost thousands of dollars per set, winding up in the collections of a few erudite European collectors. The publications were rare in Europe and all but unknown to scholars in America. Experts have determined that a single set of these volumes may have found its way to the United States by 1843, when serious exploration of Maya cities began to take shape.

The works containing invaluable knowledge of the Maya had a way of going missing in archives and libraries; the invaluable works relating to Maya life during the conquest by Bishop Diego de Landa were lost in the Madrid archives and not recovered for 300 years. The effort to destroy Maya books was complete, with the exception of four Maya codices that are known to survive. In the mid-19th century the Dresden Codex had not been recognized for the information on Maya script that it contained. The other three codices were not discovered until the 19th and 20th centuries. The Paris Codex was found in the Paris National Library in 1859, the Madrid Codex was uncovered in 1866 in Madrid, and the Grolier Codex was discovered in New York in 1976 and was returned to Mexico. The wonder of it all is that four survived. Could it be that the world's great libraries, including the Vatican Library, have other codices in their vaults?

Unveiling of the Maya Civilization to the World

During the middle of the 19th century, Spain's colonies in the New World won their independence. Gone was the xenophobic policy of New Spain. The Maya homeland in Mexico and Central America was opened to explorers and scholars of antiquity.

On October 3, 1839, John Lloyd Stephens and Frederick Catherwood boarded a ship in New York harbor and set sail for the Bay of Honduras. Little did this talented pair know how much this adventure would change their lives and result in the rewriting of world history.

When their ship set sail for the tropics, 34-year-old John Lloyd Stephens, a New York City attorney, and 40-year-old Frederick Catherwood, a British architect, were enthralled with their mission. The pair had met in England four years earlier and established a friendship based on mutual interests in ancient art and architecture. Both men had had extensive experience in the study of classic European and Egyptian archaeology. They had visited ruins of the ancient world, recording descriptions and illustrations of classic archaeological sites. Stephens was a successful travel writer. He had traveled the old world and had written two popular travel books: *Incidents of Travel in Egypt, Arabia, Petria, and the Holy Land* (1837) and *Incidents of Travel in Greece, Turkey, Russia, and Poland* (1838). The books were written in a style that provided a chatty narrative of everyday incidents that he encountered in his travels (Figure 2-3). Catherwood was a gifted artist with extensive archaeological experience in the Mediterranean and the Near East. He had trained at the Royal Academy of Arts in London and, following his formal training, became a traveling illustrator. Catherwood traveled extensively in Greece, Egypt, Italy, and the Near East, preparing illustrations of the ancient monuments from classic civilizations.

Stephens had learned of possible lost cities in the Yucatán and Central America from a book seller in New York and persuaded Catherwood to accompany him in the exploration of the abandoned Maya cities to record the sites with his accurate illustrations. Stephens had secured a diplomatic passport from President Martin Van Buren as the U.S. Representative to the Central American Federation. Stephens took great advantage of his diplomatic status in traveling throughout the region exploring the Classic Maya cities. The result of this collaboration was the 1841 publication, in two volumes, of *Incidents of Travel in Central America, Chiapas, and Yucatán,* followed by additional discoveries of Maya cities in the two-volume work *Incidents of Travel in Yucatán,* published in 1843.

The explorations of the Maya cities were carried out methodically and recorded with meticulous detail. Stephens and Catherwood had gained extensive experience observing Egyptian monuments and their carved hieroglyphics. This experience with similar ancient iconography provided a substantial background for their observations, narratives, and illustrations of Maya art and architecture.

The technology of the camera was in its infancy during this period, and the team had the use of a daguerreotype camera on their second journey. This type of camera could produce an image, but the technique of reproduction of photography would not be mastered for several years in the future. To capture the complex details of Maya art, Catherwood combined his natural talent for drawing with the use of a *camera lucida.* This device projected the image of a monument directly onto sheets of sectioned graph paper. Images could be accurately drawn in the correct proportion and perspective. His illustrations provided exquisite images that were reproduced as engravings in the two-volume sets (Figure 2-4 and Figure 2-5). The *camera lucida* images produced an exponential increase in quality when compared with any method of illustration that had previously been published depicting the monuments and structures of the classic Maya.

Figure 2-3: John Lloyd Stephens wrote a series of books that revealed the Maya civilization and changed world history. Wikimedia Commons.

Figure 2-4: Frederick Catherwood traveled with John Lloyd Stephens and produced accurate illustrations of Maya art and architecture. Wikimedia Commons.

Stephens's narrative of the art and architecture of the monuments in the classic cities, and the daily incidents of the adventure are well organized and clearly written. Stephens was familiar with the recent decipherment of Egyptian hieroglyphics by the French scholar Jean François Champollion, who had decoded the Rosetta Stone. Stephens was convinced that the carved inscriptions on the monuments were a hieroglyphic script that described the historical records of the civilization that had constructed the cities. This leap of consciousness was a direct link derived from to his knowledge of the writing systems of ancient civilizations that he had observed in the ancient cities of the Old World. Stephens stated, in Volume One of *Incidents of Travel in Central America, Chiapas, and Yucatán*, "One thing I believe, that its history is graven on its monuments. No Champollion has yet brought to them the energies of the inquiring mind. Who will read them?" Stephens's concept was well ahead of his time; however, his conception of the inscriptions of the script was to be criticized as erroneous by Mayanists for decades into the future. However, history and hard work by epigraphers would prove him to be correct.

Previous European volumes on the Maya had cost thousands of dollars each. In 1841, Stephens's two-volume sets sold for five dollars and were affordable to the general American reading public. *Incidents of Travel in Central America, Chiapas, and Yucatán* sold 20,000 copies in the first three months of publication. Stephens's clever narrative and the precise engravings by Catherwood produced works that became best-sellers throughout the world. In 1843, the pair published a second two-volume set relating to the Maya, *Incidents of Travel in Yucatán*. The second set, equally popular as the first, related to their exploration of Maya sites in the Yucatán. Though not covering the distances reflected in their first effort in Maya exploration, the second volumes explored a greater number of abandoned cities. These volumes are masterpieces of accurate visual and narrative descriptions of Maya cities (Figure 2-6).

Stephens's conclusions included his theories of the substance and age of the Classic Maya cities. Unlike European scholars, Stephens hypothesized that the ruins were of recent origin and had not been constructed by travelers from ancient Mediterranean cultures. Furthermore, he concluded that the inscriptions carved on the monuments constituted a writing system and recognized that the writing at different sites was apparently of the same language. He further concluded that the script carved on the monuments

Figure 2-5: View of El Castillo at Chichen Itza by Frederick Catherwood, the first images the world saw of the Maya civilization. Wikimedia Commons.

Figure 2-6: The Maya arch at Labná by Frederick Catherwood. Wikimedia Commons.

was the same writing system as illustrated in the Dresden Codex. These popular books resulted in the rewriting of the history of the Americas and opened the Maya civilization to exploration and multiple fields of study. Today, these books are as popular with aficionados of Maya archaeology as they were in the 19th century.

Stephens and Catherwood never returned to the Yucatán after the success of their books. However, their final collaboration made another significant impact on American life and history. Stephens had grown wealthy from the sale of his books. In the late 1840s, he helped fund the construction of the famous Panama Railroad, and Catherwood joined the effort as the civil engineer for the design and construction of the roadway line. The Panama Railroad transported gold prospectors from the east coast of Panama across the isthmus on their way to the gold fields of California. The railroad was a success and is still operating today. However, as the Trans-Isthmus project was completed, tragedy struck both players. Stephens was injured in Panama and died in New York City in October 1852. Shortly afterward, Catherwood followed him to the grave in 1854. While returning on the steamship *Arctic* to New York from England, the ship was struck by a French freighter. He went down at sea off the coast of Labrador, with many of his drawings and daguerreotypes.

The Collection of Data and the Unraveling of the Maya Code

After the Mexican-American War in 1848, travel in Mexico became hazardous. The rate of exploration was reduced by the civil strife, but some adventurers were able to travel with the protection of small armies. The technology of the camera had improved, along with the ability to record photo prints, and the Yucatán became a hunting ground for adventurous explorers traversing the rainforest seeking new finds. They were equipped with the new type of camera to record their discoveries. The explorers used photographic images and narrative descriptions of their discoveries. Though the corpus of descriptions and imagery of the ruins grew, there were few attempts to decipher the script and disclose the secrets of the Maya, including those of Constantine Rafinesque and James McCulloh.

Traveling in Mexico from 1857 to 1861, French adventurer Claude-Joseph Désiré Charnay used the new invention of reproducible photography and an efficient method of plaster casting using lightweight molds to produce three-dimensional copies of Maya art. The two innovations created a tremendous visual impact on the recording and dissemination of Maya art. In 1862, Charnay published his findings in Eugène Viollet-le-Duc's volume *Cités et Ruins Américaines* (*American Cities and Ruins*). He patterned his work after that of Stephens, employing a running narrative with clear photographic images. He returned to Mexico from 1880 to 1883 to visit the ruined cities, and published *Les Anciennes Villes du Nouveau Monde* (*The Ancient Cities of the New World*) in 1887. The development of the photogravure printing process had enhanced the reproduction of photography. This allowed his published works to be available to the same wide public readership as the works of John Lloyd Stephens. The lost cities of the Maya became popular again.

Born near London in 1850 to a wealthy engineering family, Alfred Percival Maudslay led a life of scholarship and adventure, and left a significant mark as a leader in Maya archaeology. Maudslay attended Cambridge University and then joined the diplomatic service. He served as a British diplomat in the South Pacific, where he was involved in subduing rebellious tribes in Fiji. After that posting, he was appointed British Consul to Tonga and Samoa. He resigned the British Diplomatic Corps and traveled to Mexico to begin the major archaeological work that is his legacy. He was first drawn to the ruins of the Maya cities by reading the works of John Lloyd Stephens. Maudslay carried out seven explorations in Mexico and Central America. During his first trip in 1881, he set a goal of providing a complete and accurate record of the architecture, art, and inscriptions of specific Classic Maya cities, including Chichen Itza, Copán, Palenque, Quiriguá, and the river city of Yaxchilan. Maudslay used the newly developed wet plate photographic process and made paper-mâché casts of the monuments. The work at the sites was carried out under conditions of great hardship, and the effort of transporting the voluminous results of his works back to London was a considerable task.

Maudslay retained an artist, Annie Hunter, to prepare lithographic plates of the photographs and casts he had made of the monuments and inscriptions of the Maya ruins. His work was the first to depict accurate, large-scale details of Maya script. Maudslay published his work as an appendix to the multi-volume work *Biologia Centrali-Americana* (*Central American Biology*). Previously, the only available works for the monuments were the prejudiced and amateurish illustrations of Almendáriz and Waldeck. For the first time, Maya epigraphers had concise and accurate representations of Maya hieroglyphics to study and decipher. The total of Maudslay's work was available by 1902. Maudslay moved back to London in 1907, and became the president of the Royal Anthropological Institute. He died in 1931 and is buried in Hereford Cathedral.

Augustus Le Plongeon was a highly eccentric amateur archaeologist of the late 19th century. Camera technology and lightweight casting techniques had made further advances by his time, and Le Plongeon carried out studies, made molds of art and architecture, and took innovative photographs at Palenque and Chichen Itza. He published several works from 1880 to 1896. Although his published works were failures with the public and with critics, the quality of his molds and photographs was unparalleled by 19th-century standards. He pioneered concise, close-up photography, and established the use of panoramic photography and photography from elevated vantage points. He added to the growing corpus of visual and narrative information on the Maya. Le Plongeon sold his large collection of casts to the Metropolitan Museum in New York City. The molds were never used for making replicas and met the destiny of other Maya artifacts: they have disappeared from the museum, and their fate is unknown.

Teobert Maler was born in Rome in 1842 to German diplomat parents, and studied architecture and engineering in Vienna. He took a job as an architect in Vienna. Anxious to see the world, he traveled to Mexico as a soldier in Emperor Maximilian's army during the French Intervention in Mexico (1862–1867). He quickly rose from private to captain, but then his life took a turn when Mexico won the war. Teobert surrendered his troops to the Mexican Army. Rather than be deported as an exile, he elected to stay in Mexico and became a Mexican citizen. Teobert became Teoberto.

In 1876, he visited Palenque and fell in love with the Maya. He learned the Maya language and set up a photo studio in Ticul, a small town in the Yucatán. Using a large format camera and the wet plate process, Teobert Maler made a huge contribution to the detailed records available to Mayanist scholars. Maler recorded the fine details on monuments at a wide range of Maya sites. He had a unique and clever system of revealing undiscovered sites. He was a pioneer in using *chicleros* to locate unknown Maya sites buried deep within the rainforest. These wide-ranging chicleros extracted *chicle*, the basic ingredient in chewing gum, from the *chico zapote* tree scattered throughout the rainforest. Maler offered a reward to the chicleros if they detected an undiscovered site. This yielded a world of lost cities that went undiscovered by Stephens, Catherwood, and Maudslay. Maler explored a great number of sites and recorded the carvings on the monuments in significant detail. This fine detail added greatly to the graphic corpus of the Maya monuments and, with the published codices, formed the basis for the initial partial decipherment of the Maya hieroglyphics.

Maler's voluminous work was published by the Peabody Museum of Archaeology and Ethnology of Harvard University until 1912 and later published posthumously in the 1970s and 1990s. In his later years, Teoberto lived a quiet life at his home in Mérida. His money gone, he survived by selling photos to tourists and teaching young archaeologists. He died in Mérida in 1917 at, age 75.

The Beginning of Decipherment

Along with the graphic and narrative images produced by Stephens, Catherwood, Maudslay, Maler, and other recorded collections, the last half of the 19th century saw the discovery and publishing of the lost works produced by Maya scribes, as well the lost works of Bishop Diego de Landa. A treasure trove of original material vital to the decipherment effort was discovered and published during this period.

In 1861, the *Popol Vuh*, considered to be the greatest work in Native American literature, was discovered by Abbé Charles Brasseur de Bourbourg in a private collection in Guatemala City. Brasseur possessed an amazing trait as an archival "bird dog" that enabled him to sniff out and uncover lost works of the Maya. In 1862, he unearthed the manuscript of de Landa in the Royal Academy of Madrid. The precious work had lain un-catalogued for 300 years until Brasseur discovered the document in a dusty corner of the archives. His astonishing skills of detection continued in 1866. During a visit to Madrid, Brasseur was shown a Maya book, by a descendent of Hernán Cortés. The document was considered to be a family keepsake. Brasseur recognized the work as a Maya codex. Then in 1875, another fragment of a codex turned up. Research by Leon de Rosney, the French orientalist who discovered the Paris Codex, indicated that the two Madrid finds were part of the same Codex. Together they constitute the largest known Maya book and are known as the Madrid Codex. The fourth known Maya codex, the Grolier, was not discovered until the 1976.

With the wealth of new and rediscovered information, why did deciphment of the Maya script not proceed? Why didn't some modern Champollion of Rosetta Stone fame set up shop and decipher the code with an early Enigma machine? Mayanist Michael Coe correctly hypothesized that the decipherment was hampered by the lack of linguistic training and clarity of vision in early Mayanists, traits that enabled the clever Jean François Champollion to make the leap of consciousness that achieved his monumental breakthrough of deciphering the Rosetta Stone.

Aside from Rafinesque and McCulloh, the first attempts at decipherment that bore fruit were carried out by newspaperman Joseph T. Goodman. Goodman was the classic "crossover" Mayanist, having come from a non-archeological background. Goodman was owner and editor of the *Territorial Enterprise* newspaper in Virginia City, Nevada Territory, the site of the fabulous gold strike known as the Comstock Lode. Goodman became rich on his Comstock Lode investments. Tiring of the desert dust, he moved west to San Francisco, where he took a seat on the Pacific Stock Exchange and became managing editor of the *San Francisco Post*. He later retired to his raisin ranch and began his Maya studies in the 1880s. Goodman relied on the recordings of Maudslay and Dr. Gustavus Eisen to carry out analysis and decipherment of the Maya Long Count calendar. Goodman announced in the 1897 edition of *Biologica Centrali-Americana* that he had deciphered the Maya calendar. Controversy immediately raged over the ability of a California raisin grower to achieve such a discovery, but history has proved him to be correct. The calendar tables he published in *Biologia Centrali-Americana* are still in use by scholars calculating Long Count dates. Furthermore, Goodman discovered the "head variants," mathematical hieroglyphs that can be substituted for the bar and dot dates in Long Count dates. However, his most significant discovery, announced in 1905, was the correlation between the Maya Long Count calendar and our present-day Julian calendar. With this discovery of correlated dating, the dates on Maya monuments could be deciphered with accuracy and identified with the time period that was concurrent with the history of that site. Goodman's amazing discovery was scorned by Maya scholars and lay forgotten until 1926, when Juan Martinez Hernandez recovered it and gave proof of its correctness.

The Decipherment of Maya Hieroglyphics

The decipherment of Maya hieroglyphics was impeded for nearly a half century by professional jealousy and potential for reprobation by archaeologist Eric Thompson. Eric Thompson dominated Maya studies during the mid-20th century with his overbearing personality, intellectual influence, and force of will. He used his knowledge of Maya calendrics in 1915 to gain a position with the Carnegie Institution in the excavations at Chichen Itza, where his talents were wasted as a field archaeologist. In 1926, he separated himself from the Carnegie Institution and accepted a position with the Field Museum of Natural History in Chicago.

Thompson attacked Maya scholars who developed concepts that did not agree with his case for Maya script being solely calendric. However, Thompson was an efficient iconographer and developed accurate insights into Maya religion and mythology. His monumental work, *Maya Hieroglyphic Writing*, was not a primer for Maya decipherment but constituted an impediment that retarded the Maya script for a generation of Maya scholars. Young Mayanists were cowed into subscribing to Thompson's ideas by his imperial arrogance and vicious criticism.

Thompson's willful determination to misguide Maya scholars has resulted in the tendency of today's younger Maya scholars to dismiss Thompson's contributions to the field. It is true that Thompson was wrong about the intent and characteristics of Maya hieroglyphic writing. However, Thompson made certain momentous discoveries in deciphering the Maya glyphs.

Tatiana Proskouriakoff was born in 1909 in Tomsk, Russian Empire. Her father, a chemist, was requested by the tsar to oversee the production of munitions for World War I. His duties involved travel to the United States, and his family were visiting Philadelphia in 1915 when the Russian Revolution changed the character of Mother Russia. The stateless family made Philadelphia their home. Proskouriakoff graduated from Penn State University in 1930 with a degree in architecture. Fate destined that the young architect would not be bound into the peonage of an architectural office but assumed a position as an archaeological artist at the University of Pennsylvania Museum.

Proskouriakoff's unique talents in detailing archaeological artifacts attracted the attention of Linton Satterthwaite, the director of the museum's investigation at the Classic Maya city of Piedras Negras, Guatemala, sited along the shore of the mighty Usumacinta River. She toiled at Piedras Negras from 1934 to 1938. Her job was to produce architectural restoration drawings of Structure P-7 and perspective reconstruction drawings of the acropolis as it might have appeared during the height of power of Piedras Negras. Proskouriakoff's excellent renderings were admired by the Carnegie Institution. She was retained as a Carnegie employee with a mission to prepare architectural reconstructions of significant classic Maya sites.

In 1950, during the time of the "dictatorship" of Eric Thompson, Proskouriakoff discovered a pattern of dates by using comparative observations and logical structural interpretation of glyphs during her work on the monuments at Piedras Negras. She discovered that the inscriptions carved on the stele at Piedras Negras described the history of the rulers and the accomplishments of the city. The glyphs did not relate to astronomy, religion, or similar sacrosanct subjects dictated to be the sole subjects of Maya script by Thompson, though he later agreed with her. The carved figures on the stele and lintels were mortal men and women who had ruled the city. They were not gods, priests, or mythological figures, but represented real people who had led their lives at Piedras Negras. The inscriptions described the history of the rulers of the city-state. Michael Coe, in his book, *Breaking the Maya Code*, stated that because "this extraordinary woman cut the Gordian Knot of Maya epigraphy...the Maya had become real human beings." They had actual names with personalities, achievements, and lifestyles.

Proskouriakoff published a paper in *American Antiquity* relating her discovery of the real content of Maya inscriptions written in stone. Her logic was exactly right when she stated, "In retrospect, the idea that Maya texts record history, naming their rulers or lords of the towns, seems so natural that it is strange that it has not been thoroughly explored before." She is truly a giant in the decipherment of Maya hieroglyphics and a perceptive artist in the reconstruction of Maya structures. Her ashes are buried among the ruins of Piedras Negras on the banks of the Usumacinta River.

The academic world was blindsided when the cracking of the Maya code was announced from isolation behind the Iron Curtain. The brilliant work of decipherment was carried out at a university, during the height of the Cold War, deep in the heart of Russia. The university is located 10,000 miles from the tropical rainforest of the Yucatán.

The initial phase of the most brilliant breakthrough in Maya decipherment and the greatest linguistic achievement since the translation of the Rosetta Stone did not come to pass in the hallowed halls of a great museum or in the ivory towers of an Ivy League university, but started in the war-torn streets of Berlin. In May 1945, the Soviet Army had overrun the city and was sacking the capital of the Third Reich. On that night, Yuri Valentinovich Knorosov, a young Russian artillery spotter, found himself in front of the Prussian National Library, which was being pillaged by the victorious Red Army. That fiery night in front of the library, Knorosov encountered his comrades throwing thousands of rare books into the burning pyre. It was fate that guided his hand to a book lying at the edge of the conflagration. He snagged the book from the inferno and slipped into the darkness. The book that Knorosov collected was a rare 1933 publication containing facsimiles of the Paris, Dresden, and Madrid Codices written by Antonio and Carlos Villacorta. Yuri was a student in ancient languages at Moscow State University when the war interrupted his studies. He knew that the book was unique. He secured his find in his knapsack and transported his trophy back to Russia. This serendipitous retrieval of a precious book changed the course of Maya scholarship.

In autumn 1945, the 23-year-old Knorosov returned to his studies of ancient writing systems at Moscow State University. His main interest was in Egyptology, but he was also interested in the writing systems of China and ancient India, the Arabic language, and Japanese literature. His advisors recommended that he concentrate on Egyptology. However, motivated by the contents of the book that he had recovered in Berlin, Knorosov pursued his interest in archaeology, ethnology, and the decipherment of the Maya script. Sergi Alekandrovich Tokarev, his professor, encouraged Knorosov to crack the Maya writing system, challenging him with an enticing question: If you believe that any writing system produced by humans can be read by humans, why don't you try to decipher the Maya system?

Knorosov rose to the challenge. He taught himself Spanish in order to undertake a translation of de Landa's *Relación de las cosas de Yucatán* for his research into the decipherment of Maya glyphs. He used the translation and the copies of codices to work on the decipherment of the Maya script. This work became his doctoral dissertation. He completed his studies at Moscow University and then moved to Leningrad, where he assumed a research post in the Institute of Ethnology.

Knorosov, a scholar in various ancient written scripts, was well prepared to decipher the Maya code. His knowledge of the structure and composition of early historic scripts combined with his brilliant mind enabled Knorosov to recognize the stages and evolution that are mutual developments in all early scripts. He categorized the comparative scripts as hieroglyphic and identified the Maya writing as being in this category. In these systems, he identified syllables. He recognized that the phonetic meaning of de Landa's signs were exactly as de Landa had transcribed in his manuscript. He also recognized that glyphs can sometimes be phonetic or other times can represent a morpheme (the smallest unit of meaning in a language). Knorosov also understood that the order of writing script may be inverted for use in calligraphy as well as other more complex methods to reduce ambiguity in the reading of the scripts. He used the scientific method to establish a logical methodology for decipherment.

Knorosov's brilliant work became the most significant effort in deciphering the Maya script. In 1952, when he published the paper "Ancient Writing of Central America," he presented the argument that Bishop de Landa's manuscript was made of syllabic rather than alphabetic symbols. He further improved his decipherment techniques in his 1963 monograph "The Writing of the Maya Indians" and translation of Maya manuscripts. In 1975, he published "Maya Hieroglyphic Manuscripts." Knorosov's methodologies would lead the way to full decipherment. De Landa's work had turned out to be his Rosetta Stone.

Eric Thompson attacked Knorosov with vigor starting in 1953, claiming, among other things, that the Russian claim to decipherment should be placed with other Soviet boasts of the era, including the invention of the game of baseball, the airplane, and other "firsts." The great Mayanist Thompson had decreed that Knorosov's decipherment was another hoax by the Iron Curtain masters of propaganda.

In 1955, archaeologist Michael Coe came upon an unauthorized Spanish translation of Knorosov's 1952 seminal work in a bookstore in Mérida, Mexico. This was the first review by a Western scholar of the groundbreaking work. Knorosov's doctoral thesis on de Landa's work was published in Russian in 1955. Sophie Coe, Michael's wife, was bilingual in English and Russian; she translated a new paper by Knorosov in 1958, assuring a wide audience of Mayanists. The 1958 translation describing Knorosov's methods and decipherments appeared in *American Antiquity*. Michael Coe states in his seminal book, *Breaking the Maya Code,* that Thompson was completely off track and Knorosov was right on the point. The decipherment of Maya script accelerated after Knorosov's 1963 work "The Writing of the Maya Indians," with the real lift-off taking place after Thompson's death in 1975; within four years the tide for acceptance of Knorosov's work had turned and as many as 135 participants attended a conference on Maya hieroglyphic writing in Albany, New York.

In the annals of Maya hieroglyphic decipherment, the contributions of a group of like-minded scholars including archaeologists, epigraphers, linguists, and crossover experts are difficult to separate. The group contributed to the process of interpreting the script and subsequent revelation of the history, sciences, and technology of the ancient Maya.

Further progress in the decipherment accelerated exponentially during the 1960s and 1970s, with a multitude of methodologies, including pattern analysis, de Landa's "alphabet," and Knorosov's breakthrough. Breakthroughs in reading the Maya script were advanced by a series of conferences that assembled talented epigraphers and Mayanists. These conferences, including the Palenque Round Table and the Texas Maya Meetings, combined with a new breed of "young Turks" and "born-again" veterans, created unique and advanced breakthroughs in unveiling the secrets of the Maya. These creative epigraphers included Michael Coe, Ian Graham, Nikolai Grube, Norman Hammond, Peter Matthews, Stephen Houston, Linda Schele, David Stuart, and Karl Taube. Decipherment had achieved an international status with major contributions from Maya scholars, many of them quite young, originating from such places as Canada, Germany, France, and Guatemala. Maya epigraphers can now read 85 percent of the glyphs in the codices, inscriptions, and painted vases.

As explorers and archaeologists located the remnants of this intellectual culture and reported the glory of the art and architecture of the cities and their scientific accomplishments, readers across the globe became intrigued by the Maya. During the past century, universities, museums, foundations, and governments have cleared the sites and consolidated the monumental structures to permit a view of the ancient Maya cities. Tourists and aficionados of Maya culture have flocked to the sites to gaze in awe at the skyscraping pyramids and ornate sculptures constructed by ancient artisans. The number of international visitors now counts in the tens of millions each year paying homage to the Maya. This popularity has earned the pyramid of Kukulkan at Chichen Itza, Mexico, the title of one of the new Seven Wonders of the World.

3

Creating a Scientific
Civilization in Tropical Isolation

Strolling through the emerald rainforest amid the ruins of the ancient Maya city of Cobá, Emilio Ek, a Maya guide, turned to the American engineer.

"How much time passes when your plane flies from here to Atlanta?"

"Two hours."

"When I walk from here to my home village, two hours also pass."

He paused for a moment and said, "We both live the same distance from Cobá."

His comment, though strange, was understandable. Contemporary Maya, like their ancient predecessors, are motivated by the quality and quantity of time. Temporal cycling, based on cosmic order, has governed the Maya civilization since its origin.

The origin of the Maya civilization, their cosmic philosophy, and their scientific advancements have remained an enigma since their rediscovery in the 19th century. The profound thought process that motivated Maya intellectuals to develop high levels of pure sciences have not been examined by archaeology. The process of speculation upon the roots of the Maya mystery would require multiple hypotheses that may not mesh with accepted archaeological theory, and speculative theories would be met with scathing criticism by scholars.

The question has been asked, Why were the Maya so different than other ancient civilizations? They appear out of place in time and space, with no preceding or contemporary neighboring cultures possessing similarly sophisticated sciences and technology. By comparison, the science and technology applied by the Roman, Egyptian, and Greek civilizations relied on past and contemporary cultures for scientific and technological input, which they incorporated into their own concepts and applications.

An isolated tropical rainforest environment is an unlikely setting for the incubation of a great civilization. By comparison, all other great ancient civilizations developed in the northern hemisphere between latitudes 30 degrees north and 60 degrees north. These northern latitude cultures developed in arid landscapes based on the elite management of water systems and irrigated systems of agriculture. The common element linking these ancient civilizations was a riverine subsistence; they emerged along great rivers of the world including the Nile in Egypt, the Indus River in India, the Tigris and Euphrates rivers in Mesopotamia, and the Yangtze in China. In contrast to these ancient cultures, the Maya civilization emerged in the verdant rainforest of the Yucatán Peninsula without the benefit of great rivers. The Maya homeland lies well below the Tropic of Cancer at 20 degrees north latitude, a great distance south of the other Classic civilizations, and is sited in a tropical environment largely devoid of rivers or other surface waters. The environmental and geographic location of the nascence of the Maya civilization defies conventional anthropological wisdom.

The ancient Maya were avid sky-watchers. After millennia of observations and study of the heavens, they gained an uncanny knowledge of the harmonious composition of the cosmos. Their keen interest in the vast expanse and wonder of the universe and the interlocking movement of astral bodies evolved into their quadripartite philosophy of the cosmos. This philosophy, combined with their fascination of the periodicity of astral bodies, motivated them to develop scientific disciplines that enabled them to track heavenly bodies and mathematically calculate the quantity and quality of time, predict astronomical events, and maintain accurate written records.

Maya Cosmic Philosophy

The ancient Maya peered with fascination and awe into the transparent night sky. For 1,500 years before the Classic Period, they observed the panoply of brilliant lights arrayed across the firmament and studied the roaming motion of the planets, the orb of fixed stars, the most remote of celestial spheres, and the slow motion of our own galaxy. Zealous sky-watching and understanding the complex periodic roaming of astral bodies, combined with a millennium of profound thinking, generated a knowledge of astronomy and the principals and dimensions of time. These ancient stargazers became the ancient world's greatest astronomers. Their knowledge of time and the universe grew into the veneration of the cosmos and the development of their cosmic philosophy.

The Maya quadripartite cosmic philosophy combined space and time into a single concept similar to the space-time idea of modern physics. This is a mathematical model that unifies space with time as a four-dimensional continuum (thus the term *quadripartite*). To visualize the concept, its spatial geometry can be characterized as a four-dimensional body composed of the three spatial directions plus time (x, y, z, t). An event is specified by its time and place.

The Maya were obsessed with time, which they viewed both as linear and cyclic. They were interested not only in the quantities but the qualities of time, believing that it was a living being that had a personality. The Maya viewed time as the undifferentiated past, present, and future. These principles enabled scientists to calculate simultaneous projections of astral movements with their quality and quantity of time: forward (positive time) into the future and backward (negative time) into the historical past. Their mathematical capabilities expanded to include calculations that created large array numbers enabling the projection of positive time millions of years into the future and negative time millions of years into the past. This belief system became a precept that recognized linear time, which is similar to viewing historical time periods, as well as the cyclical characteristics of time. Today, we would view the concept of cyclical time as "history repeating itself."

The cosmic philosophy, with its elements of temporal cycling, was the basis for Maya political, theological, and economic organization. The planning of seminal events and activities in politics, theology, economics, and everyday life were based on the principles of temporal cycling. The Maya used their astronomical capabilities to forecast future and past celestial events. These predictive capabilities became a mandate for elite decision-making and were applied for the scheduling of salient future events. These same skills were used to look backward in history, mathematically projecting back into the past with negative time. This enabled the Maya to look back and identify and date cosmic and historical events, which were then cycled forward to future dates, and establish place marks in time for scheduling important events. This sophisticated scientific discipline enabled the Maya to "remember the future and to anticipate the past."

The Maya cosmic philosophy motivated their requirement for calculating time and events millions of years into the past and astral movements millions of years into the future. These practices required knowledge of higher mathematics and became the stimulus for development of their elegant mathematics and astronomy. The need for accurate records of narrative astronomical findings and mathematical accounts of past and future events resulted in a sophisticated written language. The skills of Maya scientists in astronomy, calendrics, mathematics, and the application of a concise comprehensive written script enabled the preservation of records including calculations of astronomical tables, astral observations, historical narratives, and scientific practices. The written language enabled the Maya to enhance their scientific skills and preserve their knowledge for future generations.

Maya Scientific Achievements

The Maya were the last of the ancient civilizations to flower on our planet and were the last of the "overlooked" civilizations. Scientifically, the Maya were never succeeded and barely influenced by another indigenous culture; the remains of the Classic Maya culture are intact and fixed in time. The primary scientific disciplines developed by the Maya were interrelated and interfaced with the tenets of their cosmic philosophy. Maya sciences included astronomy, mathematical computation, calendrics, and a concise written script that unveiled the capabilities and accomplishments of a sophisticated and highly developed civilization. The Maya scientific achievements developed in the near isolation of the rainforest were remarkable.

Maya Astronomy

The Maya were ardent watchers of the night sky and became devout horologists. Their advanced knowledge of astronomy and calculations of astronomical periods were not surpassed until later centuries. Maya astronomers achieved accurate reckoning of time periods through the calculation and prediction of the movement of astral bodies, eclipses, and precession of the earth's axis without the aid of optical instruments. They developed accurate constants using naked eye observations aided by simple instruments, specialized astronomical structures, and careful visual observations over lengthy time periods. The instruments employed by Maya astronomers included handheld sighting tubes, vertical alignment tubes in the roofs of buildings, and vertical poles to ascertain the zenith passage of the sun and planets. Building alignments and articulated openings in buildings were employed to align and measure line of sight astronomical events.

Maya astronomers computed the time period of the earth's rotation around the sun with an accuracy that is comparable to that of modern astronomers with sophisticated optical and digital instruments. For example, the Maya calculated the length of the solar year to be 365.242 days; modern astronomers calculate the solar year to be 365.242198 days. This is only a difference of 0.000198 days per year. The Dresden Codex tracks the moon over a period of 405 lunar months or 11,960 days. These calculations produce an accurate period of 29.5302 days for a lunar month. Modern calculations yield a period for a lunar month equal to 29.53059 days. This a minute difference of 0.00039 days. Their calculations of the synodical period of Venus were calculated as 583.92027 days, compared to 583.93 days by modern calculations. Their uncanny capabilities also included the synodical period of Mars, which was calculated by the Maya to be 780, days compared to modern calculations of 779.94 days.

The Maya were among the only ancient astronomers to quantify and recognize the relevance of the wobble or period of precession of the earth's axis. They introduced this phenomenon of time and motion into their calendrics and cosmic philosophy. They accurately calculated the period of precession at approximately 25,800 years. The Maya divided the time of the earth's precession into five periods and introduced the periods into their calendrics as world ages. The present period of world age initiated on August 28, 3114 BC and will terminate on December 21, 2012. Then the new world age will initiate on December 22, 2012 (Figure 3-1).

The Maya knew that the earth was round and that the sun was the center of our solar system. To our modern technological culture, the extraordinary accuracy of Maya astronomers appears to surpass belief, considering their sophisticated knowledge of the astronomical sciences was achieved without the aid of optical instruments, chronometers, and digital tools. Their success at accurate astronomical calculating, although appearing implausible, was the result of millennia of time in a long-term thought process, native ingenium, and mathematics inspired by their cosmic philosophy.

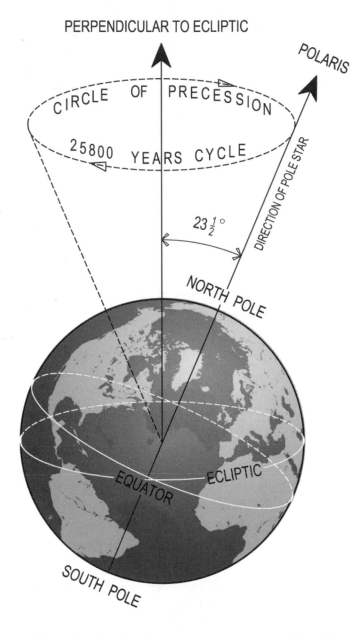

Figure 3-1: The Earth's precession was calculated by Maya astronomers. Image by Alex Tuan Nguyen.

Maya Mathematics

The mathematical system of the Maya was initially developed to track astronomical events and was then extrapolated to track quantities of time, designating place marks in future and past time periods. Their system was then adapted for practical use by technicians, engineers, bureaucrats, and merchants.

The Maya mathematical system was unique, flexible, and incredibly simple. The system used a vigesimal base of 20, rather than the decimal base of 10 used in Western mathematics. Maya mathematics was sophisticated enough to calculate and track massive numbers with the use of just three basic symbols: a dot, a bar, and an ellipse. The Maya mathematical system made possible the basic mathematical functions of addition, subtraction, multiplication, and division, as well as enabled functions using positional systems to develop calculations of large numbers. Advanced functions of Maya mathematics included the concept of the number zero and a positional system enabling large numbers. Carved symbols on Maya monuments have indicated large array numbers well beyond the range of 41,943,040,000,000,000,000,000,000,000,000. It is not known how these massive numbers were applied to Maya life and philosophy; they must be related to time and cosmic matters, because these numerical values were larger than those that could be related to measurable earthly commodities.

The Maya mathematical system was vastly superior to those of the Romans, Greeks, and Egyptians, which were limited to calculating limited magnitudes and numbers in the positive range. The manipulation of numbers by the Classic civilizations was limited to addition and subtraction. Maya mathematicians developed the concept of the number zero 1,200 years before Europeans learned of the concept from Arab scholars (Figure 3-2). The Maya mathematical system is highly flexible and is exquisitely proportioned for astronomical calculations, large array calendric numbers, and practical applications for technical matters, engineering analysis, bookkeeping, and census tabulations. Europeans did not use large array numbers until Isaac Newton invented calculus to calculate astronomical synchronization.

Additionally, the Maya number system was used in speech and written communication. Though traces of their mathematical calculations in books or on paper did not survive the conquest, it can be logically assumed that the mathematical system was used to generate the numbers indicated in the script carved on monuments and contained in codices.

Maya Written Script

The Maya developed a complete writing system, which enabled them to write anything they wanted in their own language. The Maya script is considered to be one of the world's five original writing systems, as well as one of the most complex written languages. The written language is a combination of syllabograms (phonetic characters) and logograms (characters expressing meaning).

The writing system was probably first generated as a recordkeeping process for astronomical purposes, then became intertwined with the other sciences by embedding mathematical symbols into the script. The writing system then evolved to include diverse applications associated with the scientific, technical, socio-political, artistic, religious, and historical aspects of the Maya culture. The combination of the script and the Long Count calendar enabled the Maya to provide dates on documents and monuments, allowing them to dispatch dated, long-range communications in writing.

Examples of the hieroglyphic writing are rare in Maya literature, considering only four Maya books survived the Spanish conquest. However, hieroglyphics are carved into the artwork that adorns the facades of the architectural wonders flanking the plazas of the great cities, and glyphs are painted on ceramic vases and wall murals. All of these contributed to the decipherment and offered up the secrets of the Maya (Figure 3-3).

Maya Achievements in Technology

As the Maya scientific culture developed and the affluent elite classes became more sophisticated and wealthy, Maya towns expanded into cities and then evolved into sprawling metropolitan power centers. The needs and wants of the stratified urban society became more defined as the cities burgeoned and became more complex. Urban areas needed to construct monumental and multipurpose buildings, served by a sophisticated infrastructure that included water-management systems and efficient transportation.

Inventive Maya technologies were used to overcome the difficulties of the natural environment, develop high-strength materials for construction, invent innovative structural mechanics for long-span structures, devise

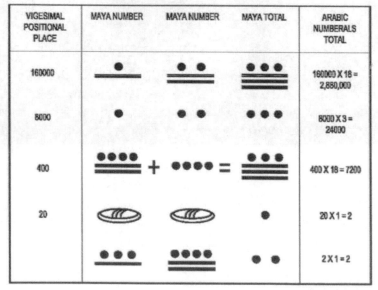

THIS IS THE BASIC MAYA NUMBER SYSTEM

MAYA NUMBER CHART

VIGESIMAL POSITIONAL PLACE	MAYA NUMBER	MAYA NUMBER	MAYA TOTAL	ARABIC NUMERALS TOTAL
160000				160000 X 18 = 2,880,000
8000				8000 X 3 = 24000
400				400 X 18 = 7200
20				20 X 1 = 2
				2 X 1 = 2

TOTAL = 2,911,222

EXAMPLE OF MAYA MATHEMATICS
ADDITION OF TWO NUMBERS USING THE MAYA POSITIONAL SYSTEM OF MATHEMATICS.
EACH VERTICAL LEVEL INCREASES THE PREVIOUS LEVEL BY 20 FOLD.
ADDITION IS SIMILAR TO STANDARD MATH, CARRY OVER SUMS GREATER THAN 20 VERTICALLY.

MAYA MATHEMATICS

Figure 3-2: Maya mathematics were vigesimal, or based on 20, and not 10 like our mathematics. Image by Alex Tuan Nguyen.

durable substitutes for metal tools, construct efficient transport systems, and create agriculture systems that enhanced food production. The Maya, the Americas' first civil engineers, combined these innovations to implement the structures and infrastructure systems that created the sophisticated urban fabric of the world's largest cities of their time.

Tool Fabrication

Maya technology overcame the lack of native metallic ore. They developed specialized tools, harder than iron, for the fine working of stone and wood. These tools enabled Maya technicians and artists to create great works of finely detailed art and architecture. Specialized tools fabricated from jadeite, a material harder that steel, enabled Maya builders and artisans to construct structures of grand architecture replete with finely carved stone friezes. They made the world's sharpest cutting blades from obsidian, a volcanic glass. This Maya technology has extended to contemporary medical practice: obsidian is currently used for scalpels in surgery.

Hydraulic Cement and Cast-in-Place Concrete

Maya technicians invented the methodology for producing hydraulic cement from native limestone. This cement was used as the basis for the production of cast-in-place concrete, which was used to construct strong and durable structures that were the hallmarks of Classic Maya cities. Cement was also the base material for the stucco that coated the Maya structures and the mortar that was vital to the construction of masonry structures. Cement was the technological "glue" used to hold the Maya cities together and enabled their structures to withstand 2,000 years of a harsh environment. This technologically innovative material enabled Maya high rise cities to remain standing today as a tribute to the glory of Maya technology.

Long-Span and High-Rise Structures

The Classic Maya cities were the world's most populous of their time in history. High-rise buildings reaching into the tropical sky presented a spectacular profile against the backdrop of the rainforest canopy. These momentous landmarks would not have been possible to construct without the structural mechanisms developed by Maya engineers. These innovative technicians invented the vaulted arch, high-rise structural systems, and other mechanisms that enabled the construction of long-span, high-rise buildings which characterized the skyline of Maya power centers.

Figure 3-3: Maya developed one of the world's five original written languages. Illustration by Mark Van Stone.

Water-Management Systems

The Maya population and its grand cities existed in a harsh natural environment that divided the year into wet and dry seasons. In response, they developed a series of unique technical solutions to satisfy the constant threat of thirst for the large cities, as well as water for agriculture irrigation systems. Maya engineering solutions included shaped cityscapes designed to divert storm water into storage facilities, underground reservoirs for urban water supplies, water filtration systems, and efficient irrigation systems for agriculture. These civil engineering systems enabled the survival and prosperity of the Maya power centers.

The Maya Superhighway System

The difficulty of travel through the tangled roots of the dense jungle environment was a laborious effort that was made more difficult by the quagmire created during the rainy season. An efficient all-weather transport system was absolutely necessary to maintain levels of power and wealth, while operating an efficient government for the city-states. To solve transport issues relating to commerce, military movements, agriculture, and general travelers, Maya engineers developed a system of elevated paved highways that connected their power centers. All-weather roads, known as *sacbeob* (singular *sacbe*), or "white roads," provided the Maya with a reliable road system that could be used as year-round transportation. Hundreds of miles of these roads were constructed during the Classic Period.

Maya Bridge Engineering

The rainy season brought needed storm water for replenishment of precious water supplies in the cities and for irrigation in the hinterlands. However, the rainy season, with its heavy amount of storm water, caused flooded rivers for a period of six months. Maya engineering rose to the occasion by producing creative bridge designs of various types and spans, including cast-in-place concrete bridges, timber bridges, and long-span rope or cable suspension bridges that crossed broad flooded rivers. The Maya constructed a long-span suspension bridge across the wild Usumacinta River at the city of Yaxchilan. This bridge, constructed with a center span of 63 meters, is considered to be the longest bridge in the ancient world.

The Maya Transportation System

The North American continent and the area of the Maya world did not evolve native animals that could be domesticated as beasts of burden. The horse, oxen, and other beasts of burden were European imports to the Americas. However, large amounts of manpower were available for power applications. Maya technology understood the principle of the wheel, using them on toys, but the wheel was not viable for use on carts using manpower. Instead, they creatively developed man-powered transport systems that were more efficient and economical than animal-powered transport. The adventurous and resourceful Maya were also sea traders who developed seagoing cargo vessels that enabled long-range trade routes.

How Did They Know What They Knew?

Epistemology is the study of the nature, methods, and validity of knowledge and belief. It deals with the production of knowledge and asks the question, How do we know what we know? In the case of the scientific knowledge of the Maya, the question can be asked, How did they know what they knew? A hypothesis could be developed that argues the stimulus for the development of knowledge can be assumed to be their belief in a quadripartite cosmic philosophy. Further, the Maya had real time working in their favor; they efficiently applied 1,500 years of Pre-Classic and 600 years of Classic Period studies to elevate their knowledge of the sciences.

The methods used by the Maya to acquire new levels knowledge are familiar to scientists and researchers today. These techniques include the scientific method, heuristic methodologies, *a priori* knowledge, and comparative studies. These methods were applied to enhance the development of the basic scientific disciplines espoused by the Maya. Additionally, comparative studies, similar to logic developed by modern anthropologists, are theories based on the discovery that different cultures on similar levels of cultural complexity will solve similar solutions when faced with similar problems. This includes the invention of writing and mathematics when the society has reached a level that requires these knowledge tools

When considering the wealth of scientific disciplines cultivated by the Maya, astronomy was obviously the first of the sciences to be developed. The light show featuring heavenly orbs shining above the Maya world were on revue on a nightly basis millions of years before their time. The dazzling sight of the light show filled the ancient observers with wonder and fascination. The Maya studied the galaxy for centuries and embedded the complexities of the cosmos into their accumulated knowledge.

The results of astronomical studies and observations were first transmitted by oral tradition. The movement of planets eclipses of the sun and moon, as well as the names of stars, planets, and constellations, were passed down by orally until writing was developed. Astronomical knowledge was enhanced during the centuries of the Pre-Classic Period, and Maya astronomers pooled their ideas, enabling them to generate intellectual concepts of the qualities and quantities of time and introduce this concept into their philosophy of life.

The process of counting the days and years of astral periods led to the development of mathematics. The study of astronomy and calendrics spawned and stimulated a need for numerical recordkeeping. This led to the manipulation of numbers for mathematical computations of astral cycles and time periods, and then evolved into a complete mathematical system. Initially, mathematics used the dot and bar symbology, but advancement in the capabilities and complexities of mathematical functions such as the application of negative numbers required the introduction of the number zero, so the shell symbol came into being. It is interesting that this symbol forming an oval shape representing "nothing" is very similar to the Arabic symbol for zero, which has been adopted by international mathematicians. It has been suggested that the basic mathematical symbols were derived by the use of a pebble for a single unit and a line or stick to represent five units. This use of only two symbols was practical when low value numbers were involved, but the system of pebbles and bars became cumbersome when large numbers were enumerated.

Maya mathematicians used their intellect to develop more concise methods of interpreting and recording large numbers. Recordkeeping methodologies could have taken several formats, including the use of slates for marking the counts of days, then stucco walls marked with graphite crayons serving as tote boards for recording larger tallies of heavenly activities. As time passed, necessity ultimately led to the invention of paper, symbology, and the ink brush, and the development of the book for recordkeeping. This led to the production of numerous books relating to various matters and gave rise to the libraries

The need to express large array numbers led to the development of the positional mathematical system, in which each vertical level of mathematical notation was increased 20 fold. This system permitted Maya mathematicians to raise their calculations to 160,000 after five levels, to 3,200,000 after six levels, and to 64,000,000 after seven levels. The application of this method of calculations led to concise calculations that would require minimum space on a leaf of paper. With the positional number system and the concept of the number zero, it became possible to calculate and project time periods millions of years into the future and calculate negative umbers representing millions of years into the past.

The tie that bound the integral sciences together was the development of a precise written script. This script intertwined astronomy, mathematics, and the narratives required to record the activities of Maya science in order to provide students and future generations with guidelines and direction for the application of science, laws, and practical matters. The production of subsequent written records was not maintained by a single person but by generations of sky-watchers. As their corpus of knowledge grew, the specialists in astronomy developed the need to accurately describe the motions of astral bodies. The scenario for the development of Maya script paralleled the sciences of astronomy and mathematics. Both sciences required sophisticated symbology for recording the cycles of astral bodies, recordkeeping, calculations, mathematics results, and practical terminology.

The development of the script could have started as a method for naming astral bodies, stars, and constellations, and then evolved to include numbers relating to periods of time and other astronomical terminologies. As part of learning to interpret the symbols used to describe an activity, the reader became a party in the development of the symbology. The contribution of new symbols to the corpus of known and accepted symbols introduced new concepts and enhanced the script into an efficient communication system. The symbols served to objectify the elements of astronomy, mathematics, history, and the other sciences. The creative power of scientific terms and words converted to symbols enhanced the scope and abilities of the script as a medium of communication. The dissemination of the Maya script, acceptance of known symbols, and introduction of new symbols caused the script to evolve into a concise, phonetic written language. The scientific arts, philosophical ideas, and conventional discourse communicated by the Maya script enabled permanent recording of these concepts for contemporary use and future application for the intellectual elite, power elite, technological society,and merchant classes.

The Maya script, calendar, and mathematics were developed prior to the Classic Period. The first known Maya script was from 250 BC and was found on painted walls in San Bartolo in Guatemala. At this time, the Maya script, system of mathematics, astronomical sciences, and cosmic philosophy appeared to be fully formed. There is little evidence of the formative stages of Maya script or other sciences.

This scenario describing the development of the Maya scientific society is based on research, comparative studies, and knowledge of Maya achievements, tracing it from a group of from ancient sky-watchers, to fledgling scientists, to interdisciplinary scientists. It is apparent that as the sciences developed through the Pre-Classic Period, Maya society became more stratified and sophisticated as the classes of power elite, intellectual elite, the class of specialists, as well as a merchant class grew into prominence. With their growing sophistication and wealth, Maya villages grew into towns, the towns expanded into cities, and the cities blossomed into the world's largest urban centers, which were built and maintained with sophisticated, innovative technology.

4

What Are Stone Age People Doing With the Number Zero?

World-famous archaeologists have described the Maya civilization using various retrogressive anthropological terminologies including Stone Age culture, early Neolithic Age culture, and brilliant aboriginal people. Yet, the question may be asked, If the Maya were an aboriginal, Neolithic culture without metallurgy or practical use of the wheel, what were they doing with a mathematical system of exquisite refinement, other pure sciences, and technical capabilities that surpassed that of Western civilization by more than a millennium? The archaeological classification of the Maya as a Stone Age people compares this civilization with a cultural time period that had terminated in Europe some 10,000 years before the golden age of the Maya. Is the classification of the Maya as a Stone Age culture the fault of the Maya for not having a natural source of metal available for tool fabrication, or is it due to a flaw in the standard archaeological nomenclature for defining the cultural and technical sophistication of a society with the material used to manufacture tools, weapons, and other implements?

Archeology has adopted a badly skewed nomenclature for the classification of ancient cultures, but then how do you classify a unique culture that prospered long after the fall of the Roman Empire and was ascending to greatness when Europe was wallowing in a period of political disarray and educational morass? Furthermore, this lost civilization was discovered intact with its art, architecture, and literature preserved for collection and study by scientific disciplines. The answer to the intellectual levels and achievements of the Maya are well known, but the classification of their technological level has not been upgraded.

This archaeological nomenclature for the classification of cultures includes a three-age system of developmental levels, with subsequent ages identified by the type of material used to fabricate tools and weapons used by that culture. This archaeological nomenclature was not derived from the collected wisdom of archaeological studies, but was adopted from a system of age classification used to curate the ancient tools and weapons at a 19th-century Danish national museum. This work was developed during the early beginnings of archaeology and today is still part of the basic conceptual imagery of defining the intellectual level of a culture.

The Growth of Archaeology and Its Audience

The discipline of archaeology had roots that grew out the interests of a few erudite scholars. The initiation of the study of antiquities began more than 500 years ago and has matured into a well-respected field of study, one that has captured the imagination and interest of the public, caught up in the thrill of archaeological discoveries. The studies of classical antiquity emerged in Italy during the 15th-century Renaissance. Initially the interest in antiquities was purely literary. This interest led to the desire to identify the actual sites of the references in the texts. During the 16th century, architects were exploring the ruins of Roman buildings and collecting ancient statues to embellish the palaces of their patrons. Antiquarian research resulted in the excavation of Herculaneum in 1709 and Pompeii in 1748.

Classical antiquity aroused the intense curiosity of scholars across Europe. Scholars wrote volumes that proved to be milestones in art history, with narratives and illustrations of monuments with origins in ancient cultures. Meanwhile, individuals and government collectors looted the sites in Italy and Greece of vases, statues, sections of buildings, and other antiquities.

The organized scientific study of ancient civilizations began with Napoleon's invasion of Egypt in 1798, allegedly to conduct a comprehensive survey of Egypt antiquities. In 1799, the French brought 167 archaeologists and scientists to the region. The most noted archaeological finding of the survey was the discovery of the Rosetta Stone. This Ptolemaic Era stele is composed of granodiorite and carved with a bilingual inscription in ancient Egyptian, in both hieroglyphic and demonic script, and the same passage written in ancient Greek characters. The Rosetta Stone became the possession of the British in 1801, as part of the Treaty of Alexandria; it was transported to London, and placed in the British Museum.

Credit for the first full translation of the Rosetta Stone was carried out by the French scholar Jean François Champollion in 1824. The feat earned him a place in history, and his name is a synonym for code breakers. He became the patron saint of epigraphers, and the Rosetta Stone became an icon of epigraphy. The breaking of the code of the mysterious Egyptian hieroglyphics caught the attention of the public.

The Rosetta Stone was not the only archaeological discovery that interested the world. Many more followed. Heinrich Schliemann (1822–1887) is justly hailed as the founder of Aegean archaeology. Fueled by a large business fortune, Schliemann could afford to pursue his passion for archaeology. Convinced of the accuracy of the Homeric epics, he carried out excavations identified in the epic poems. His pioneering paved the way for excavation of long series of Pre-Classic sites. Schliemann's discovery of Troy and the romance of finding the jewelry of Helen of Troy held the public in rapture.

The 1842 discovery of the lost pre-Colombian Maya civilization caught the interest of the world and ignited the imagination of the reading public. The chatty narrative of John Lloyd Stephens and the meticulous drawings of Frederick Catherwood are some the finest pre-photographic records of archaeology. The two-volume sets of their discoveries became runaway best-sellers, spreading across the globe and rewriting history. Similarly, the discovery of the boy-king Tutankhamun's tomb in 1922 by archaeologist Howard Carter caught the world's fancy. Archaeology began to mature, and with its maturation brought a growing market demand for books, films, and touristic visitations to archaeological sites.

The Development of the Three-Age System

The initial effort toward creating order out of the chaotic nature of prehistoric antiquity came from Danish antiquarian Christian Jorgensen Thomsen. In 1806, the Danish government established a commission, of which Thomsen was secretary, to assess the geology and natural history of the area. In 1816, the Danish crown established a national museum, and Thomsen was selected as its first curator. The collection in the museum included a large and eclectic array of ancient tools, hunting weapons, and other artifacts. Thomsen surveyed the collection of weapons and tools and made the logical decision to display the artifacts based on the materials from which they were made. He separated the artifacts into three types of material: stone, bronze, and iron. With the tools and weapons divided into these three divisions, Thomsen then determined that the three categories represented consecutive time periods for the ordered sequence of the technological development of a culture. Thus the three-age system of nomenclature was established. The Thomsen "three ages" concept was adopted in 19th-century Germany. The three age concept became widely used by scholars, museums, and the discipline of archaeology.

In 1865, John Labboch published what was considered to be one of the finest archaeology theses on pre-historic times, a seminal book that further advances the three-age concept by subdividing the Stone Age into a Paleolithic phase and Neolithic phase. Paul Reinescke (1872–1958) further embedded the three ages into archaeological theory when he developed a sequence for the Bronze Age and the Iron Age of Central Europe. The concept of the three ages became incorporated into archaeology theory, while subdivisions of the three ages into successive stages have remained the standard for classification of cultures.

The three-age system is either too vague or not applicable for the classification of a complex civilization. Although the three ages of stone, bronze, and iron made sense to the emerging discipline of archaeology in the early 19th century, the classification system was based on insufficient data. It measured only material artifacts and did not consider socio-political, artistic, architectural, scientific, and economic aspects of a society. The concept is Eurocentric and is difficult to apply outside of Europe and the Mediterranean. It totally fails when assessing a civilization without access to metal ores. Furthermore, the three-age system of civilization relative to the progress of their technology can be misinterpreted. The Stone Age of European cultures from 12,000 BC was not concurrent with African or American cultures. Moreover, some societies skipped the Bronze Age and went directly from Stone Age technology into the Iron Age.

Since Thomsen formulated the three-age concept, archaeology has adopted numerous scientific methodologies for researching the age and origin of a culture and its artifacts, including amino acid dating, radiocarbon dating, thermoluminescence, magnetic dating, and DNA analysis in the fields of paleo-botany, paleo-climatology, archaeo-astronomy, paleo-ecology, paleo-entomology, and paleo-ethnology. However, archaeology has not advanced a comprehensive methodology for classifying the technology of cultures based on their overall intellectual and societal development.

Unfortunately, archaeology has inadvertently misled the public in defining relative technological levels of our ancient past. This is the public who constitutes the clientele and market for archaeology. The credo of science is "stick to the facts." Archaeology can't draw an accurate picture of the capabilities of a culture from a bare minimum of facts. The public has been left with the impression that stone tools and the Stone Age appellation represent the total extent of Maya technology. The lack of an advanced system of nomenclature may be because the majority of ancient civilizations had been discovered and studies of their development had been well advanced before the rediscovery of the Maya civilization was introduced to the world in 1842.

The market for archaeology has grown into a multibillion-dollar business. The tourist business attracting visitors to archaeological sites has become the premier financial source in many countries. For the older traveler, few experiences can match the pleasure of archaeological sites set in exotic places with strange-sounding names. The younger traveler is attracted to archaeological sites located in ecologically protected environments. The hospitality business in these areas is booming and creating employment for thousands of local workers. The film industry has capitalized on the glamour and thrills attached to romantic adventures and discoveries of lost civilizations.

However, little of the funds from tourists interested in archaeology are directed to the bank accounts of dirt archaeologists. These devoted individuals survive by university teaching part of the year and spend the remainder of the year excavating archaeological sites. This dichotomy is part of the reason that research necessary for establishing a clear, concise, and logical set of archaeological guidelines for defining levels of civilization has not progressed. The guidelines would be based on intellectual and scientific achievements, societal advancement, technological accomplishment, and division of labor. The nomenclature for a culture should not be based on the materials they used for tools and weapons.

The Stone Age Mindset of Maya Archaeologists

When Stephens and Catherwood stumbled on the power centers of the Classic Maya, 170 years ago, they had indeed found a lost civilization, but one that was "lost" only in the eyes of the beholders. Exploration and investigation of this brilliant civilization was slow to start, and then it was retarded by professional arrogance.

By the end of the 19th century, scientific archaeologists such as Alfred Maudslay, Joseph Goodman, and Herbert J. Spenden had analyzed the Maya mathematical system and published seminal works. The correlation between the Maya calendar and the Gregorian calendar was verified and completed in 1927. Maya archaeologists had explored many of the great Maya cities, and views of their art and architecture were published and recognized to be unlike any styles in the world. Maya mathematics and astronomical systems were becoming recognized as brilliant representations of an advanced society.

However, fathers of Maya archaeology were confined by the three-age system and its Eurocentric attitudes toward levels of civilization. Sylvanus Griswold Morley, one of the most sensitive of the early Maya archaeologists, in his publication *Guidebook to the Ruins of Quirigua*, established the groundwork for a negative archaeological attitude and represents the prevailing view of the Maya at that time. In this volume he stated:

> When the material achievements of the ancient Maya in architecture, sculpture, ceramics, the lapidary arts...are added to their abstract intellectual achievements—invention of positional mathematics with its concomitant development of the zero, construction of an elaborate chronology with a fixed starting point, use of a time count as accurate as our own calendar, knowledge of astronomy superior to that of Egyptians and Babylonians—and the whole is judged in the light of their known cultural limitations were on a par with those of the early Neolithic age in the Old World. We may acclaim them, without fear of successful contradiction, the most brilliant aboriginal people on the planet.

Morley has high praise for their intellectual and scientific achievements. However, he considered the Maya civilization to be Neolithic and aboriginal. These terms conjure up images of cave men living off insects and using stone axes to bash heads rather than the reality of a scientific, intellectual society living in large cities with high-rise structures that would not be replicated for another millennium. The use of these terms relegates the Maya civilization to the lowest rung on the civilization ladder. Morley did not observe metal tools, therefore the Maya were classified as Neolithic. Actually, using the three-age system, the status of Neolithic was high praise. He could have called them Mesolithic or just plain old Stone Age.

In Morley's book *The Ancient Maya*, published in 1946 and still in print as a basic textbook for archaeology updated by Robert Sharer, he continues to refer to the Maya as a Stone Age people. He viewed Maya technology as Stone Age technology. It was obvious that archaeologists did not uncover metal objects or a practical use of the wheel. To Morley's astonishment, the Maya were able to create elevated levels of science, art, and architecture of a harmonic aesthetic that surpassed Old World civilizations. After decades of discovery and study, Morley continued to reference the Maya civilization as "primitive."

Eric Thompson, a giant in Maya archaeology, was Morley's contemporary. Thompson, who is discussed in Chapter 2, controlled the process of decipherment of the Maya script and is considered to have repressed the advancement of decipherment for nearly a half century. Eric Thompson is the author or two seminal works: *Maya Hieroglyphic Writing* and *A Catalogue of Mayan Hieroglyphics*. Thompson wrote from his ivory tower at the Carnegie Institution. His disdain for the achievements of the Maya was apparent. He considered the Maya to be a culture of idiot savants. He could not envision how or why the Maya created esoteric astronomical calculations, higher mathematics, or a concise calendar. He considered their sciences to be an obsession, but could not envision the purpose for their work. He did grasp the concept of the Maya cosmic philosophy. Thompson judged the Maya's accomplishments by the measure of European Renaissance civilization.

The use of the three-age system continues today. If an archaeologist does not encounter metal artifacts in his studies of a culture, then by the rule of the trinity of the three ages, the culture must be Stone Age. What other alternative does the researcher have as a reference for a cultural technology? The multitude of works published by the new generation of Mayanists praise the sciences and philosophy that constitute the knowledge of the Maya, but prejudice the general public and archaeology by referring to the Maya as a Stone Age people. Change in archaeology is slow. The three-age system is in effect, and no archaeologist wishes to have academic criticism come crashing down on him or her for publishing revisionist nomenclature for classifying a culture. A classification that reflects a civilization's achievements in abstract intellectual attainment, sciences, technology, mathematics, calendrics, astronomy, writing systems, divisions of labor, management systems, and the sensitivity of its art and architecture, is needed, and one such classification exists.

Morley and Thompson, as well as other leaders in the archaeological field, never missed a chance to defame the Maya for their known "cultural limitations," including the lack of metallurgy and the practical use of the wheel for transport. As it has been pointed out, the karstic limestone geology of the Maya zone did not include ore from which iron can be extracted. The closest deposits of iron ore are 1,500 miles to the north. The Maya overcame this shortfall of Mother Nature by exploiting the unique materials that are products of the subduction zone of tectonic plates. These materials were harder than iron and sharper than steel. To recognize these technical achievements of the Maya, an active imagination and a rich engineering background are required. An archaeological education has not equipped the practioner to recognize these technological breakthroughs that bypass the technology of the Iron Age and venture into an advanced level of science and technology.

The Definition of a Civilization

Archaeology has had its opportunities to develop a logical and comprehensive system of nomenclature for the level of civilization in a culture. Vere Gordon Childe may be the world's most renowned archaeological theorist and a popularizer of archaeology with the public. His many publications presented a synthesis of archaeological knowledge in this vast and complex field in an authoritative and unique manner. Childe was a professor of archaeology at the University of Edinburgh and later the director of the Institute of Archaeology at the University of London. Childe coined the term *urban revolution* to define the change in a civilization from village-based societies to a science-based civilization living in large cities with a complex economic structure and social organization. He was one of the greatest archaeological synthesizers, attempting to place his archaeological observations on a wider world scale. Childe did not include the three ages in his definition of advanced civilization. He referenced bronze and iron metallurgy, but only as a measure of scientific progress rather than the standard that defined the level of achievement of a civilization. Childe's studies of ancient civilization included the Maya. Childe described the urban population of a city as the result of a progressive stage in the economic structure and social organization of communities. For Childe, it was the invention of writing, not the material of the tools of a civilization, that was the defining index of a civilization. He contended that the invention of writing coincided with a dramatic threshold in the economic and demographic structure of a civilization. Further, population growth and the development of sciences evolved into the growth of urban places with an advanced socio-political organization. Childe used the term *civilization* to define the critical turning point in a culture. He believed that the features that comprised a civilization evolved in a "revolutionary" fashion and is present in a culture that has reached a critical mass of complexity.

Childe believed that the development of an urban civilization was the result of the evolution of a society based on progressive change in the economic structure and social organization of a culture. He established guidelines that identify a civilization based on its level of technical advancement, its sciences, its cities, and urbanism:

1. Large urban centers.
2. Monumental architecture.
3. Ruling class that is exempt from manual labor.
4. Sophisticated styles of art.
5. Craft workers, merchants, officials, priests, supported by surplus food produced by farmers.
6. Systems for recording information (writing).
7. The development of exact sciences.
8. Long-range trade with the importation of materials both as luxury (prestige) goods and as raw materials.
9. Resident specialist craft workers politically and economically under the control of political officials.
10. Permanent and dominant state organizations.
11. Social solidarity of the community as represented by the preeminence of temples.
12. Primary producers paying surplus to a deity or a divine ruler (central authority).

The Maya civilization meets or exceeds the criteria for a civilization as defined by Childe. It is apparent that the use of the anachronistic and misplaced three-age system is not a measure for the civilization level of a culture. The lack of iron ore within the Maya zone was one of Mother Nature's practical jokes. Without iron ore you cannot make iron tools, but the Maya bypassed the Bronze and Iron Ages by their use of jadeite as a material for the fabrication of their tools. Archaeologists should consider the adoption of the Gordon Childe definition of civilization, which elevates the Maya to the top of the civilization scale, but if they insist on using the three-age system, they should consider classifying the Maya as "technolithic," a technologically advanced culture that did not have metal tools.

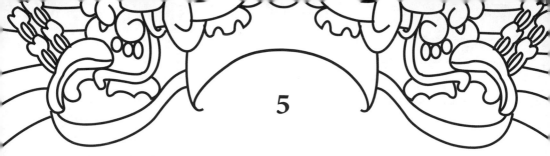

5

Building a Civilization

The artistic legacy of the Maya is one of the richest in the world. Their architecture, sculpture, and applied arts reached an extraordinary level of refinement and splendor during the Classic Period. The accumulated cultural wealth of centuries was expressed in the elaborate art styles of the monuments, sculpture, and refined architectural details of their cityscapes. Archaeologists, architects, and art historians have long been astonished by the sophistication of the artwork encountered in the high-rise cities of the Maya, as well as the sensitivity of their artistic work. The execution and integration of their graphic arts into the architecture of monumental buildings is unparalleled. The quality of Maya artistic skills in art and architecture rival the artistry produced by ancient civilizations of the Old World, and their accomplishments have established a stylistic framework that continues to inspire contemporary artists (Figure C-3).

Architecture as a Sculptural Art Form

The architectural design of the facades and the sculptural detailing of structural elements of the monumental buildings of the Maya were expressed as a cultural art form. Maya monumental structures were designed for practical applications and served as functional spaces, but were conceived as the symbolic representation of authority and economic power. Maya architects displayed a cultural uniformity in the functional space planning of their buildings. However, the most powerful and influential cities and regions developed distinct artistic styles that reflected localized concepts of philosophical symbology. As a result, art and architecture styles expressed regional differentiations, although the primary spatial design and structural elements of a specific building type remained somewhat similar throughout the Maya world. Trademark elements of regional style were reflected in the design of building facades, geometrical architectural patterns, pyramid massing, temple roof comb configurations, articulated stairways, column detailing, door lintels, stele, and carved pavement stones.

The monumental buildings are wonders of art and architecture; facades were lavishly decorated with finely carved sculpture that reflected the design style of that region and the artist's ability in composition and execution of detail. Facades in certain regions displayed sophisticated sculptural designs that depicted elaborately detailed supernatural monsters and dragon masks whose open jaws framed the entrance to the building. Other facade styles were resplendent with three-dimensional repetitions of effigies of gods, carved niches, stone columnettes, or complex geometrical latticework intertwined with three-dimensional representations of supernatural deities and bas-relief carvings of historical figures. Door lintels, constructed of stone or timber, were carved with stylistic depictions of gorgeously attired personages surrounded by script, scrollwork, serpents, jaguars, and other figures symbolizing the power of the rulers (Figure C-4).

Maya art and architecture were the centerpieces of the large verdant plazas sited at the center of their cities. The plazas were surrounded by prominent government buildings, palaces, temples, and universities. These architectural masterpieces were the palette on which Maya architects applied their most sophisticated style and complexity of design.

The most dramatic and easily recognized structure produced by the talents of Maya architecture was the Classic Period pyramid. The design of these towering structures relied on intricately worked sculptural stonework to create an upward stepping profile for the monolith. The top of the pyramids featured a platform supporting a vaulted temple structure. The temple was crowned by an elaborate roof comb soaring above the temple structure. The open latticework of the roof comb served as an armature that supported decorative figures and sound and light devices. The festooned roof comb included sculptural figures, reflecting mirrors, and wind chimes. The concept of a finely sculpted pyramid, with its dazzling roof comb towering high above the plaza, was intended to develop a sense of wonder in the eyes of the populace and enhance the power of the city-state.

The Sophistication of Maya Sculpture

The skilled stone-cutters and sculptors of the Maya construction industry worked as close-knit teams to create the unique artistic and architectural stonework that became the signatures of Maya cities. Talented sculptors were responsible for creating the complex architectural details that configured the structure of the buildings as well as the artful applications of regional style that adorned the facades of Maya structures. The intricate sophistication and detail of sculptural and carved stonework required hardened tools of varied size and geometry that met the high criteria for carving meticulous artwork.

Maya skill at sculptural art was unrivaled; experts in the world of art and architecture agree that the Maya mastered all the sculptural procedures and techniques that are accomplished by modern sculptors as well as the Old World artists. Artisans exhibited an extraordinary degree of sophistication in realism when representing the human figure. Three-dimensional facades of figures sculpted with poise and anatomically correct proportions became popular in the late Classic Period. Artistic expression in these works of art may represent supernatural figures participating in complex sequences in which they interact with human figures. The sculptures celebrated naturalistic styles.

Whereas their uncanny skill in realistic art was used for major works, bas-relief or low relief techniques were popular with Maya sculptors. Bas-relief is a sculptural technique wherein symbols or figures are raised above a flat background surface to give a three-dimensional effect to the work. Recessed relief, another carving technique, was used to provide a three-dimensional sculptural effect with the carved details recessed below the plane of the surface. In addition, a technique similar to intaglio was used. This technique creates an incised carving where images and symbology is finely engraved below the surface matrix of the stone.

Individual genius was encouraged and was clearly reflected in the artist's work. Sculptors were permitted to sign their finished work. The high social standing of leading artists is made clear from their titles included in the signatures. Their titles show that they were members of the nobility. It is apparent that there was a lively industry in sculptural studios and stone workshops. The production of art and architecture components developed as a major industry and became a major part of the broad range of Maya commerce.

Based on artistic and technical analysis, it is apparent that the complex and sophisticated Maya sculptural repertoire required specialized tools. These tools would be fabricated from a hard material shaped for specific carving tasks. Maya sculptors used tools with functional shapes that varied with the level of sculptural detail and finesse of the carving to be accomplished. For delicate dressing of stonework and for final shaping of a sculptural work, chisels of various sizes were used. These specialized chisels were used in conjunction with drills, awls, gouges, and mallets to execute a fine work. Archaeologists suggest that this complex sculptural work was done with chert and wood tools; however, art experts agree that this sophisticated artwork could only have been accomplished with specialized tools fabricated from a hardened material.

Carving Stone in the Stone Age

During the 170 years since the rediscovery of the lost civilization by John Lloyd Stephens and Frederick Catherwood, erudite scholars, accomplished sculptors, recognized art experts, and Mayanist archaeologists have closely studied the art and architecture bequeathed to the world by the ancient Maya. Experts have admired the sophisticated style and exotic mastery of the skilled and concise stone carving of their art and the intricate artistry of architectural detailing. Sophisticated and advanced as the Maya art and architecture have appeared, archaeologists have taken their artistic achievements for granted and ignored the obvious application of advanced technical methodology and specialized tools that were employed by Maya stone cutters and artisans to create the unparalleled works displayed on Maya monuments.

As discussed in Chapter 4, archaeologists have classified the Maya as a Stone Age culture. With this archaic mindset, the archaeological discipline has taken for granted the world-class art mastery and sculptural techniques used to create the monuments and monumental structures. They have not properly investigated the technology that fabricated the tools required to execute these fine art works. Because evidence of metal tools has not been detected *in situ*, archaeologists have assumed that Maya sculptural art was executed with rudimentary tools. Archaeological textbooks and lectures declare that the finely executed art and architecture of the Maya were executed with Neolithic tools.

On the other hand, experts in the fields of sculpture, art history, and architecture have closely studied the artistic works of the Maya. They consider it incomprehensible that these magnificent cities, towering architectural wonders, and sculpted monuments could have been executed with primitive tools. Their opinion is that the works of art created by Maya stone-cutters and artisans rival the finest art of Old World civilization and the notion of using Stone Age tools is an archaeological fairy tale. They opine that the monumental works of Maya artisans exhibit a special talent and artistic technology that is impossible to replicate without the use of specialized, high-strength tools, including chisels, drills, files, and gouges.

Archaeological textbooks barely mention the existence of Maya tools. However, when tools are referenced in textbooks, they describe Maya tools as flaked stone implements of chert, but the descriptive drawings on many of the same pages show smoothly shaped tools that are obviously fabricated of jadeite. Many of these books were published before 1950 when, as we shall see later in this chapter, geologists and archaeologists did not believe that sources of jadeite were located in the Americas. They believed that jadeite found in pre-Columbian sites was imported from the Orient. Therefore, an archaeologist would be up the archaeological creek without a paddle if he postulated that Maya tools were made from a material that was not native to the Americas. He would be criticized by the academic world even if he was right.

The Geology of the Maya World

The geological nature of the Maya zone ranges from a stable deep platform of karstic limestone beneath the Yucatán Peninsula, to an active volcanic belt stretching along the Pacific Coast, to kinetic and subduction movement between adjacent tectonic plates extending in an east-west direction across the landmass of Guatemala. The raw materials produced from these diverse geologic features were exploited by Maya engineers, and their unique characteristics benefited the development of their technology.

The porous limestone shelf that comprises the majority of the 125,000-square-mile area of the region had a negative factor on the environment; the porosity of the matrix quickly absorbed storm water, which deprived the region of surface water. On the positive side, limestone also provided an unlimited supply of raw materials for construction of the cities. Maya engineers exploited the unique products of volcanic and tectonic activities to develop and fabricate tools that built the Maya civilization.

Obsidian: Blades Sharper Than Steel

The arc of active volcanoes extending along the Pacific Coast produces lava flows containing a blend of minerals, including obsidian, a naturally occurring glass formed as an extrusive igneous rock. This rock is produced when felsic lava is extruded from a volcano and cools without crystalline growth. Obsidian is classified as a mineraloid because of its lack of a crystal structure. The presence of impurities, including iron and magnesium, in the matrix of obsidian give the material a dark green to brown and black color. Obsidian is harder than iron, with a hardness of 5.0 to 5.5 on the Mohs scale of mineral hardness, whereas iron has a relative hardness of 4.0 to 5.0 on the same scale. The source of the material is found in the volcanic highlands of Guatemala and is collected several ways: mined at source sites, recovered as nodules from riverbeds, or taken from fractured lava outcroppings. Obsidian became a valuable commodity, and trading flourished during the late Classic Period. The unprocessed material was transported overland and by trading vessels plying jungle rivers and the Caribbean to overseas markets.

Maya technicians recognized the valuable and practical physical characteristics of obsidian, including its ability to be fractured to produce ultra-sharp blades for tools and its capacity to be knapped to make decorative objects. Obsidian tools were applied to technical and utilitarian tasks that required a keen cutting edge. Its hardness and prismatic workability enabled Maya creativity to produce fine carving blades, knives, lances, projectile points, and other bi-facial tools. In addition, the attraction and luminosity of obsidian colors enabled craftsmen to fabricate luxury artifacts including labrets, pendants, figurines, ear spools, mirrors, and vases. Hafted obsidian tools with keen cutting edges were used for carving artwork, medical procedures, food preparation, agriculture, hunting, and multiple industrial applications.

The mining, transportation, fabrication, and distribution of obsidian products developed into a prosperous industry that contributed to the wealth of Maya city-states. The tools and artifacts shaped from obsidian offered numerous technical, ritual, and domestic applications, creating a broad market among the Maya and their trading partners. The plentiful products crossed all social-economic lines, and obsidian tools found their way into Maya homes, both elite and commoners. Obsidian technology was inexpensive, while requiring only the raw material and the skill of a knapper; it required a minimum of steps to fabricate an ultra-sharp tool. Obsidian was actually an economic alternative to the expensive and intensive labor enterprise of processing metal ore for tools.

Maya technicians unknowingly produced the world's sharpest blades from obsidian. The cutting edge of a well-crafted obsidian blade is much sharper than blades of modern, high-quality steel. The edges of obsidian blade approach molecular thickness with an edge honed to only 3 nanometers wide. When viewed through a microscope a steel blade has an irregular, jagged edge, an obsidian blade has a smooth, regular edge. The advanced cutting tools used by Maya technology have been adopted by modern surgical medicine. The unique cutting capabilities of obsidian blades are prized in surgical techniques where extremely fine cutting action is required or for scientific studies where trace metals from standard steel scalpels cannot be tolerated. Obsidian scalpels are so fine that they are preferred to steel scalpels in human surgical procedures where scar tissue might result from a coarse blade. Furthermore, healing time is reduced because of the finer incision by the use of obsidian. Plastic surgeons, cardiothoracic surgeons, and eye surgeons use scalpels and surgical knives made from obsidian. Obsidian blades can be 100 times sharper than traditional steel scalpels. The techniques for fabricating the modern obsidian blades use the same techniques developed by Maya technicians; a skilled knapper fabricates the scalpel blades using ancient techniques.

Jadeite: Tools Harder Than Iron

The Maya zone is divided into two tectonic plates: the North American and the Caribbean. These plates are part of the mosaic of interlocking crustal plates that constitute the earth's surface crust. The edges of adjacent plates form a boundary or fault line. The Maya fault line constitutes a subduction zone that extends in an east-west direction through the Montagua Valley in present-day Guatemala. Jadeite is formed under high pressure and relatively low temperatures in metamorphic rocks located up to 15 miles deep in subduction zones. Jade is the generic term describing two distinct minerals: nephrite and jadeite. Though the two are visually similar, they have different mineral characteristics. Nephrite and jadeite are both white in their pure state with colors caused by inclusions of other minerals. Jadeite has a more brilliant range of colors, and it is the more precious of the two.

Jadeite is a pyroxene mineral found in quantity in only two locations throughout the world: the Union of Myanmar and Guatemala. Maya technicians recognized the physical properties of this mineral; long used as a gemstone, jadeite has proved to be harder than iron and its tough structure is difficult to fracture. It has the capability to be shaped into specialized tools for a variety of technical applications.

The popular green jadeite is sodium aluminum silicate of relatively great purity. It is a member of the pyroxene family of minerals ($Na\ Ai\ Si_2\ O_6$). Black jadeite or chloromelonite, an iron rich black isomorph, is produced by a minor substitution of silicone (Si) by aluminum (Ai) as well as limited replacement of the aluminum (Al) by iron (Fe+3). Black jadeite has unique physical properties. On the Mohs Scale of mineral hardness, iron has a hardness of 4.5 to 5, jadeite has a hardness of 6.5 to 7.0, and diamond has the hardness of 10.0.

More important is jadeite's toughness or resistance to breakage. The mineral has an equigranular intergrowth of prismatic crystals, which are 10 times more resistant to fracture than quartz. Because of its hardness and toughness jadeite required considerably more skill for shaping and artistic elaboration than other gemstones. For thousands of years, this hard and tough material had been worked and shaped by Mesoamerican artisans including the Olmec into beautiful jewelry, figures, masks, and other prestige goods, and the skills continued with the lapidary skills of Maya artisans.

Large quantities of jadeite in a rainbow of colors have been mined in Guatemala since the Olmec era, and it has been the source of all jadeite used and traded by Mesoamericans for 3,000 years. Quality jadeite was cut and polished by Olmec and Maya artisans to create finely carved jewelry and other exquisite valuables. The Olmec preferred the jadeite color known as Olmec Blue, whereas the Maya preferred the brighter green color of jadeite. The green color was associated with life, fertility, and power. The association of green jadeite with Maya elite indicated that they valued jadeite above all other materials, even gold. Maya elite and royalty possessed a wide range of green jadeite prestige goods including jadeite

THE LOST SECRETS OF MAYA TECHNOLOGY

Credit: Digitized Sky Survey, ESA/ESO/NASA FITS Liberator.
Author: Davide De Martin (www.skyfactory.org)

C-1: Orion's Belt. Maya obsession with the cosmos and time helped their technology evolve.

C-2: The grand cathedral in Mérida was constructed from stone taken from Maya buildings. If you look closely, you can still see the evidence.

C-3: The facade of dragon mouth architecture exhibits the talents of the Maya sculptors at Chicanná.

C-4: Masks of Choc carved in stone create an intricate facade at Kabah.

C-5: Interior view of room in Xtampak palace with Maya vault. Plaster covers the wall, and 1,400-year-old timber thrust beams and lintels survive.

C-6 (above):
Carved facade at
the triumphant,
long-span arch
at Kabah.
C-7 (right):
The grand
portal arch that
marked the
entrance to the
sacbe from
Labná to Uxmal.

C-8: Five-story Edzná palace with stepped structural arch configuration.

C-9 (above left): Edzná vault stair bridge. Maya arched vault supports stairs over interior passageway at multistory palace at Edzná. C-10 (above right): Edzná beam stair bridge. Concrete beams span stairs over passageway.

C-11: Elegant circular astronomical observatory at Chichen Itza .

C-12: The astrological observatory at Mayapán is a circular building.

C-13: Elegant three-story palace at Xrampak. Columns created a veranda on the exterior set of rooms on each level.

suits, rings, and necklaces. The living elite were adorned with jadeite ear spools, necklaces, pendants, and teeth inlaid with the gemstone. On the other hand, they considered jadeite in colors other then green to be of little value. Black jadeite, while possessing all the strong physical characteristics of green jadeite, was considered to be of little value. Therefore, by default, black jadeite became the preferred material for tool-making.

Maya artisans created finely carved jewelry and other exquisite jadeite valuables from green jadeite. Maya technicians made the transition of converting lapidary skills into techniques for shaping black jadeite into specialized tools for sculpture, construction, architectural details, woodworking, agriculture, and myriad other disciplines. It was a logical transfer of lapidary skills to create the industry for manufacture of a variety of specialized tools. Maya technicians took advantage of the characteristics of the tough material and combined their lapidary skills to produce tools for executing a variety of practical tasks.

Thousands of examples of specialized tools have been recovered *in situ*. These tools were not the province of the elite and were not included in the personal possessions or votive deposits that were placed in the tombs of the elite. Archaeologists have not discovered this black jadeite artifacts *in situ* within the tombs of elite persons. The jadeite tools were, however, invaluable assets belonging to Maya artisans. The implements were passed down from father to son within families practicing the artistic and stoneworking trades.

During the Classic Period jadeite mining, transport, trading, and lapidary skills were big business, and demand for jadeite products was extensive. The jadeite industry that had flourished for 3,000 years fell from grace when the Maya civilization degraded in the 10th century. With the collapse of the civilization and the abandonment of the cities, construction, sculpture, and the lapidary industries ceased, and the demand for jadeite and its products was extinguished.

There is evidence that jadeite jewelry production had terminated with the Classic Period. Jadeite was not being mined and products were not produced during the Post-Classic Period. Jadeite artifacts excavated from Post-Classic sites were heirloom treasures apparently inherited from the Classic Period. As time passed the memories of the sources of jadeite, already a secret, as well as the lapidary skills of Maya artisans, disappeared into the mists of time. The location of jadeite mines was lost to the collective memory in Mesoamerica and the world from the Classic Period until the mid-20th century. The Spanish conquistadors, questing for gold, had little use for jadeite, dismissing the treasured stone as just green rocks. However, the name of this gemstone can be attributed to the Spanish. The name *jade* is derived from the Spanish *piedra de ijada*, meaning "loin stone." Jadeite had been long recognized by the Maya as a cure for kidney ailments and the remedy was adopted by the Spanish. The word was absorbed into English as "jade."

The source of Mesoamerican jadeite was so lost to history that in 1875 famed German mineralogist Heinrich Fischer declared that ancient jadeite objects found in Maya sites were not fabricated from jadeite mined in America but were actually imported from the Orient. During this period Maya archaeology was a developing discipline and, based on these scientific geologic reports, archaeology came to the conclusion that natural jadeite sources were not found in Mesoamerica. This misconception was taught to young archaeologists. It is easy to realize that archaeology would fail to visualize that specialized Maya tools would be fabricated from a precious gemstone, especially since jadeite was not native to Mesoamerica. It was not until the 20th century that scientists began to investigate potential sources of Mesoamerican jadeite. This theory that jadeite was imported to Mesoamerica was challenged in 1900 by Thomas Wilson. While noting the natural occurrence of nephrite in Alaska and British Columbia, Wilson stated that the source of jadeite in Mesoamerica would eventually be located.

The fairy tale that jadeite sources did not exist in America was proven to be fictitious in the mid-20th century. Scientific work carried out after World War II by Robert Foshaq, the Smithsonian Institution's curator of geology, led to a renewed interest in the quest for a source of jadeite. The first documented incident of a jadeite source in Mesoamerica occurred in 1952 when Robert Leslie discovered a field of jadeite boulders in the Montagua River Valley. In addition, Leslie discovered an ancient jadeite workshop along the Montagua River with an abundance of debitage as well as worked beads and the tools for jewelry-making.

One of the most intriguing stories surrounding the search and finding of the enigmatic source of jadeite reads like an adventure novel. It is a real-life account that weaves a mixed blend of adventure, scientific discovery, and romance, combined with financial success. Mary Lou Ridinger, a noted archaeologist and Jay Ridinger, a geologist, met while investigating the source of jadeite in the Montagua Valley. They were not only successful in their search for the mother lode, but they became husband and wife. The Ridingers explored the canyons and hills of the Montagua for the source, they hit pay dirt in 1975 when they discovered *in situ* jadeite boulders in the hills overlooking the Montagua River. Their success continued over the years, and the team went on to uncover numerous jadeite sources including the source of the rare Olmec Blue. The discovery of the source of the coveted blue jadeite proved that Olmec and Maya technicians had mined native jadeite in the Montagua Valley for 3,000 years and that jadeite was not been imported to Mesoamerica by seagoing traders. The success of the Ridinger team continued in their commercial ventures. They operate a viable jadeite mining and lapidary enterprise in Antigua, Guatemala. Their factory produces jadeite jewelry, carvings, and museum replicas of Maya masterpieces.

The fine carvings produced in Jade S.A., the Ridinger studios, are crafted by descendents of ancient Maya artisans. The contemporary artisans at Jade S.A. utilize diamond saws and high-speed hardened steel drills to work the tough jadeite into works of art. The traditional techniques of working jadeite are not used; these ancient skills remained a mystery.

The Ridingers and their crossover scientific colleagues have made large advances in identifying the sources of jadeite. It is ironic that these rediscovered sources are providing raw material for the descendents of ancient Maya artisans to assume their place in the world of art by creating jadeite masterpieces. The mystery of the source of jadeite led to the assumption by early-20th-century archaeologists that Maya tools were just "stone." It would have been preposterous for archaeologists to identify the tool material as jadeite. That is why conventional doctrine stated that jadeite was not native to Mesoamerica. However, the ancient Maya techniques of shaping jadeite into tools remained a mystery until a fortuitous encounter deep in the rainforest of Chiapas.

The Rediscovery of Maya Tool Technology

At first the hum of the aircraft engine was barely audible above the omnipresent cacophony of millions of insects and birds dwelling in the surrounding rainforest. A gap in the rainforest canopy gave me a fleeting glimpse of the low flying Cessna 172 as the aircraft traversed its downwind leg, paralleling the broad river in preparation for landing. A wingover on its base leg lined up the red and white aircraft with the narrow slot hacked from the tangled jungle growth. The cleared swath formed a verdant tunnel that served as the landing strip at the ancient Maya city of Yaxchilan. The pilot expertly guided the aircraft through the precarious slot, which barely permitted wingtip clearance, for a safe landing. He touched gently down on the grass surface and rolled to a stop.

I watched this demonstration of precision flying in admiration. "Wow, that's the way to travel in the jungle," I mused. My back was stiff from traversing the Usamacinta River in a dugout canoe. It had been a two-day trip traveling downstream from Sayaxché, Guatemala to Yaxchilan. Two men climbed out of the aircraft, secured the plane to its moorings, off loaded their gear, and began to set up camp. I learned later that the taller man was the pilot. Rick Muyers, a Canadian bush pilot on a busman's holiday, was wisely avoiding Canadian winters and spent these days traversing tropical archaeological sites by air. The passenger was an energetic man with an athletic appearance and confident movements. This was my first glance of Philippe Klinefelter, architect, sculptor, and the world's foremost expert on Maya tool technology.

Later during that evening in March 1989, as the members of the expedition relaxed around the campfire, the two fly-in visitors joined our group. Philippe and I introduced ourselves, and we chatted about our interests in Maya archaeology and the fates that brought us together at Yaxchilan. Philippe immediately grasped the concept of my search for the lost technology of the Maya; it soon became apparent that we shared similar quests in probing for the lost secrets of the Maya. He recounted the decades of revelations he had experienced investigating and researching the enigma of ancient Maya tool technology. When

Philippe described his success in uncovering the utilitarian character and composition of Maya tools, I was stunned with an overpowering thought! During all my research into Maya science and technology I had completely overlooked the one obvious point: None of the advanced construction engineering and fine artistry of the Maya that I had encountered could have been accomplished without the use of specialized tools. I now knew why the fates had brought us together at the ancient City of Yaxchilan.

All the great civilizations had special tool systems that were used to construct their cities. The Egyptians, the Greeks, the Romans, as well as the modern construction industry has specialized tool systems for all phases of construction: heavy tools for large jobs, hand tools for fine work, tools for lifting operations, and tools for transport. Maya engineers were no exception. I had overlooked a technological absolute that was the base requirement for the construction of engineering works as well as the art and architecture of the Maya. I had never considered the specific, specialized tools that were used by the Maya to create their wondrous cities. I soon learned that the study of tools was a common oversight in Maya archaeology, which never looked at the tools of the common laborer. Fate had been kind to bring us together and had presented us the opportunity to work together. For all my expertise in Maya technology, including cement fabrication, engineering mechanics for large structures, water-management systems, highway systems, long-span bridges, and transportation systems, I realized that I had allowed a black hole to reside within my cognitive system. I had overlooked the crucial system of mechanisms that unified the components of Maya technology into a whole: the specialized tools that shaped their scientific civilization. And here before me was the leading expert in that area that would provide not only the examples of Maya tool systems, but the sources of the raw material and the re-creation of ancient Maya techniques for tool fabrication. This work would solve the mysteries of Maya tools and would assist the Maya in changing their classification as a "Stone Age culture." Our conversations initiated a whole new level of forensic engineering research to the lost technology of the Maya and became an integral part of my search for the truth.

Philippe Klinefelter lives in Austin, Texas. His studio is located at the rear of his spacious property and is housed in a large, high-roofed structure offering light-filled interior space; the walls of the studio are flanked with broad entrance doors. The volume of the space and the oversized doors are required to permit the movement of large megaliths that are part of his work in creating monumental stone structures. The walls are covered with an array of shiny steel sculptor's tools. Using these tools, huge colored stones, and creativity in this spacious studio, Philippe creates monumental sculptural works out of hard rock. His grand scale sculptures, some weighing 30 tons, have been installed as landmark centerpieces in parks and urban spaces, where they serve as fountains or memorials. Philippe also executes fine sculptures influenced by the style of Maya art. These works adorn the passenger terminal at Austin International Airport and serve as the artistic theme of multimillion-dollar residences designed around Maya architectural styles.

During my first tour to Philippe's studio, we strolled through the cavernous space. I was enthralled with his style and the scope of his marvelous works in progress—maquettes of past and future projects were situated around the studio—but most of all I was intrigued by the vast array of steel sculptor's tools available for his disposal. The racks on his wall were covered with specialized steel tools employed for the carving of hard igneous stone of contemporary sculptures The array included shiny steel implements of every shape and purpose, including chisels, awls, gouges, rasps, and levers of all sizes and shapes. These steel tools are examples of the highest quality of work fabricated by master tool-smiths of the Czech Republic. The gleaming steel tools were arranged on wooden peg boards in a rank and order that reflected their function and service application for fashioning stone into fine artwork.

Philippe guided me into another space adjacent to his studio. This display space was conformed and illuminated for a special purpose. In this inner sanctum, Philippe introduced me to the analogous tool technology accomplished by Maya craftsmen. He introduced me to the world of precision tools crafted by Maya artisans; the walls on this room are covered with a display of the diverse geometry of Maya tool fabrication.

The display features hundreds of Maya tools, including chisels, gouges, drills, axes, adzes, blades and other tools fabricated from black jadeite and obsidian. I strolled around the room permitting my eyes to wander over the marvelous examples of the priceless treasures that Maya lapidaries and technicians had fashioned into specialized tools. These tools were used for the myriad variety of tasks required to build the Maya civilization. My observations recognized specific chloromelonite tools that were designed for various tasks, including fine sculpture, stone cutting, construction, mining, agriculture, and numerous other technical applications. The task of recognization was easily accomplished because the tools of Maya craftsmanship replicated the functional geometry of modern instruments.

To be introduced to the fine workmanship of ancient technicians and being able to observe the diverse array of black jadeite tools was a unique opportunity. However, Philippe had another mind-boggling demonstration for me. He reached into the collection and selected ancient Maya tools of various sizes and functional shapes; he laid these tools on the work table. He then selected modern hardened steel tools from the studio walls and placed them alongside the black jadeite tools. The tools were produced a thousand years apart but they were of similar shape and size! The ancient jadeite tools and the modern steel tools that he had selected were comparative examples of similar tools of a different age and culture that had been fabricated for similar stone-working tasks. He was demonstrating how ancient tool-makers and modern tool designers solved their approach to a similar stone-cutting task by creating tools of similar sizes and shapes.

Without an audible explanation, Philippe clearly made his point. His demonstration made visible the anthropological logic termed *comparative studies*. When a civilization reaches a specific level of sophistication, it will develop similar solutions to similar problems as that of parallel cultures. Maya technicians had developed the same type of tools to carry out their tasks a millennium prior to the time period when the modern steel tools were designed and forged. Tools have been an integral supplement to the human hand since the beginning of civilization. The geometrical shape of Maya tools appeared to be discipline-specific, and their functional characteristics appear to be driven by ergonomics required to perform a task. The approach to a specific design solution has not changed in a thousand years. The geometrical design of the chloromelonite tools were shaped by the logic demanded by the scale and quality of the task proposed for that tool. From the evidence of the comparative work products laid on the work bench before us, it was apparent that skilled Maya sculptors and stone-cutters had encountered similar issues as modern tool-makers and they achieved a viable solution in the same manner. The comparisons made it apparent that the Maya craftsmen shaped their tools in the same series of geometrical sets as modern tool designers.

In the decades since our fortuitous meeting at the ancient city of Yaxchilan, Philippe has expanded his knowledge of the ancient crafts by replicating the technical means and methods used by the ancient ones in fabricating the vast variety of Maya tools uncovered by Philippe. During this period I have joined him in his quest to advance the knowledge of Maya tool technology, the methodology used by Maya sculptors in carving stone and supports his efforts to find the source of tool materials. I have researched the methodologies used by Maya stone-cutters in the construction of the monumental stone and concrete structures. My contribution is based on the application of my background in forensic and structural engineering, the physical sciences, and Maya building construction technology. Philippe has greatly advanced the knowledge and awareness of Maya tool materials, fabrication, and technology, and has led the research and investigation effort as a hands-on sculptor and an innovator in replicating the ancient methods of Maya tool fabrication. The search has led him on a long and winding trail, following a path has been steeped in intrigue. We have followed the mysterious quest into the basements of museums, disseminating information on tools by delivering scientific papers and demonstrations of tools and tool fabrication at international symposia, filming demonstrations of tool-making for the History Channel, field expeditions to the sites of jadeite sources, and investigation of ancient Maya jadeite workshops.

Our quest for the source of Maya jadeite exploitation has taken us to the Montagua valley, where we observed ancient jadeite mining sites, ancient workshops with jadeite debitage, and ancient tool-making, and we have investigated the ancient Maya city of Guyatan, a city that was a center for mining and the lapidary production of jadeite jewelry and tool production. At Guyatan we examined a green jadeite boulder that had been partially worked, then abandoned. The methods of working and shaping the boulder were similar to the techniques that Philippe had reconstructed in his tool-making research. During our survey of the nearby jadeite sources we encountered jadeite boulders where "blanks" for making tools had been incised in the boulder and then abandoned. Philippe's research on Maya tool technology was featured on a History Channel production. During the filming of that production he demonstrated Maya tool-making technology before the cameras. Philippe's ground-shattering research and techniques into Maya jadeite has not been one-dimensional. He not only collected and assessed the capabilities of Maya tool production, but he has become a master at replicating the original techniques for fabricating Maya tools made from jadeite and obsidian materials. All the while he has maintained his initial quest; Philippe's goal is to completely understand the techniques used by the Maya sculptors and how they used their tools to produce their sculptor's art.

Revealing the Secrets of Fabricating Ancient Maya Tools

Philippe uses tools that were once well-kept secrets of Maya artisans and, after the Classic Period, their use was lost to living memory. He has mastered the process of Maya tool-making and the techniques of carving stone and wood used by Maya sculptors. He locates and collects raw tool material at the source, prepares the materials used for tool-making, and fabricates the tools using the same ancient techniques employed by Maya craftsman, but the ancient skill did not come easily. The role of becoming a master craftsman of Maya tools was a difficult journey to follow. The lack of academic studies, artifacts, and materials research on Maya tools made finding the starting point difficult. The clues to the truth were difficult to find and, as one can assume, fate had to take a hand in finding the solution. Philippe has always had an interest in art and architecture; his architectural training at the University of Texas and his training as a sculpture honed the passion for his quest.

His interest in the Maya culture led him to move to Mexico. He resided in southern part of Mexico in the state of Quintana Roo. His home in the outskirts of the city of Chetumal was located on the Hondo River. In the 1970s, tropical hardwoods were harvested in the rainforest and floated down the Hondo River to the saw mills near Chetumal. Philippe was sculpting works from tropical exotic hardwood. His raw material was readily available from the salvaged log ends and burls that he hauled from discards at the local sawmill.

The area was populated with living Maya, and sites of ancient Maya cities were located nearby including Bacalar, Kohunlich, and the Rio Bec sites. As Philippe worked on his sculptural projects, he also spent time exploring the Maya ruins. It was while examining the sculptural works in the ancient cities that he began to wonder how the ancient Maya could cut and carve hard wood and stone sculptures with such style and accuracy without the use of metal tools. What were their tools like and what were the unique techniques of carving used to produce the exotic art? He had no guidance from archaeological disciplines because Maya tool making and their uses had not been explored.

While visiting Antigua, Guatemala, he had a breakthrough experience that accelerated his quest for knowledge of Maya tools. Philippe was visiting the jadeite carving shop owned by Jay and Mary Lou Ridinger. An unusual tool was displayed in a glass case. The tool was a dark green jadeite gouge of ancient provenance. It matched the size and style of modern steel gouges that Philippe used for sculpting wood and stone. This was a moment of truth that opened a new world of opportunity. The tool was a compass that gave Philippe directions of where to look for the tools of the Maya.

Philippe did not miss this opportunity to pursue the secrets of Maya tool-making, and he has spent decades exploring the methodologies used by Maya sculptors to carve stone and wood. Over the years he searched newly opened ruins of Maya sites where he could observe and photograph the sculpture and stonework found in these ancient cities. He carried out close examination of the surface of carved stone that showed visible tool marks that remained on the craved works. The search for actual samples of Maya jadeite tools led him to museums and private collections. The jadeite artifacts were called "Celts" from the Latin, *celtis*, which means "chisel," but these artifacts were not conceived as tools by archaeologists. As his investigation continued he was able to search out all the types of tools that were needed to cut and carve examples of wood and stone that Philippe had seen in ancient ruins and in modern museums.

Philippe has been a sculptor for decades. He has worked with Maya tools for thousands of hours and has come to appreciate the efficiency and exquisite beauty of Maya jadeite tools. It has long been known by archaeologists that jadeite chisels were used in carving Maya stele. Eric Thompson noted that thousands of jadeite tools were encountered at archaeological sites. He reported that the artifacts he encountered were of many shapes and sizes, and were in various stages of wear. However, the investigation of the nature of these unique tools was never pursued. Philippe's studies into the character and materials used for Maya tools gave him an educated start to his ability to replicate ancient Maya methods of sculpture and of tool fabrication.

In the Montagua River Valley of Guatemala, Philippe found the appropriate materials to work jadeite into shaped tools. Jadeite is found as a water-worn stone cobble along the banks of the river and *in situ* in outcroppings. Quartz and quartzite are common in the area can be used for hammer stones and drill bits. The maguey plant grows bountifully throughout the area, the fibers of this plant have a very high tensile strength, and cords made of this fiber are excellent for saw-cutting of jadeite using quartz or garnet sand as an abrasive.

After replicating some of the jadeite chisels (using jadeite courtesy of Mary Lou Ridinger of Jades, S.A.), he was able to use these tools to carve wood and limestone. The process of working material with jadeite tools was a sculptor's dream; the tool was efficient and carved the materials with ease.

On each trip to Guatemala, Philippe searched for examples of jadeite tools. To assist in identifying the tools, he drew outlines and displayed photos of the tools to potential sources. He visited native markets, museums, and private collections. Over the years, his research into the type and variety of Maya tools paid off and yielded a wide range of shapes and sizes of tools. He has collected or created what can be described as the basic toolkit of a Maya sculptor.

He has classified the tools into a system of nomenclature that varies with the type of tool, its method of being held while being utilized, and the method of percussion used to apply pressure of the edge of the tool to the object being carved. To illustrate the wide variety of shapes and purposes,

Figure 5-1: Maya tools, handheld, hafted, and finger-held.
Photo by Miguel Alvarez, courtesy of Philippe Klinefelter.

the method of holding these tools, and the types of percussion used with each, Philippe assembled the tools into groups and photographed the collection for an overview of their characteristics. Philippe has used the finger-held tools and instruments for carving and believes that they were custom-fitted for the fingers of each sculptor. In using finger-held tools, he began to appreciate the value of jadeite as a tool material and the advantages jadeite held over modern tools. Their advantage lies in the ways they perfectly fit in the fingers of the working hand. It appears that handheld tools were custom-made for the individual. The merging of the handle and blade into a single instrument provides a great advantage over modern tools.

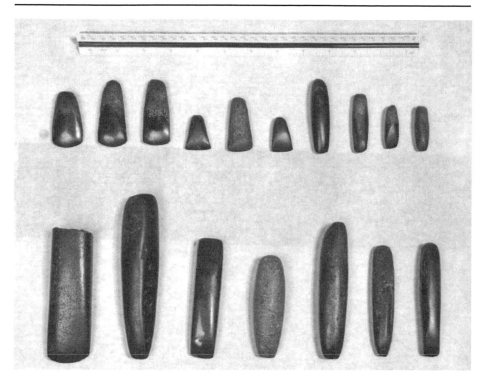

Figure 5-2: Various Maya jadeite tools with 1-foot scale shown for size.
Photo by Miguel Alvarez, courtesy of Philippe Klinefelter.

Figure 5-1 indicates three rows of jadeite chisels. They are grouped by the method of holding the tool while working with the tool. The top row is of larger tools to be held in the hand, the middle row is of finger-held tools, and the bottom row consists of tools that are hafted. The wooden haft would be attached to the jadeite with Maya rubber or latex cement.

Figure 5-2 is an array of two types of chisels. The top row is of smaller tools and is to be hafted with a wooden handle. The larger chisels on the bottom row are held in the hand. Figure C-23 shows an array of finely made gouges. The top row represents hafted gouges, the middle three are finger-held gouges and the larger gouges on the bottom row are handheld.

In his work as a sculptor, Philippe works with handheld, finger-held, and hafted tools. In Figure C-24, Philippe demonstrates the carving of limestone using a handheld chisel and in Figure C-25, he demonstrates the use of a hafted fine chisel while carving a limestone block. Philippe has replicated Maya methodologies for drilling limestone. He is able to develop open holes in stone using a solid drill bit or closed shapes using a hollow reed and abrasive quartz or garnet sand. His bow drilling equipment is shown in Figure C-26.

Philippe has mastered the use of the total range of Maya tools and feels he has learned the techniques used by the ancient Maya master builders and carvers. It is possible that Philippe can bring these ancient tools and his Maya carving techniques back to the Yucatán and develop young Maya sculptors that can learn to replicate the exotic styles of their forbearers.

6

Maya Cement:
Holding the Civilization Together

During the Classic Period the population of the Maya urban power centers expanded, as their wealth, prestige, commercial, and religious power flourished. The city-states, with their towering pyramids, multi-story palaces, monumental buildings, and infrastructure projects enjoyed a continuous construction program of building, rebuilding, and expanding their urban matrix. The height and span of massive buildings owed their strength and structural capacities to advanced Maya building technologies. These monumental buildings were constructed of cast-in-place concrete set into a facing of well-cut limestone. The cast-in-place concrete, a strong and durable structural material, was made with Maya cement, which was also used as stucco coating, mortar, paving, and other building applications. Fabrication of cement was developed by Maya technicians before 250 BC using an innovative fabrication process that was in use until the 20th century.

It is easy to imagine how these monumental structures, testaments to brilliant Maya technology, would have disappeared if the structures had not been constructed of strong and durable building materials. If the Maya construction materials had consisted of timber, bricks, or stone masonry alone, they would have almost totally degraded by the constant attack of the forces of the natural environment. The prying roots of the jungle, earthquakes, and hurricanes during the past 1,200 years would have caused the total disintegration of less durable materials. However, Maya engineers constructed the cities of structural materials that survived the millennia. Explorers encountering the ancient cities found their structures to be principally intact. The durable cast-in-place concrete construction of the monumental structures and their survival is a testimony to Maya building technology.

Archaeo-engineering investigation reveals that Maya technicians were producing cement and constructing cast-in-place concrete structures before 250 BC. The process of fabricating cement by Maya technicians is similar to the process used in modern cement production. The raw materials, including limestone, are elevated to high temperatures in order to induce the chemical process that converts the raw materials to cement.

The Maya developed true hydraulic cement; this is cement that reacts with water to form silicate hydrate crystals. These crystals grow and interlock to create the bond between various components making up the concrete mix and produce the hard, durable construction material known as concrete. The cement paste in the mix glues together the aggregate, fills the voids, and allows the mix to flow more easily. The compressive strength of concrete initiates with the stiffening and increases with further consolidation, called "setting," after which the strengthening process begins. Maya cement had a chemical makeup similar to modern Portland cement; both are materials that have valuable characteristic of "setting up," gaining strength and durability when placed and permitted to harden under water.

The History of Cement in Construction

The history of construction using cement harks back to construction during the building of the Roman Empire. Romans used cement-based concrete on a large scale. Roman cement was not a fabricated material but was based on a natural volcanic material called pozzolana ash. This natural cement was exploited from the earth near the town of Pozzuoli in Italy. Roman engineers combined the pozzolana ash with additional materials, including crushed brick. It has been determined that Roman engineers discovered the method of using this natural cement to formulate concrete in approximately 200 BC.

Roman concrete, *opus caementicium*, was made from pozzolanic ash, crushed aggregate, and quicklime. The use of concrete enabled Roman engineering to depart from low strength masonry and rectilinear structures, and permitted them to develop designs using the compressive strength of concrete for new structural mechanics of diverse geometry and greater dimensions. These Roman structures included arches, vaults, and domes. Roman concrete lacked the strength of modern Portland cement, but its strength was sufficient to construct the dramatic structures built for the Roman Empire. The average compressive strength Roman cement is 2750 psi (200kg/cm^2) after 2,000 years of curing. The initial strength of the Roman concrete was closer to 1,500 psi (120kg/cm^2) when placed in the original construction. The Romans added other materials to their concrete mix to improve performance. Horsehair was added to reduce cracking, and the addition of animal blood to the mix enhanced the concrete to be resistant to freezing. In lieu of wood forms, Roman engineers often used brick as formwork, placing cast-in-place concrete in the interior between the rows of brickwork to develop structural elements.

After the collapse of the Roman Empire in AD 476, the secret of cement for the production of concrete was lost in Europe for 1,400 years, with the exception of 1547, when the brilliant Michelangelo Buonarroti executed the design of a thin shell of Roman concrete for the dome of Saint Peter's Basilica in Vatican City in Rome. The history of the production of cement fast-forwards to 1824. The invention of the process for fabricating modern Portland cement was patented by Joseph Asplin, a British stonemason from Leeds. Asplin developed the process for producing cement by heating finely powdered limestone. He then ground the resulting "clinkers" into powder, producing hydraulic cement. Asplin named his product "Portland cement" because its color resembled the stone quarried on the Isle of Portland, a peninsula off the English coast.

In 1848, Joseph Asplin's son William developed an improved version of the cement that produced true hydraulic cement. The process of producing Portland cement involves the elevation of raw materials to their melting point, inducing the chemical reaction for conversion to cement. The improved version required a higher temperature to induce the chemical reaction for the process. This process produced the building material known as modern Portland cement. Joseph Asplin's invention has enabled concrete to be the most popular building material in the world, with more than 1.75 billion tons produced each year.

Calcium is the essential chemical component in cement production. Calcium can be derived from a variety of raw materials, the most common raw material being limestone. The mixture of limestone and other constituent materials are heated to temperatures of 1450–1600 degrees Celsius in the sintering process. These temperature levels are capable of melting limestone and inducing a chemical reaction to form calcium silicate (3 CaO.SiO2). The product then assumes the form of globules known as "clinkers." When cooled and ground into powder, the product becomes Portland cement.

The parallel between modern concrete–based structures and structures produced using Maya cement is apparent. However, Maya technicians developed their process independently. Maya engineers developed cast-in-place concrete structures to build their high rise cities and sophisticated infrastructure. Maya technicians produced the same chemical process for fabricating hydraulic cement as that used by modern technology, but the Maya technical achievement was more than 2,100 years in advance of modern technology.

The Maya Process for Producing Cement

The geologic composition of the Yucatán Peninsula is well suited for the exploitation of raw materials for construction. The Yucatán is a limestone platform that juts out into the waters of the Gulf of Mexico and the Caribbean Sea. The limestone strata extend down more than 2,500 meters in depth from the surface to the basement layer of sedimentary rock formed 540 to 245 million years ago during the Paleozoic Era. The geologic layers resting upon the basement include a 100-meter-thick stratum from the Mesozoic Era and are made up of materials that include sandstone, gypsum, salt, and silt formed 245,000,000 to 144,000,000 years ago. The third stratum is a layer of limestone, with a thickness of 1,300 meters, formed during the Cretaceous Period, 136,000,000 to 65,000,000 years ago. The upper stratum is a 1,000-meter thick stratum of limestone that rests upon the Cretaceous layer. This layer of Tertiary Period material was deposited 65, 000,000 years ago.

A 15-meter-layer of Oligocene to Pliocene epoch limestone, approximately 90 meters below the surface, was formed 38,000,000 to 5,000,000 years ago. The surface layers consist of Quaternary Epoch limestone, some 60 to 80 meters thick, formed 2,000,000 to 10,000 years ago, and a 10-meter-thick surface layer of Holocene Epoch limestone formed less than 10,000 years ago. The geologic composition of the Yucatán shelf provided the Maya with an unlimited supply of raw materials for the production of strong and durable building materials.

The basic principles required to produce hydraulic cement consist of two major efforts: the mining of limestone, the raw material (Figure 6-1), and the ability to elevate the temperature of the limestone to a temperature

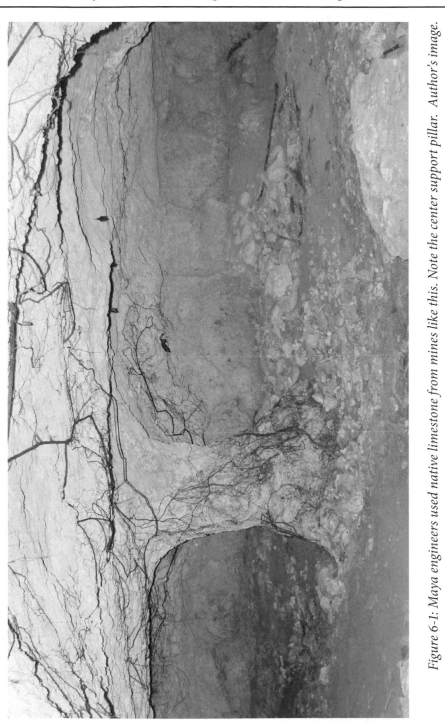

Figure 6-1: Maya engineers used native limestone from mines like this. Note the center support pillar. Author's image.

level that will melt the raw materials and induce the chemical conversion into cement clinkers. In modern cement fabrication, the raw materials are very similar to those that were available to Maya technicians. However, the Maya natural environment did not offer fuels that burn at high temperatures, such as coal or natural gas. The only major fuel source available to the Maya was the timber, which grew abundantly in the forest. The use of timber alone, as a fuel source, cannot achieve the 1,450 degrees Celsius temperature required to melt limestone. Wood burns at 300 to 500 degrees Celsius, much lower than the threshold for melting limestone. A physical mechanism was required to enhance the thermodynamic process for the combustion of wood fuel and elevate the combustion to the required high temperatures for a specific time period in order to achieve the desired chemical conversion to melt limestone.

It is unknown how Maya technicians developed the geometry of the ingenious cement kiln assembly that enabled them to convert raw limestone into hydraulic cement. The process was in use by 250 BC and most probably was developed in a heuristic process of numerous trial-and-error developmental efforts for producing higher temperatures, until the optimum prototype of the classic cement kiln was developed. This kiln was used by Maya construction until the 20th century, when modern industrially produced cement became more cost effective. This process is still in use today in remote locations and for consolidation of Maya archaeological structures.

The cement firing kiln assembly developed by Maya technicians was a basic blast furnace that applied similar thermodynamic and chemical applications to those used by Henry Bessemer when he invented his blast furnace in 1856 (Figure 6-2). To achieve the requisite high temperatures for melting limestone, the Maya developed an assembly constructed of self-consuming timber fuel into a geometric configuration that induced elevated temperatures using the same process as the Bessemer blast furnace.

The timber kiln assembly serves multiple purposes: It functions as a platform for stacking the raw limestone material on the top, provides the requisite fuel for the combustion process, and develops a geometrical configuration that enables the assembly and its timber fuel to perform as a thermodynamic reactor, producing elevated temperatures at the centroid of the kiln. The streams of super-hot air are exhausted upward via the open cylinder in the center of the kiln, introducing high-temperature heat flow

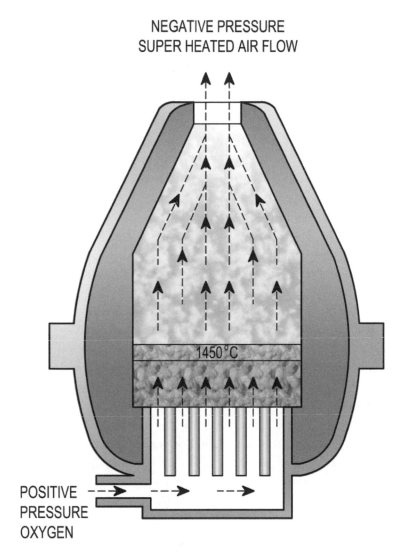

NEGATIVE PRESSURE
SUPER HEATED AIR FLOW

1450°C

POSITIVE
PRESSURE
OXYGEN

BESSEMER BLAST FURNACE

Figure 6-2: Maya engineers developed a thermodynamic
process in their cement kilns that is similar to the
modern blast furnace. Author's image.

for melting the raw materials at the top of the kiln. The physical process of achieving these high temperatures is accelerated by the induction of cool, oxygen-rich outside air, which elevates the temperature in the center core while reducing the ambient pressure in the center core. In turn, the low pressure at the center core induces a rapid flow of cooler, oxygen-rich air from the exterior of the kiln, which increases the ambient temperature of the core center, causing super-heated air to dynamically exhaust upward (in a chimney-like effect) into the limestone material. The cycle of increased interior temperatures and the inflow of oxygen-rich air continue until the process is optimized, and the limestone is melted and converted into cement clinkers.

The cement fabrication process was in use as part of the consolidation and restoration of major Maya archaeological sites well into the 20th century, including, but not limited to, Uxmal, Calakmul and Chichen Itza. Figure 6-3 is a photograph of Maya workers applying the final adjustments to a cement kiln at Chichen Itza during the early 20th century. The cylindrical assembly, which provided the platform for the limestone and the fuel to achieve the desired final product, is constructed of locally acquired green timber. The geometrical configuration of the assembly clearly indicates the opening in the center of the kiln that served as the vertical flue and combustion chamber for the kiln.

Figure 6-4 is a graphic of the thermodynamic flow chart of the kiln assembly and the combustion and heat transfer process used by the Maya to produce a successful cement fabrication operation. The process applied the thermodynamic reaction provided by the geometrical configuration of the kiln and the fuel materials.

The diameter of a typical kiln was approximately 6 meters across the width of the assembly. The assembly was constructed of small-diameter wood logs of less than a meter in length. The logs were stacked horizontally in a radial pattern, with large logs infilled with smaller logs and chinked solid with chipped wood. The center of the kiln was open to the atmosphere, with a vertical cylindrical shaft of 8 inches in diameter. The central shaft extended from the ground level to the top or platform level of the kiln. The height from the ground level to the top of the platform is approximately 2 meters. A passageway for the flow of outside air to the center is located at the bottom of the kiln. When the kiln has been assembled, limestone is deposited on the top level of the platform formed by the timber logs. The

Figure 6-3: Nineteenth-century cement kiln at Chichen Itza used for consolidation of the site. The process was thousands of years old at this time. Courtesy of Carnegie Institution.

raw limestone material is cut into small blocks and stacked to a height of 0.75 meters. The process is started by igniting easily combustible material in the form of dry leaves, dry decayed wood, or resinous wood that is deposited into the core center. This material is the tinder that is easily ignited and burns quickly to initiate the chemical reaction for producing cement.

The process involves a logical procedure that applies sound physical and chemical procedures, combined with ritual that has become a part of the cement-making process. To assure a long-term source of heat the logs must contain sufficient moisture content to control the time of combustion. Heat generated by the process will produce requisite high temperatures while assuring a long-term period of regulated temperatures. Wood that is very dry will ignite and burn too quickly. The timber logs must be green or soaked in water to impede the combustion process to the desired time of 24 to 30 hours. The atmospheric and meteorological conditions are also

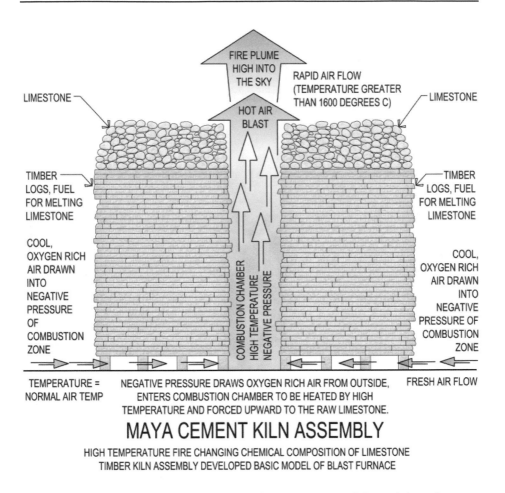

Figure 6-4: Thermodynamic diagram of a Maya cement kiln with heat flow into the limestone raw material. Author's image.

important. Clear weather is required for the burn; the chance of precipitation should be zero. A rainstorm during the process would result in failure, and it would have to be restarted. The process must be carried out in level terrain configurations and weather conditions without wind. The presence of wind will result in an unequal combustion process and cause the windward side of the kiln to burn at greater rate than the leeward side. The uneven burn will result in collapse of the windward side and a failure of the cement-making process. Under optimum conditions, a narrow tongue of flame will soar skyward as the flames extend to a height of 30 meters, resulting in a unique pyrotechnic manifestation. As the fire becomes very hot, the flame color changes with the temperature, from red to orange, then yellow, and finally to blue. A blue flame indicates a temperature of 1,600 degrees Celsius, which is sufficient temperature for melting limestone.

The kiln burn process has certain ritual or superstitious attendants to the procedure. The Maya cement makers do not permit the presence of women during the burning of the kiln. This superstition could be akin to sailors on ships that forbade women to board their vessel. They believed it was bad luck, even though the sailors always referred the ship in feminine terms. The Maya cement kilns were also considered to be feminine. They believed that the kiln would become jealous if another woman was present during the burn and the kiln may refuse to operate properly.

When the burn is complete, the clinkers and cinders are allowed to cool. The mass is then allowed to cool. The cement clinkers are allowed to be exposed to dew and rain. The mass will expand into a dome of fluffy, white powder that is five or six times its original bulk. The cement can then be collected and ground into a fine powder. This powder is hydraulic cement that could be combined with water, admixture, and aggregate to create cast-in-place concrete for structures, concrete for pavements, mortar for stonework, and stucco for plastering the interior and exterior of their magnificent buildings. The cast-in-place concrete mixture was one part cement, three parts loosely ground limestone, and water. The process required five tons of wood to produce one ton of cement.

Forensic Analysis of the Chemical and Physical Properties of Maya Cement Compared With Modern Portland Cement

Archaeologists, when describing Maya structures and architectural components, freely use the terms *mortar*, *stucco*, and *concrete* interchangeably. These descriptions are intended to identify applications of cementitious materials in the construction of Maya buildings. However, nowhere in published work do archaeologists investigate the sources and methodologies for the fabrication of cement or cast-in-place concrete. Several references on the Internet relating to archaeological discussions of Maya building materials state the Maya used a material that "mimicked" concrete, but was not concrete. As the old saying goes, if it feels like concrete, looks like concrete, and holds like concrete, then it must be concrete.

Archaeology has not properly investigated sources of cement or the application of cast-in-place concrete in Maya structures. However, there have been attempts to probe the issue, and research indicates that in "The Engineering Knowledge of the Maya" in *Contributions to American Archaeology* (Volume II, 1934), the Carnegie Institution published the results of chemical tests on Maya cement. Analysis was carried out on three samples of concrete taken from the structure known as the Casa de Monjas at Chichen Itza. Tests showed that the samples were quite close to each other in percentage of calcium oxide and carbon dioxide. These tests did not include comparisons with Portland cement or physical tests for strength. Archaeologist Lawrence Roys, who directed the tests, did make the observation that the Casa de Monjas may have been constructed during a period of 150 years and the quality of the cement over that time appeared consistent. The testing, though ambitious, did not indicate the exact source of the cement or its strength.

It was not until 1999 that a science-based, chemical, and physical testing program was carried out on Maya concrete. A team of scientists from the Autonomous University of the State of Mexico under the auspices of the National Institute of Archaeology and History carried out a field collection of samples and laboratory testing of Maya cementitious materials including concrete, stucco, and mortar. The team was led by Dr. Horacio Ramirez, and included Ramiro Pérez and Heriberto Diaz. They successfully carried out the testing program and published their results in a paper entitled "El cement y el concreto de los Maya" ("The Cement and Concrete of the Maya") in the Mexican scientific journal *Ciencia Ergo Sum*.

Samples of Maya concrete, mortar, and stucco were collected for the testing program from the ancient Maya cities of Palenque and Colmalcalco, as well as concrete from Yaxchilan. The ancient concrete samples were evaluated using standard laboratory testing procedures for cement-based materials. The results were compared with similar standardized test results derived from samples prepared from modern commercial Portland cement. The testing included chemical analysis, defraction of the matrix, and physical analysis, including unit weight and compressive strength.

The properties of the Portland cement, the international standard for hydraulic cement, were selected as the baseline for the comparative analysis versus Maya cement. The results indicated in Table 6-1 show a close similarity in the chemical composition and relative percentage of these materials between Maya cement and Portland cement. Physical testing of the mechanical properties included compressive strength of the concrete samples and unit weight of the samples made with Maya cement. It must be noted that the test samples were collected from degraded Maya structures. It is probable that the ancient concrete test samples included minute fissures in their matrix, which would lower the compressive strength testing. The results of the testing program conclude that though the chemical composition of Maya cement is slightly different from that of Portland cement, it should be considered as having the same chemical composition as the advanced quality control of Portland cement. This quality control meets strict international standards for manufactured cement.

The pozzolanic index is an important measure of the character of cement. The test analysis of oxides for Maya cement samples indicated a pozzolanic index of 0.12. This value is greater than the pozzolanic index 0.05, which is the lower limit acceptable in modern concrete, and indicates that pozzolanic activity was significant. The team concluded that this level of a pozzolanic index was produced intentionally and did not occur by chance.

Table 6-1: Comparative Chemical Analysis

Element	Maya Cement	Portland Cement
C	13.17	12.67
O	38.42	44.24
Mg	5.48	1.37
Al	1.17	2.70
Si	2.82	9.58
Ca	38.01	22.66
Fe		1.25
Na		3.31
K		0.92
S		1.30
Y	0.93	
Totals	100.00	100.00

In an additional experimental program, carried out at a later date and conducted by Dr. Horacio Ramirez and Heriberto Diaz, undamaged samples of ancient concrete were collected for testing. The samples were collected from an ancient slab at Palenque and from the wall of Temple No. 6 and Structure No. 5 at the city of Yaxchilan. The samples consisted of eight specimens of Maya concrete of approximately 61 mm in size. The program included testing for measurements of pulse velocity, compression strength, modulus of rupture, and modulus of elasticity, and was carried out in the civil engineering laboratory of the CFE (Comision Federal de Electricidad) in Mexico City. The testing produced the following results:

1. Average pulse velocity: 4.16×10^6 mm/s (horizontal), 3.3×10^6 mm/s (vertical).

2. Average compressive strength: 1330 psi (93 kg/cm^2) with a max of 2430 psi (171 kg/cm^2).

3. Average modulus of rupture for concrete: 260 psi (18 kg/cm^2).

4. Modulus of elasticity: E = 1,970,000 psi (138,504 kg/cm^2).

These results indicate that the strength of ancient Maya concrete is more than adequate for resisting the loads superimposed on Maya structures. Structural analysis of Maya structures by the Ramirez team indicated that concrete in these structures was acting under a maximum stress of approximately 350 psi (25 kg/cm^2). The results of both tests indicate that Maya structures were constructed of cast-in-place concrete with a much higher strength concrete than was required. The conclusions of the authors indicated the following:

1. The advanced materials of construction fabricated by Maya engineers, including concrete, have a remarkable ability to resist severe environmental exposure due to these significant mechanical properties comparable to modern standards.

2. The values of compressive strength of concrete samples are higher than reported than tests on other ancient American cultures.

3. Maya structures were designed by Maya engineers with a sufficient factor of safety.

4. As a result of the testing program and studies, a procedure for formulating cement with the characteristics of the ancient

Maya cement has been developed. In the future, this blend of cement will be used by INAH in the restoration of Maya archaeological sites.

The result of the testing program concludes that the chemical composition of Maya cement is only slightly different from that of Portland cement. The study concludes that Maya cement, though not a perfect chemical match with Portland cement, is a true cement and can be defined as a building material very similar to modern cement. The authors of the study also concluded that Maya cement has cementitious properties that characterize the material as true cement and chemical agglomerate with properties that bind the constituent components of the concrete mix together into a strong matrix. The report states that the Maya cement was well compacted, and the aggregates were well graded, with a maximum size of 40 mm, similar to modern concrete.

The unit weight of Maya concrete determined by the study falls within the range of unit weight for modern Portland cement. The unit weight of Maya concrete was 112 pcf (pounds per cubic foot), or 1.8 gm/cm³, whereas Portland cement concrete varies from 110 pcf to 150 pcf depending on the mix of aggregate. The compressive strength of Maya concrete averaged 1,300 psi, or 93 kg/cm², in the testing program. This is a lower strength than contemporary concrete, but would have been an acceptable level of compressive strength in the early 20th century, and was definitely acceptable as a structural material in the type of buildings designed by Maya engineers. The use of unreinforced mass concrete structures by Maya engineers applied this durable, low-strength concrete for use in a variety of purposes. The conclusions of the study were clear: the cement fabricated by Maya technicians was true cement, and concrete made with this Maya cement possessed the chemical and physical characteristics to develop cast-in-place concrete structures, mortar for masonry construction, and stucco for surface applications. Maya cement proved its capabilities by modern scientific analysis and indicated that it was the structural building material that held Maya cities together against all odds.

Testing the Capabilities of the Maya Cement Kiln

The ingenious cement kiln, with its special geometry, enabled the forced flow of oxygen-rich air into the interior of the kiln and fire cylinder, which elevated temperature in the kiln to 1,450 degrees Celsius in order to melt the limestone and induce the chemical change from limestone into cement. An actual test of the capabilities of elevating temperatures by the timber kiln would be a positive proof of its thermodynamic capabilities.

The opportunity to construct a scale working model of a Maya cement kiln came about during the filming of a production for the History Channel. I had the chance to carry out the test in conjunction with sculptor Philippe Klinefelter. The History Channel was filming a segment relating to the technology of the Maya. This sequence of the production covered the fabrication of cement utilizing Maya techniques. We started our test with intentions of using the full-scale Maya design for the blast furnace. We soon realized that if we used the full dimensions for a typical Maya cement kiln, it would require 22 cords of wood, or 11 truckloads of wood, each with a 10-cubic-yard capacity. Not only would the logistics and economics of the project be a daunting issue, but we also would be the object of special attention from the City of Austin Fire Department when the flames soared 20 to 30 meters vertically into the sky. Considering the alternatives, we choose the better part of valor and selected the scientific route for the test. We decided to build a working scale model.

We determined that our scale model would be one-fifth of the full size timber kiln, an achievable task. We set about collecting the raw materials for the scale model. Building the scale model kiln required a surprisingly large amount of materials. When we purchased the limestone and wood for the cement kiln a large truck was required to transport our load.

"Okay," I said to Philippe. "Here is the design sketch; we need to split the timber into appropriate sizes for the kiln. It would be great to use some of your jadeite Maya tools." However we settled for a steel hatchet and a wedge. The construction of the 4-foot-diameter and 2-foot-high timber kiln went smoothly. Philippe chopped wood into appropriate modules, and I arranged them in the appropriate Maya manner. When the timber array was in place, we stacked the limestone on top around the center of the fire cylinder. We added some pine kindling to the center of the fire cylinder to aid the initial combustion of the thermodynamic system. The scale model that would prove the effectiveness of the Maya blast furnace was now ready for the filming of the demonstration.

The film crew and the host of the documentary assembled, and we went over the script for filming the performance of this Maya invention. When all was ready, the cinema professionals were set to roll the cameras. We had exactly followed the ancient Maya procedures for building the kiln and were proceeding with traditional methods of ignition and burning of the timber blast furnace that would convert the limestone into cement clinkers. We knowingly only violated one of the traditional rules of Maya cements technicians: women were not permitted to be present at a burn, and we had women on board as crew members. We were not going to test modern mores by clearing women from the filming. "Oh, what the hell!" I thought. "This is a scientific experiment. What could go wrong?" It is better to face the anger of the gods than the wrath of an angry female crew member, so I shouted, "Let her rip!"

Philippe had prepared a metal scuttle with hot coals to start the procedure, staying within the Maya "rule book." A deviation from the standard was the attachment of a pyrometer to the interior of the fire cylinder to monitor the levels of burn temperatures. "Action!" shouted the director. Cameras rolled and the test initiated, with the host pouring hot coals into the fire cylinder.

There was an immediate ignition of the pine kindling, as the rosin-filled slivers of wood pyrolyzed. Gases from the kindling streamed up and ignited. The flame in the center of the cylinder began to shoot upward in a column. We observed the meter on the pyrometer as the needle crawled to the right of the scale indicating higher and higher temperatures. The camera kept rolling. The center of the fire cylinder was now in full combustion. The thermodynamic action of the kiln was driving the red flames higher and higher. The needle on the pyrometer crawled to the right as it registered higher temperatures. The fire grew hotter, and the flames turned to orange as the wood began to release gases that increased the rate of combustion, lowered the interior pressure, and sucked oxygen-rich air from the exterior into the bottom of

Figure 6-5: Flames soar as a scale model Maya cement kiln operates.
Author's image.

the cylinder. The flames roared upward to a height of 2 meters (Figure 6-5). The host of the History Channel film maintained a running narrative of the testing activities, describing the color and height of the flame and the temperature reading. The flame turned a light red as the system began to burn hotter. There was no smoke from the burn, due to the highly efficient thermodynamic reactions developed by the Maya kiln. The upper scale of the pyrometer was calibrated in Fahrenheit and the lower scale indicated the Celsius scale. The needle moving to the right indicated higher temperatures. The crew urged the needle to higher temperatures: 200 degrees Celsius, 400 degrees, 600 degrees.... The increase was slowing, but still moved upward.

There had to be a limit to our test. The high temperature of the fire was quickly consuming the dry oak timber. The temperature rose to 800 degrees and stalled at that temperature level. The combustion stabilized as the wood fuel became expended and the temperature began to drop. We had not soaked the wood fuel in water. (Our test actually combined show biz with scientific principles. The director wanted a dynamic blaze, and we did not know how much the soaked wood would affect the burn.) The reduced size of the timber-powered reactor and dry fuel supply resulted in a short burn and reduced temperature. As the brave little Maya blast furnace began to reduce its temperature, the director called out, "Cut!" The crew filmed some B-rolls, then slowly began to gather their gear and pack it up. There were hearty goodbyes as they sped into the night.

After their departure we assessed the performance of the scale model. First, the filming was a success, even with dry wood. Second, Maya technology attained another proof of its capabilities. The scale model was able to validate the thermodynamic performance and capabilities of the Maya timber kiln. The scale model performed as described by the ancient Maya cement fabricators. The flames shot skyward in a vertical column. The temperature of the scale model kiln was elevated to 800 degrees. This is twice the burning temperature of wood. My calculations of this heat level and the model's similitude indicated a potential temperature production of well over the 1,400 degrees required to transform limestone into cement.

I guess the Maya fabricators were wrong about allowing women to be present at a kiln burn.

7

Towers in the Forest

The 1842 landmark publication *Incidents of Travel in Central America, Chiapas, and Yucatán* became an immediate best-seller. John Lloyd Stephens's chatty prose and the crisp illustrations of Frederick Catherwood spurred the imaginations of its readers on flights of fancy to the lost civilization set in a tropical paradise. This masterpiece of prose that introduced the Maya to the world is considered to be a more learned and illuminating work than many dissertations on the Maya published by later scholars. Stephens offered the world its first glimpse of the intellectual, artistic, and engineering masterworks of the Maya culture. The pair was the first foreigners to observe and describe the strange architecture, rich ornamentation, and soaring structures that were the legacy bequeathed by the collective genius of the Maya civilization.

Until the end of the 19th century, scholars and archaeologists held forth multiple theories relative to the origin of the Maya. Opinions relative to their origin were strongly Eurocentric, and scholars offered theories that claimed the origins of the Maya to be Greek, Roman, Chaldean, Phoenician, or even Egyptian. Scholars also perceived that the ruined cities were thousands of years old. Stephens, with his level-headed thinking, and his knowledge of classic civilizations and languages, made logical postulations about the origin of the Maya: 1) the cities were hundreds of years old, not thousands, 2) the builders were not travelers from afar but were the ancestors of modern Maya living in the Yucatán at the start of the Spanish conquest, and 3) the hieroglyphics seen carved on stone throughout the region indicated the same culture and belief values throughout the Maya area. John Lloyd Stephens was "spot on" when he correctly theorized the age, cultural consistency and the origin of the Maya civilization. Yes, the Maya civilization was homegrown, all natural, purely domestic, indigenous, and born in the Yucatán.

Catherwood's illustrations and vivid descriptions of the ancient sky-scraping towers and exotic palaces looming above the emerald forest were proof that the cities had resisted the test of time, the attack of the tangled jungle environment, the tropical heat and rain, and countless hurricanes and devastating earthquakes. The resilient structures were mute testimony to the skilled technology of the Maya. The buildings in the sprawling cities had resisted degradation because the large structures had been constructed of durable building materials and formed in unique structural geometries. These unique structures were constructed with cast-in-place concrete structures that were erected more than 1,800 years prior to similar western technology. If Maya technology had not achieved elevated standards that were capable of constructing high-strength structures, but instead had constructed their cities of timber, brick, and thatch, Stephens would have encountered completely ruined and degraded cities that would have been buried deep below the jungle surface. No obvious evidence of these Maya cities would have been found.

The Maya applied innovative methods of agriculture technology including agronomy, terraces, raised fields, and efficient irrigation systems. This enhancement of agriculture products and yield was achieved, against all odds, in a fickle environment with poor soil, tropical heat, and a seasonal desert due to cycles of a rainy season followed by a dry season. The development of Maya civilization and its sciences, technology, and sophisticated city-states can be traced directly to the food surplus produced by efficient Maya agriculture. The abundant food surplus enabled sedentary lifestyles and encouraged the Maya to build villages and towns that support full-time artisans and technicians. These specialists were not required to grow their own food and so had adequate time to develop special industrial skills. The Pre-Classic sky-watchers, artisans, and technicians evolved into the astronomers, mathematicians, scribes, physicians, and engineers that expanded into the collective intellectual genius of the Maya civilization. Maya agriculture had set them free.

The variety of industrial skills and numbers of technicians and artisans expanded. The burgeoning of this multi-tasking society and its need

Figure 7-1: A typical Maya house that has been in use for thousands of years.
Author's image.

to operate as an efficient urban entity elevated the role and organization of the political elite and the management bureaucracy that was required to govern the population centers. The population centers became more defined, villages grew into towns, and towns into cities. As the cities grew in parallel with the scientific and technical character of the culture, the basic Pre-Classic building consisted of a timber skeleton frame lashed together and covered with a thatched roof and wattle walls (Figure 7-1). This basic structure then evolved into more permanent and sophisticated structures that were able to resist the harsh environment, earthquakes, and wind storms while minimizing maintenance requirements. Specialized technologies were required to construct larger and taller buildings, and to create an infrastructure that satisfied the demands for water resources and transportation needs of the urban population. Maya engineers enhanced their capabilities in hydraulics and water management to collect, store, and distribute large volumes of potable water that enabled a safe and comfortable life style in Maya urban centers. As the power elite, scientific, technical, and merchant classes grew, they set up shop in the city center to be close to economic activities and the market place for trading operations. The growing wealth of the urban centers enhanced the need for specialized building systems. Buildings grew in size and configuration, and became more elaborate.

Their invention of a self-sufficient city, with supporting agriculture in the hinterlands, was not a new idea in historical terms. However, unlike cities in other civilizations, Maya cities became more independent, becoming incubators of trade, sciences, technologies, learning, and specialized trades. City-states, bound together by the mutual goals of trade, a common culture, and scientific concepts, developed into a political network, a logical evolution. The cities grew stronger and created an integrated network of commerce.

The Growth and Development of City-States

City building had expanded throughout the Maya zone by the late Pre-Classic Period. The Maya gravitated toward a political model of power and economic wealth based on a city-state concept. During the Classic Period, more than 50 independent Maya power centers evolved into a network of autonomous city-states. This political phenomenon of independent city-states morphed into a successful intra-city trade and political network. The city-state network became the locus of political, intellectual, and economic power throughout the Maya world.

Why city-states? We can attribute this to the individuality of the Maya to choose independence over being controlled by outside influences. The civilization would not have had its longevity and character if it had chosen another course of political organization. The route of the empire as a political organization, as was chosen by the majority of other great civilizations, including the Roman, Egyptian, and Aztec civilizations, forced a widespread territory to operate under a lone power center. The empire had requirements for a large-standing army to control its wide-ranging territory and systems to collect the tribute paid by the conquered people. Empires tended to be single dimensional in many aspects, and the cost of large-standing armies to maintain control reduced the economic power that could be applied to science and technology.

The city-state political system enhanced the urban fabric of each city, as well as the intellectual capability of individual Maya cities. Maya city-states enjoyed an advantage over the economics and politics of an empire. They were self-reliant centers of administrative, commercial, scientific, and technical activities that capitalized on the diversity of industry and market opportunities contributed by other city-states within the trade network. They were spared the expense of a large, wide-ranging, standing army. The alliances of the city-states were generated from the lucrative trade and cultural exchange, rather than from external conquest. There were, of course, exceptions. Larger city-states drawing on their great wealth and greater political power commanded smaller cities within their sphere. Larger and more powerful city-states were able to conquer other weaker city-states and create regional city-states.

The further advantage of the network alliances of city-states lay in their synergistic enhancement as incubators of scientific and technical concepts. A certain city-state would collect ideas from the other city-states, then enhance the concept in their own in-house "think tank." The borrowed concept would be assessed, then nourished, improved, and disseminated other city-states via the interchange of commercial trade activities. Multi-city political systems relied on this reciprocal system of trade, and the diffusion and dissemination of technological concepts. By contrast, an empire with a single central city would likely have a single center of learning and could not be adaptive to outside ideas.

The various divisions of labor and industrial disciplines required specialized, functional buildings with vertical and horizontal functional spaces designed to satisfy the operations of each industry or activity. There was also a need for urban traffic circulation, open space plazas, and an efficient infrastructure. Specialized structures were constructed for specific functions and tailored to the needs of the city. City planners and engineers met the challenge of the burgeoning population with a never-ending construction program and an enhanced water-management system. (In the late Classic Period, Maya cities boasted populations of 100,000 people. At the same time, the city of Rome had a population of 35,000 and the city of Paris was home to 20,000 inhabitants.) The infrastructure included the construction of an ample water management system with water collection, storage, and delivery systems that enabled the survival of the densely populated cities during the seasonal drought. This infrastructure became an integral part of the design of the cityscape. Plazas, hardscapes, roadways, and buildings all became part of the water collection system. The roofs of structures, roads, and plazas were designed and constructed to slope toward water-collection channels.

A typical classic Maya polity was a self-reliant city-state governed by a lord who served as the ruler. The domain of the city-state consisted of a capital city with a finite territory comprised of smaller towns and villages surrounded by the farmland that supported the population with its agricultural needs. In most cases, the capitals of city-states were not at great distances from each other. The cities seldom required more than two to three days travel between them. The closeness of the cities enhanced technology, trade, and, most importantly, the exchange of ideas. Each of the various city-states possessed valuable natural resources that were special to that city and provided a wide variety of industrial products that formed the basis of their viable trade network. The commercial network that developed between the larger and smaller city-states was based on the trade exchange and the need for specific products that were unique to a certain city-state.

The flow of commercial goods and materials between the city-states and the lively traffic activities between them resulted in the need for the construction of a network of all-weather, paved highway system connecting the city-states. The network of Maya roads featured long-span bridges, rest stations, and drainage structures.

The growth of specialized disciplines in each city resulted in the development of nodes or precincts in the cityscape devoted to specific disciplines or industrial functions. These specialized disciplines required different types of structures to serve their needs. City planners met this need by establishing sectors or neighborhoods within a city for these disciplines. Urban planning and technology were required to construct the functional structures for the cities and develop corresponding infrastructure. The resulting functional forms of buildings had requirements in the size of plan, interior space, and height of floor levels, interior light, and geometry. Applying multi-discipline technologies, Maya engineers created functional buildings using their durable construction materials. These materials included cast-in-place concrete, high-strength timber, and composite stone and concrete structures that were formed in a variety of innovative geometric shapes.

The grand plazas in the cities were the center of the activities and functions that gave energy to the city. These large greenswards and hardscapes of the urban centers were surrounded by large-scale monumental buildings. The buildings housed administrative, economic, religious, educational, and scientific functions. The plazas were replete with large stone stele covered with carved hieroglyphics and figures of personages that described the historic sagas of the city. During a typical day in the life of a Maya city, the populace would stream into the plaza, carrying out their business, shopping, trading, and sharing gossip while traversing the wide open space that became the crossroads, as well as a place of assembly, for the denizens of the city. The plazas served as the venue for large assemblies of the faithful for public manifestations of pageantry, ritual, ceremonial rites, and celebration that were carried out and performed on outdoor platforms and the temples encircling the plaza. The tropical climate made the construction of large, enclosed structures impractical for the gathering of crowds. Moreover, though only hundreds could gather in overheated interior spaces, thousands could assemble in the cool evening air of the plaza. This led the Maya engineers to design interior spaces for more traditional applications, in a size and volume similar to their traditional houses or *ná*. Long-span structures were reserved for monumental statements such as entry arches to cities.

There is evidence that the Maya developed prefabricated structures for construction efforts and transported them some distance to selected construction sites. This was a part of the commercial matrix of Maya culture. Buildings have been excavated that were abandoned in an unfinished condition. The various stone element of the facade had been laid out on the ground at the front of the building ready to be installed, when the construction was abandoned.

It is known that Maya possessed a lucrative market in the construction industry. It is logical that smaller urban centers, without specialized building trades, would rely on a larger construction center with specialized trades to produce the building components for a widespread market. Shipping would be carried out by manpower with components sized for tumpline use. Again, the Maya were ahead of their time: the first references in Europe for the case for prefabrication came from Leonardo da Vinci. Many facades of elegant Maya buildings were constructed of mosaics of carved stone that were prefabricated off-site and transported to the site to complete the facade.

High-Rise Buildings in the Rainforest

"Build it and they will come" may be an older catchphrase than we know. The attractions and comfort of the city life increased migration away from the hinterlands and into urban centers. As cities grew, there was a constant demand for new workers and expansion of the urban core. Maya engineers developed structural engineering mechanisms, which they combined with innovative, high-strength building materials, to meet the demand for monumental buildings that engendered the magnificent Maya cities.

The Maya structures were constructed of high-strength materials using a hybrid of linear and circular structural mechanisms that generated graceful buildings towering above the sprawling cityscape. These unique structures, unlike any other style in world architecture, represented a diverse variety of monumental buildings including pyramids, palaces, temples, observatories, administrative buildings, and ball courts. The buildings featured creature comforts and amenities including plumbing, potable water, ventilation systems, and sewerage disposal systems.

The sophistication of Maya structural engineering was a synergistic product of high-strength building materials and engineering mechanisms that resisted seismic events, hurricanes, and the harsh environment, while solving the complex geometries required by the function of the building and by the exotic style of monumental buildings.

Maya High-Tech Building Materials

Maya engineering technology exploited native resources to create high-strength, technologically advanced construction materials. These materials are quite similar to products used in modern construction technology. The range of high-strength materials of construction applied by Maya engineers greatly exceeded the capabilities of European materials of construction until the 19th century. The shopping list of materials developed by Maya engineers is extensive. The following materials of construction are native and were developed as high-strength materials used by Maya engineers:

Native Limestone

The Yucatán is an extensive limestone shelf extending deep below the surface. The native limestone is a multi-use building product and is the basis for cement, aggregate for cast-in-place concrete, and raw material for cut stone masonry and the material for carving Maya sculptures. The compressive strength of limestone exceeds 5000 psi (34.5 MPa), which is more than acceptable for structural purposes.

Hydraulic Cement

Maya technicians invented the process for fabricating hydraulic cement and applied this multi-purpose building material to construction projects before the year 300 BC. They used hydraulic cement as the principal binding substance for the majority of building materials in Maya construction, including cast-in-place concrete, mortar, stucco, and composite structures. The demand for the fabrication of hydraulic cement was continuous, and the production of cement material required a high demand for timber to be used as the fuel for the process. The collection of the timber fuel at times resulted in the clear cutting of forests and greatly impacted the environment of the hinterlands of the city-states.

Cast-in-Place Concrete

Today, the most popular building material is cast-in-place concrete. The same was true during the Maya Classic Period. This durable construction material is formed by a paste of hydraulic cement and water, which coats the surface of the stone aggregates added to the mix. The cement and water paste reacts through a chemical process called hydration. The paste hardens and bonds with the aggregate, gaining strength to form the rock-like mass known as concrete. One great advantage to constructing with concrete is that the process starts as a pliable, flowable material when newly mixed; when placed within the structural forms, it assumes the shape of the formwork. When the chemical hydration process is complete, the paste hardens and forms the hard, high-strength material known as concrete. Cast-in-place concrete was used by the Maya to construct structural members for buildings, paving, walls, and reservoirs.

Composite Limestone and Cast-in-Place Concrete

The invention of cement was a great step forward for Maya technology. However, the real breakthrough in increasing the strength of structural building materials was combining the beneficial capabilities and strength of cut limestone with cast-in-place concrete to create a high-strength composite material. This combination not only produced a strong, durable material, but also eliminated the prerequisite formwork required of Roman or modern concrete structures.

This composite system of materials used the cut limestone facing walls to develop the exterior and interior surface of the wall structure in lieu of wooden forms. When the fluid concrete is placed between the walls, the interior face of the limestone wall elements becomes coated with the concrete paste and creates a strong surface bond with the interior concrete. When the concrete has hardened, it technically becomes a part of the limestone walls and develops a composite structural system that has an exceptionally strong weight-bearing resistance and enhanced lateral resistance. The composite structure is stronger than its parts. This type of composite structure was used for arches vaults, walls, and roof structures in Maya buildings.

Limestone, Masonry, and Mortar

The application of cut limestone blocks bonded together with cement mortar was used to build load-bearing and non-load-bearing walls. Structural mortar is a homogeneous mix composed of cement, fine aggregate, and water. When water is added to the cement and aggregate and mixed, the hydration process is activated, and this malleable paste is applied to the surface of the limestone blocks. The mortar bonds the adjacent masonry blocks together to form a strong structural wall system. These walls were used as partitions in buildings to develop interior room-demising walls and exterior walls.

Stucco

Stucco is an applied plaster consisting of cement, aggregate, and water. Maya engineers and architects used the material in multiple ways for interior and exterior applications. It is generally considered that stucco was applied over the rough stone surface as a smooth aesthetic finish that could then receive paint or other finish materials. However, the waterproofing qualities of stucco are one of the major reasons that the Maya structures were able to resist the attack of their harsh environment. The application of several coats of stucco not only resisted water intrusion into the matrix of the structure, but deterred the growth of fungus, mold, and jungle vegetation that could penetrate the surface of exposed stone and pry apart the interior structure. Stucco also served as the base material for three-dimensional sculptures of Maya art and as artistic decoration on the facade of Maya structures.

Bright colors of paint were applied to the walls and facade sculptures. This presented a dramatic effect, but the impact of the painted building was accelerated by the addition of mica into the mix of the paint for the surface coating. The lustrous pigments were made with mica to give the building a dazzling effect in the bright tropical sun and generate a lustrous effect in moonlight. Studies have indicated that major buildings received numerous coats of stucco and luminous paint over the years. Each new coating of mica paint gave the sacred buildings a dazzling appearance. Again the Maya were ahead of their time: mica is used in modern paints, for the similar purpose of creating a shimmering appearance on a painted surface.

The interior and exterior coatings of stucco, and the brightly colored paints that covered the major structures, were constantly repaired and replaced during the Classic Period. After abandonment, this moisture-resistant material reinforced the battle against the onslaught of the environment, until centuries had passed and the ceaseless attack of the jungle growth finally broke through the outer barrier of stucco. The composite stone and concrete structures resisted the external environment for additional centuries after the stucco had been breached and enabled the monumental structures to survive the jungle attack.

Multiple examples of extant interior and exterior stucco are located in Maya cities. Figure C-5 indicates the stucco remaining on the interior of vaulted ceilings.

High-Strength Structural Timber

The Maya world was fortunate to be the homeland of several varieties of dense, high-strength tropical hardwoods, which were also resistant to insects and decay. Several of these timber products possessed the tensile strength exceeding that of cast iron. The wood was used for lintels and beams due to its high strength, durability, and resistance to termites and decay. Some of the timber beams survive today, 1,300 years after being installed in Maya structures (Figure C-5). High-strength, durable structural timber includes sapodilla or chico zapote (*manilkara zapota*), cedar (*cedrela odorata*), and mahogany (*swietenia macrophylla*). The tensile strength of chico zapote is more than 20,000 psi.

High Tensile-Strength Rope

Hemp rope or henequen is indigenous to the Maya world. The strong fibers of this plant were collected from the sword-shaped leaves of the *agave fourcroydes* plant. Its strong fibers were woven into high-strength rope and used in multiple applications by the Maya. This rope had a tensile strength of 18,000 psi. In construction, rope was used as a suspension cable in bridges, a hoisting cable in construction, as a trussing connection device to secure joints of timber structures, and for other construction uses, including fabrication of containers for transporting building materials. In addition to construction applications, this strong and pliable material was used for baskets, clothing, and hammocks.

This very same rope became indispensable throughout the world during the 18th and 19th centuries, when it was needed for ships, thus becoming was an extremely lucrative export from the Yucatán. It was used by the construction, marine, and other industries that required rope cable before steel or nylon cable was available. This one export made the Yucatán and its capital city, Mérida, extremely wealthy.

Latex

The milky latex of the sapodilla tree produced a natural rubber and gummy substance, which was used for several products, including chicle, the basis of modern chewing gum, and the coating for waterproof fabrics. In construction, latex was used as an additive for concrete, as an adhesive to secure jade tools to wooden handles, for the waterproofing of structures, and for gluing structural members together. Latex is a natural polymer that, when used as an admixture for concrete, enhances the bonding, durability, and workability of the concrete.

Concrete Admixtures

The use of admixtures to improve the durability of cast-in-place concrete has been identified from various sources. The addition of volcanic ashes, powder of burned clay, and a by-product of the process of making tortillas has positive effects on concrete workability, durability, and strength.

The flowers from the morning glory vine last for a single morning and die in the afternoon. However, the discovery of the merits of the chemical agents collected from the juice of the morning glory vine has been known for thousands of years. Maya engineers added the juice of the morning glory vine to the concrete mix to induce waterproofing in the concrete. Maya used the juice from the species *ipomoea alba* to convert latex gum from the *castilla elastica* into bouncing rubber balls used in the Maya ball games. The sulfides in the juice of the morning glory vine served to vulcanize the rubber when the two substances were heated together. The Maya learned this process from the Olmec, who predated the process of vulcanization by Charles Goodyear by 3,000 years.

Realization of a Maya Structure

The conception and construction of a Maya structure initiated with the patronage or sponsor of the structure. Whether the goal was to construct the tallest pyramid to enhance the glory of the city, to construct of a luxurious palace for the comfort of an elite family, or to erect a structure for commercial purposes that kept the big wheel turning, someone had to fund the project. When the purpose, size, and level of luxury had been established, the planning for the project would begin.

Remnants of fragile documents, including the plans and designs of engineers and architects, did not survive the collapse of the Maya and the ravages of time. However, it is known that the Maya were expert at paper production. They were also skilled in mathematics, written communication, and astronomy, all of which are part of the process of converting conceptual ideas into hard line drawings on paper for visualization before physically transferring the drawings of a structure into the "bricks and mortar"—or stone and concrete—of a building. To develop their drawing or plan for a project design, architects and engineers used straight-edge tools similar to those used by modern designers prior to the advent of the computer.

The layout of the building on the site would follow the guidelines established by the design drawings. The outer perimeter of the structure would be demarcated with wooden posts and "string lines" made of hemp cords or rope, and 90-degree corners were accurately defined with a string line using a set of lines and a circle. It is known that the Maya possessed a defined measurement system with units of approximately 0.96 meter. Using this system, the outer perimeter of the building would be laid out. The verticality of walls and their angular intersections would be defined using "plumb bobs." Water levels and building squares were used in "truing" the construction of the building.

Mobilization of the construction process would follow conventional standard methods used throughout the world. Because beasts of burden were not native to the Americas, Maya technology solved the issues of transportation of construction materials by using the efficiency of readily available manpower. Construction materials were transported in quantities and weight that could be transported and handled by one man. Stones cut for construction were sized to be transported by one man. The device now known as the tumpline was used for overland transport and construction lifting. This load-carrying device, which carried the Maya civilization during its glory days, is still used today for transporting loads. A look at Maya constructions makes it clear that the vast majority of the cut stones could be transported by one man and a tumpline. Loose or fluid construction materials, such as sand, cement, small stones, and wet concrete, could easily be transported using the manpowered tumpline and a container woven of sisal. This method of construction was used in Mexican construction until well into the 20th century.

As the construction of a structure grew taller, access to the upper construction levels was carried out by work scaffolds made from trussed timber poles. These cross-braced towers were stable, conformed to the geometry of the building facade, and were accessed by ladders. Maya artists did not normally depict common scenes such as construction sites. However, a mural on the wall in the temple of the warriors at Chichen Itza indicates the use of trussed timber towers, similar to scaffolding used in construction today. The mural shows the scaffolds used as a "war machine." The mural indicates a warrior using an atlatl standing on top of what appears to be a 6-meter trussed tower. The tower is being steadied by warriors at the base as the elevated hurler launches his dart into the besieged city. The height of the tower would increase the range of the atlatl by 18–27 meters; the tower had a great advantage over the capabilities of the defenders at lower levels. A similar type of scaffolding would have been used by laborers building Maya structures.

As the construction progressed upward, the ubiquitous hemp rope was used to hoist construction materials to the appropriate level for installation. The application of stucco on the facade was carried out using tools that are similar to today's stucco application. The first coat could be applied by hand and flat boards, and then finished with trowels. Murals were sketched out using graphite crayons, the colors were mixed with mortars and pestles, and the murals were applied with brushes.

Maya engineers were masters at combining high-strength materials and structural mechanics to satisfy the geometric requirements of their monumental buildings. Maya engineers invented a variety of structural systems to suit the unique style of their architecture. They capitalized on their home-grown feats of structural ingenuity, combined with high-strength building materials, to create column free interior spaces, erect multistory building, construct a skyscraping pyramid, and many other engineering feats.

The Maya Arch

The basic building block used in Maya structures was a closed structural element commonly known as the "Maya arch." This element had multifaceted capabilities and could span between supports to create interior spaces in a building, span a gateway to develop an inspiring entrance, be elongated along its longitudinal axis to develop a large vault-like interior space, or be positioned vertically to form multistory vaulted buildings.

Scholars of Maya architecture often refer to the structural shape of the Maya arch as a "false arch" or a "corbelled arch." However, as a structural mechanical element, the Maya arch is not a structural arch. This unique structural spanning system is a trapezoidal linear truss that resists gravity loads by axial force members flowing in a straight line load path within a closed circuit geometrical network from the roof to the foundation.

A corbelled arch is formed by stair-stepping successive blocks of masonry stone from the spring line upward in a manner that enables the shape of the interior structure to project up toward the center of the vault. Each supporting side will step upward and join at an intersection at the apex of the structure (Figure 7-2). The interior of the spanned space assumes a trapezoidal shape. The corbelled truss is not a true structural arch. All the interior stresses in the structure are transferred into linear compressive stresses. Corbelled arches require thick walls and an abutment to counteract the

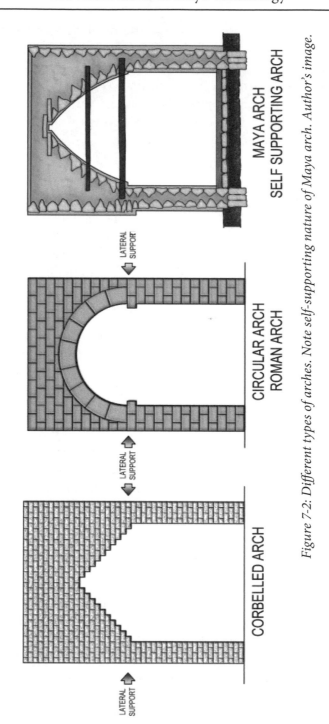

Figure 7-2: Different types of arches. Note self-supporting nature of Maya arch. Author's image.

horizontal stresses generated from gravity loads, which would tend to collapse the archway without appropriate lateral stability.

The true arch is a circular structural shape assembled of cut stone in a uniform, upward, circular curve. The arch maintains its stability through the compressive pressure of the curved stone sections against the face of adjacent sections. The true arch must have lateral resistance at the spring line (Figure 7-2). Eurocentric archaeologists have used the circular Roman arch as the prototype for a non-linear structure spanning between two supports. That is why they use the term *false arch* for the interior space formed by structures in Maya architecture. Because it is not curved, ergo, it must be a "false" arch.

The Maya truss used in large structures, though capable of doing so, was seldom used to span large interior spaces. In the tropical environment of the Yucatán, the construction of large interior spaces for assembly was impractical, with average temperature hovering near 80 degrees Fahrenheit (26 degrees Celsius) year-round, with periods of higher temperatures in the 90s Fahrenheit. The assembly area for large gatherings in the sultry tropics took place outside in the open plazas to take advantage of the cooling trade winds. A large interior space crowded with people would be stifling and impractical. The Maya trapezium arch is the primary structural element or building block of large architectural constructions. (Figure C-5, Figure C-6, Figure 7-3, and Figure 7-4).

The Roman arch or true arch took the form of a semi-circle spanning between two supports. During the course of the Roman Empire, engineers combined cast-in-place concrete with facing bricks to increase the span of the arches. However, the construction of an arch required detailed workmanship. To erect the structure of a Roman arch, it was required to erect a wooden form with a scaffold system to support the stone or brick forming the arch. The formwork was erected prior to placing concrete. The forming device for the arch is called centering.

The stones or brick of the circular arch were required to be fabricated with the sides of the arch stones sloped radially. The formwork, scaffold system, and centering provided support for the wedge-shaped masonry elements of the arch. These trapezoidal elements are called "voussoirs" until they are in place. The wet cast-in-place concrete would then be placed in the space between the brick arches. A massive centering system was required to sustain the weight of the brick arch members and the wet concrete. When

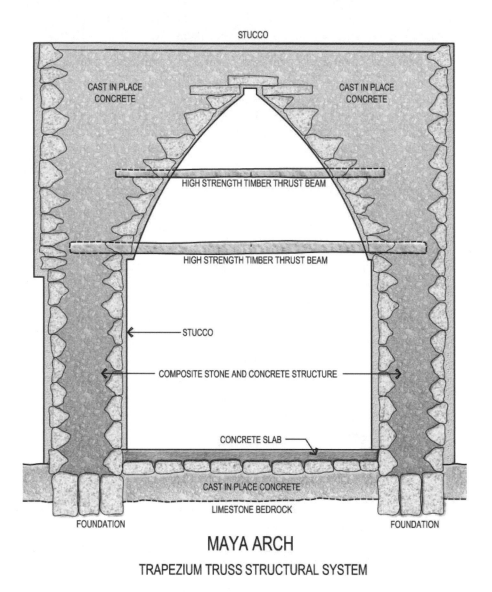

STUCCO

CAST IN PLACE CONCRETE

CAST IN PLACE CONCRETE

HIGH STRENGTH TIMBER THRUST BEAM

HIGH STRENGTH TIMBER THRUST BEAM

STUCCO

COMPOSITE STONE AND CONCRETE STRUCTURE

CONCRETE SLAB

CAST IN PLACE CONCRETE

LIMESTONE BEDROCK

FOUNDATION

FOUNDATION

MAYA ARCH
TRAPEZIUM TRUSS STRUCTURAL SYSTEM

Figure 7-3: Construction of a typical Maya arch using composite stone and cast-in-place concrete. Author's image.

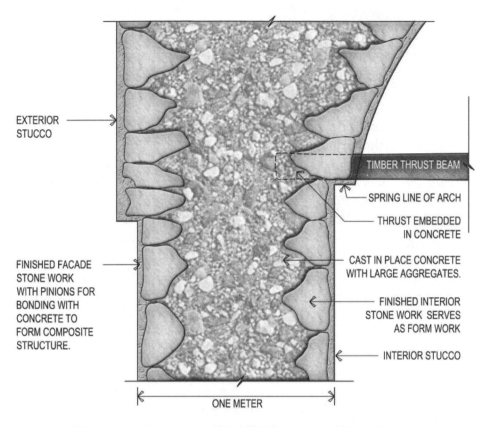

EXTERIOR STUCCO

TIMBER THRUST BEAM

SPRING LINE OF ARCH

THRUST EMBEDDED IN CONCRETE

FINISHED FACADE STONE WORK WITH PINIONS FOR BONDING WITH CONCRETE TO FORM COMPOSITE STRUCTURE.

CAST IN PLACE CONCRETE WITH LARGE AGGREGATES.

FINISHED INTERIOR STONE WORK SERVES AS FORM WORK

INTERIOR STUCCO

ONE METER

DETAIL: MAYA VAULT STRUCTURE AT THE SPRING LINE

Figure 7-4: Detail of typical arch construction at spring line and timber thrust beam. Author's image.

the concrete had gained sufficient strength, then the centering system could be removed. At this point, the arch would be self-supporting due to the composite action of the concrete and stone arch.

As a structural unit, the Maya arch resists gravity loads as a trapezoidal truss consisting of linear structural members. The nature of the Maya trapezoidal structure resists large gravity loads in pure compression and tension members. Maya engineers used this trapezoidal structure to create long-span interior spaces. The use of the trapezoidal Maya arch permits an attractive, column-free structural system and is stronger than the curved arch. Computer analysis of the Maya structure has verified its superior strength, and time has proved the test of durability and its resistance to the environment (Figure 7-3 and Figure 7-4).

The construction of a Maya trapezoidal structure is less complex than the classic Roman arch. The Maya arch does not require formwork, special scaffolding, or the shaping of stones into trapezoidal voussoirs to form the basic shape and surface of the structure. The Maya arch is constructed using a system that employs the exterior and interior stonework at each face of the wall as the formwork for the cast-in-place concrete wall interiors. Interior timber thrust beams are used as an integral part of the structure and are used as interior scaffolding during construction. The construction of the basic, trapezoidal, single-story Maya structure utilized simplistic but brilliant methodologies. The process is repeated for multiple adjacent structures on the same plane or vertically for multistory structures.

The basic construction sequence is shown and described in Figure 7-5a through Figure 7-5d, and provides an overview of the construction of a single Maya arch module. A description of each stage follows. Multiple horizontal or vertical modules are constructed in a similar manner.

Figure 7-5a

The foundation for the basic structural module is constructed as continuous stonework is laid with leveling mortar upon the shallow limestone stratum. The walls are placed in lifts of approximately 1 meter, with cut stone masonry placed on each side of the wall. The walls are filled then with wet cast-in-place concrete and large stone aggregate. Once a concrete lift has set up, the next section of cut stone masonry interior and exterior walls are installed and the interior of the walls can be filled with concrete.

When the appropriate wall height has been constructed to the spring line, a high-strength circular timber member of 5 inches in diameter, called a "thrust beam," is placed at strategic horizontal intervals along the spring line of the arch. The ends of the thrust beams are embedded approximately 1 meter into the concrete in opposing walls. The bonding of concrete to the rough surface of the timber thrust beam resists the lateral compression force generated by the structure during the construction phase. A 12.5-centimeter-diameter beam embedded 0.5 meter into the wall concrete can generate up to 30,000 pounds of lateral resistance at each end of the thrust beam.

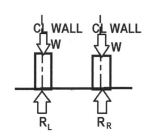

FREE BODY DIAGRAM

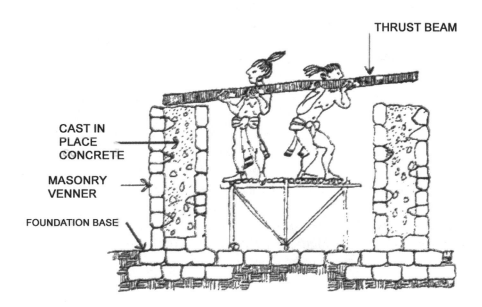

Figure 7-5a: Stage 1 in the construction of the Maya arch. Author's image.

Figure 7-5b

With the timber thrust beams in place, construction can proceed upward. The horizontal thrust beams can now be used as scaffold supports for workers to facilitate access for the construction of the inward structure element. The trapezium-shaped vault geometry is generated by installing cut limestone blocks on the outside and inside faces of the vault structure.

The interior stone is shaped with a flat face that is inclined upward. The rear of the stone is a pinion shaped element contoured to optimize the bonding surface between the stone and the cast-in-place concrete wall interior. The exterior stone facing is placed vertically. The shape is similar to the interior block, with a pinion positioned to optimize the bond between the concrete infill and the cut stone. As the upper vault wall varies in width to form an isosceles triangle, the inward leaning geometry of the vault mass will alter the center of gravity of the structure. The alignment of the centroid of the mass with the center line of the vertical support wall moves inward to a position toward the center line of the shaped vault. The inward shift of the center of gravity will induce an inward bending moment in the upper wall. The inward bending moment would create instability in the partially constructed arch and would cause a collapse without the horizontal resistance of the thrust beam. Maya engineers were aware of the stability characteristics of this construction. The installation of the timber thrust beams resulted in a compressive member that will "push" back against the inward bending tendency of the inclined upper walls of the trapezium. Therefore, the high-strength timber thrust beam serves to stabilize the equilibrium of the construction.

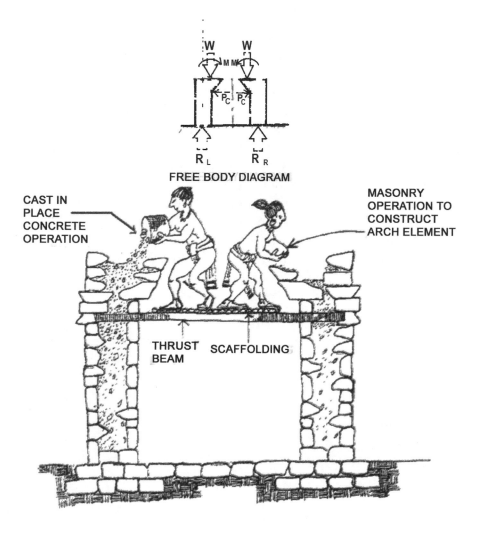

Figure 7-5b: Stage 2 in the construction of the Maya arch. Author's image.

Figure 7-5c

The construction of the angular upper section of the arch continues until the inward bending mass of composite structure again becomes unstable and an additional upper horizontal thrust beam is required. This high density timber member is a smaller diameter than the lower thrust beam, and embedding in the concrete is minimized due to the reduced levels of thrust. A 3-inch-diameter beam with an embedment of 24 inches into the concrete mass is adequate support for the upper thrust beam. The installation of the upper thrust beam enabled the Maya construction team to stabilize the structure and continue the upward development of the trapezoidal structural shape. The trapezoidal structure is completed with the installation of the horizontal capstone at the apex of the arch. The capstone and the opposite forces at the interface of the top elements of the arch structure stabilize the inward bending movement, reducing horizontal compressive forces in the system.

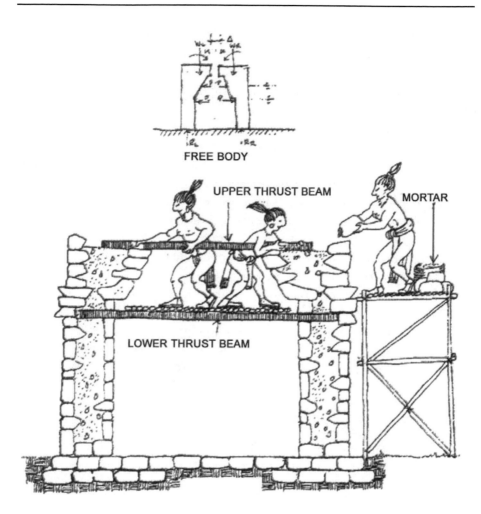

Figure 7-5c: Stage 3 in the construction of the Maya arch. Author's image.

Figure 7-5d

When the capstone and top horizontal construction have been installed, the connection of the two vertical segments of the geometry completes the closed structural circuit of the trapezium structure. The structural vertical element may now be constructed. The structure is now a stable, load-carrying mechanism. The inward bending moments are stabilized and the closed circuit of the completed geometry alters the load paths of the structure. The gravity loads will follow the load paths through the angular roof structure and be supported by the vertical walls at the base of the system. This action of load resistance of the truss action, however, creates an outward horizontal force at the spring line. The lower thrust beam now reverses the nature of its stress from a compression member and becomes a tension member, resisting the outward movement on each side. The bonded embedment of the timber thrust beam into the concrete wall resists the tension "pull out" action caused by the horizontal vectors at the spring line. The lower walls react to transmit vertical loads, and the thrust beam is now a horizontal tension member. The two components combine to resist the vertical and horizontal vectors of the truss. The composite walls and the thrust beams now complete the closed circuit that develops a stable structure.

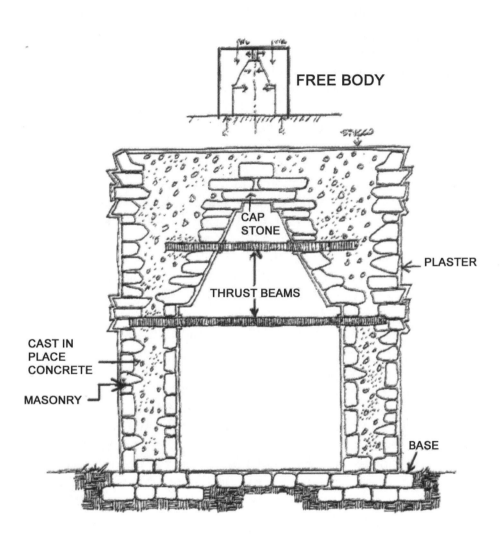

Figure 7-5d: Stage 4 in the construction of the Maya arch. Author's image.

The Resolution of Horizontal Forces Over Time

The analysis of a typical Maya trapezium arch indicates that the tension resistance of the timber thrust beam is a permanent part of the stable structural system for the arch. Maya engineers anticipated the long-term resistance of the timber member as part of the monumental structure. For this reason, the engineers selected a dense, high-strength timber similar to *chico zapote*. This wood is highly resistant to termites and degradation. In addition, it has tensile strength of more than 20,000 psi, which is a strength similar to low-grade steel. In some cases, the tension beam has degraded over the centuries; however, in specific cases, the resistant timber thrust beam has survived into the 21st century. The timber thrust beams at Xtampak (Figure C-5) are survivors of the abandonment and are still functional tension members. When the trapezium structure fails, it is usually at the perimeter of the building. Interior arches in the same structure depend on the adjacency of the exterior line of trapezium structures. In these cases, the thrust beam at the perimeter has degraded and failed, and the horizontal tension forces have pushed the exterior wall outward. The interior arches remain intact due to the lateral support from the remains of failed exterior vaults.

The presence of the surviving timber thrust beams in Maya arches has long been a mystery in the annals of archaeology. The use of the beams has been opined by archaeologists to have multiple applications. They have been considered to be devices for the hanging of hammocks, curtains, or clothing, or used as storage platforms or as granaries. Legendary archaeologist Eric Thompson suggested that the timber beams were installed to hark back to the horizontal roof beams of the native huts. To the best of my knowledge, the use of the thrust beam as a structural member was first suggested by Lawrence Roys, an engineer who wrote *The Engineering Knowledge of the Maya*, published in 1934 by the Carnegie Institution of Washington. Mr. Roys was spot on: the timber beam was not an interior design accessory, but a vital structural member.

The stability and strength of concrete trapezium arch is superior to similar structural systems. Maya engineers developed this system for permanency. Its inherent strength is capable of resisting large levels of vertical and lateral gravity loading. Its strength and function enable its use as a basic module in a stand-alone configuration or in a series of horizontal and vertical structures arrayed in buildings and other applications.

Practical Applications of the Maya Arch

The basic geometric structural module of the Maya arch was used throughout the Maya world, further reinforcing the exchange of ideas and technology within the Maya sphere of influence. The structural component was used to generate interior clear spans in single-story and multistory structures, monumental portals, triumphant arches, underground water-storage reservoirs for water, bridges and support systems for stairs, tunnels, and aqueducts.

Examples of monumental stand-alone structures using the trapezium arch include the grand arch at Kabah and the entrance portal at Labná. The grand arch at Kabah (Figure C-6) is the largest known freestanding trapezium arch. This 6 meter × 7.5 meter structure is the grand entrance to the city of Kabah. The arch connects the city of Uxmal with Kabah via a 12-mile-long roadway or sacbe. The 3 meter × 3 meter vertical members of the structure resist the lateral forces of the arch. This arch has been remediated. However, in its failed state, the 3 meter × 3 meter members did not collapse but were converted to cantilevers due the concrete construction of the members.

The portal entrance at Labná is also one of Frederick Catherwood's subjects. The portal arch is the entrance to the monumental structure to a major building group. A sacbe leads to the entrance. Catherwood's illustration shows sculpted figures in the niches below the thatched roof sculptures at each side. They have now disappeared.

The Maya Vault Structure

The Maya trapezium arch is the basic building module for the construction of the classic Maya vault. Maya vault geometry is generated by extending the trapezium arch along its longitudinal axis (Figure 7-6). The Maya trapezium arch structure was applied to develop a closed interior space in Maya buildings. The vaults ranged in size based on their uses. Vaulted spaces at the exterior of buildings tended to be larger because of the advantage of air circulation. Larger buildings with multi-vault spans varied in size from a single-level vaulted space, to large palaces of 200 vaulted rooms. In multistory palaces, the structure rose to heights of five levels, with upper vault levels connected to each other with exterior and interior stairs.

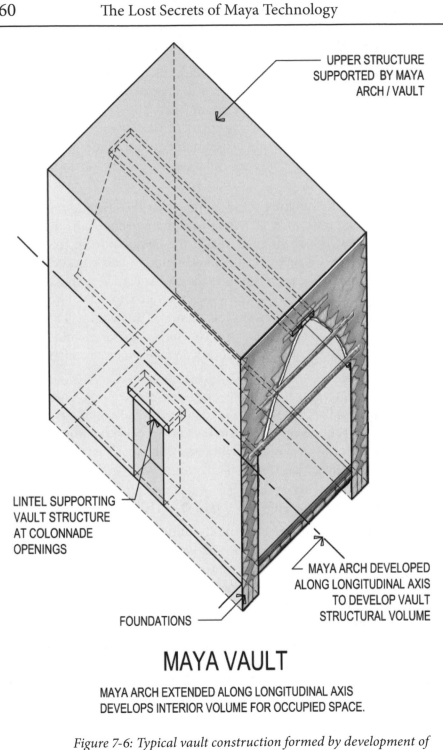

UPPER STRUCTURE
SUPPORTED BY MAYA
ARCH / VAULT

LINTEL SUPPORTING
VAULT STRUCTURE
AT COLONNADE
OPENINGS

MAYA ARCH DEVELOPED
ALONG LONGITUDINAL AXIS
TO DEVELOP VAULT
STRUCTURAL VOLUME

FOUNDATIONS

MAYA VAULT

MAYA ARCH EXTENDED ALONG LONGITUDINAL AXIS
DEVELOPS INTERIOR VOLUME FOR OCCUPIED SPACE.

*Figure 7-6: Typical vault construction formed by development of
arch along longitudinal axis of vault. Author's image.*

The design of a specific type and size of building and its function dictated the size and number of vaulted rooms and their relative geometry. Once the size and position of the vaults in a building was established, and their egress and ingress openings as well as interior circulation was established, then the structural geometry of the vaults could be determined. Large buildings tended to position their vaulted interior spaces in parallel to the long facade of the building with wider and greater number of door openings at exterior vaults to enhance air circulation. The plan of large buildings maximized the number of exterior rooms while optimizing the structural capacity of the vaults. The adjacency of the vaults enhances the resistance to lateral forces.

The ability of the vault structure to solve the requirement for various living and working functions was very flexible. Vaults were constructed with linear shapes, crossing vaults (groin vaults), and circular vaults. The linear vault had a straight centerline with demising end walls constructed of masonry. This type of vault was used to develop the typical interior space for Maya structures. It was used in single and multistory buildings by Maya engineers (Figure C-5 and Figure 7-6). Additionally, Maya architecture used vaults that crossed at right angles. The crossing vaults form architectural groin geometry at their intersection. The groin is the intersection of two perpendicular vaults and creates structural stability at the intersection, as well as serving as an attractive aesthetic device.

The Size of Maya Vaults

The size of the Maya vault in structures varied with the function of the building. The sizes ranged from small spaces to 12 foot × 20 foot interior spaces. The construction of large interior spaces for assembly was not practical—not because of structural limitations, but for environmental reasons. The lack of dynamic ventilation combined with the tropical heat made large assembly spaces a liability.

The usual size of a vault in a royal residence was approximately the size of the traditional Maya house or *ná*. It is logical to consider this living space as the prototypical living space used during the Classic Period. In modern architecture, the 12 foot × 20 foot suite is a typical room size for hotels and dormitories.

The Maya Vault as a Finished Chamber

The Maya vault is a structural element that had multiple applications and was employed to develop long-span, single-story and multistory structures. The interior spaces of vaults in Maya buildings were finished with a surface coat of stucco plaster that provided a comfortable and attractive interior space; a cool, waterproof living facility; and a safe shelter from hurricanes and tropical storms.

The finished structural stonework of the walls would have presented a rough surface even when laid up in a workmanlike manner. The interior spaces of Maya vaults were finished with a smooth plaster coat of stucco. The plaster finish included the walls, floors, and ceiling areas. After the plaster coating, the walls were polished or painted with solid colors or murals, depending on the usage of the space. Figure C-5 indicates a plaster finish basically intact 1,400 years after application. Note that the vast majority of the ceiling structure of Maya vaults had a curved surface. This is not a circular curve. When analyzed, it appears that this curve has a convex shape similar to a parabola. This ceiling shape, when coated with smooth white stucco, would have the ability to magnify and reflect a light source in the vaulted room and greatly enhance illumination. Simple lamps with fuel and a cotton wick could provide a light source, with the light magnified multiple times from the white curved surface of the ceiling and the walls. Studies of Maya life in the Classic Period have indicated they cooked with cotton seed oil. This fuel was the popular lamp oil in mid-19th-century America until kerosene became available. Cotton was a major crop for the Maya; therefore, it is logical that cottonseed oil served as fuel for Maya lamps and that the white parabolic ceiling enhanced the light source in the room.

The floor surface was paved to complete the accommodations. The door opening featured a covering of cloth, woven mat, or animal hide that provided privacy and security, while permitting air flow into the interior spaces. The sides of the door openings featured an assembly for supporting a pole or cord for hanging the cloth. These devices are recessed cord connections to hold back the closure system at the top or at the bottom.

Timber Beam Structures, Stone Columns, and Composite Columns

High-strength tropical timber was used by Maya engineers for spanning bridges, roofs, and floors. Examples of these structures include the bridge at Pusilha, the palace tower at Palenque, and the sweat house at Piedras Negras. In several cases, the timber beams were used with a concrete topping. This system then became a composite structural material, and the total strength exceeded the sum of parts.

Stone columns were used to support large door openings and the attendant stone lintels and timber roof beams. The typical stone column was assembled from prefabricated "drums" of stone and assembled *in situ* with connectors between adjacent drums. These columns were used singularly or in rows to create a post-and-beam structural system.

Column support systems were used in several applications, such as the mid-span support of lintels for large door openings and the development of openings in wall of the exterior vaults. The columns were quite large with diameters of 0.96 meters. The columns elements were constructed off-site and sized to be transported to the site by a single bearer. The column shells were then assembled and filled with cast-in-place concrete. This methodology formed a large column using smaller fabricated segments. This type of column was used at the palace at Edzná.

Special Types of Maya Structures Using Technological Magic

Maya structural engineering met the challenge of functional requirements for special structures. These special structures were configured with a unique geometry that presented challenges for Maya technology. These structures used the basic components of the arch, vault, and construction materials described previously, but each type of structure used a creative twist that set it apart.

Multistory Structures

The design and construction of Maya high-rise structures produced buildings that surpassed the height of multistory structures throughout the world. Maya engineering of multistory building construction used a step-back structural system of trapezoidal arch and vault structures. This structural technique of stepping multistory structures has functional advantages that enhance light, ventilation, and vertical access, while increasing structural capabilities (Figure 7-7). Multistory buildings, though not widespread, were exquisite examples of Maya engineering. Notable examples were at the cities of Xtampak and Edzná (Figure C-13).

The palace at the ancient city of Xtampak is a graceful structure rising to three levels in height. This landmark building exhibits Maya structural engineering technology in a multistory configuration (Figure C-13). The long dimension of the vaults is parallel with the outer facade and features a series of colonnaded openings to enhance light and ventilation. The interior vaults have typical openings between units.

The cross section of the palace clearly displays the load paths for gravity loads and their structural members (Figure 7-7). It is noted that the second and third structures are set back in order for the outer wall on the second level to bear co-linear with the inner walls of the first level. This geometry directs the forces from the upper stories to traverse axially downward through a load path down into the composite concrete walls. The upper walls do not transmit their gravity loading directly through the trapezoidal arch structure, but align with vertical walls. The core or interior of the multistory structure lies beneath the grand staircase in the palace. An interior, winding stairway traverses upward to access all levels. The five-story palace at the city of Edzná is a graceful example of Maya art, architecture, and structural engineering. The configuration of the building uses the step back structural system that aligned the walls of the vaults as the building stepped upward. This geometry developed a sound structure and delivered a dramatic architectural form. The exterior stair system is unique; the Maya trapezoidal arch and concrete slabs were used to span stairs at the floor levels producing a continuous stair system (Figure C-9 and Figure C-10).

Circular Maya Structures

A number of Maya cities boasted circular structures that are considered to be astronomical observatories. The Maya were unparalleled as astronomers, and it is logical that these scientific people would construct a structure dedicated to celestial observation and designed to functionally optimize astronomical studies. A circular structure with an unobstructed view of the horizon would be an excellent place for star-gazing.

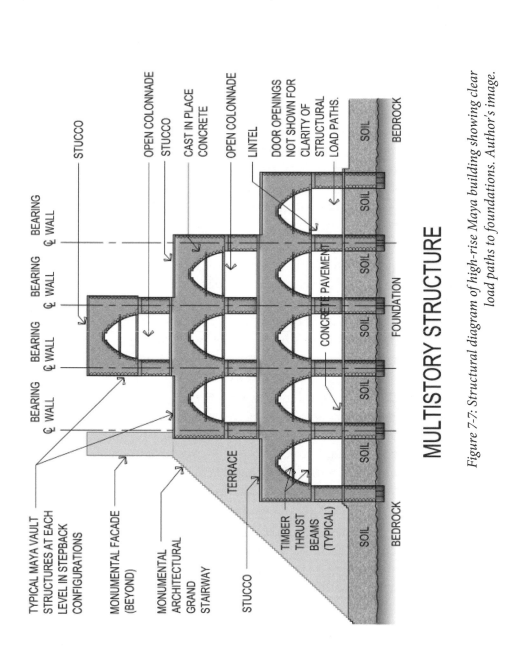

MULTISTORY STRUCTURE

Figure 7-7: Structural diagram of high-rise Maya building showing clear load paths to foundations. Author's image.

Some cities designed their observatories as circular structures with functional interior space and exterior walkways and roof platforms; others erected, tall circular structures that were constructed of solid materials, including concrete and stone, without functional interior spaces. Instead, these structures used exterior stairs and observation platforms on the top. Examples of this solid structure include the tall circular tower at the city of Cobá in the Yucatán (Figure C-14). The structure features exterior steps on the facade to the top of the tall tower. This tall structure would be a logical design to observe the cosmos over the tall rainforest trees. The basic design criteria for 360-degree fields of clear vision would require a tall structure; the cone-shaped tall structure would resolve this issue. The structure consists of exterior stonework with a mass concrete infill. This structure was first called the "sorbet" by French archaeologists due to the cone shape of the ruined structure.

The most noted Maya observatory is the circular structure termed the "caracol" at the city of Chichen Itza. The observatory at Chichen Itza applies the Classic trapezoidal arch structural system in a circular plan configuration and is a fine example of Maya engineering. The interior of this cylinder-shaped structure is formed by tall Maya vault construction in a closed circular plan with a stairway at the center column. Figure 7-8 indicates the cross section of the "caracol" structure.

The circular vault uses the Maya arch as its basic building block. However, the arch forms a circular shape rather than the linear shape used in building vaults. Observatories did not have the advantage of optical equipment for observing the stars, but the circular-shaped structure became the astronomical observation instrument. Wall openings and markers were used as fixed points for indicating certain astronomical events, calendric dates or the changing of seasons.

The city of Mayapán in the Northern Yucatán has a circular observatory with functional interior space (Figure C-12). This observatory is not a towering structure, but is sited in the middle of the city with clear views of the heavens. The terrain is flat in this area of the Yucatán, and the sight lines to the horizon are not obstructed.

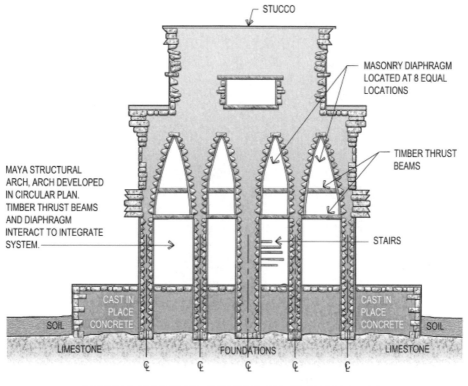

STUCCO

MASONRY DIAPHRAGM
LOCATED AT 8 EQUAL
LOCATIONS

TIMBER THRUST
BEAMS

MAYA STRUCTURAL
ARCH, ARCH DEVELOPED
IN CIRCULAR PLAN.
TIMBER THRUST BEAMS
AND DIAPHRAGM
INTERACT TO INTEGRATE
SYSTEM.

STAIRS

CAST IN
PLACE
CONCRETE

SOIL

CAST IN
PLACE
CONCRETE

SOIL

LIMESTONE

FOUNDATIONS

LIMESTONE

MAYA VAULT IN CIRCULAR STRUCTURE

Figure 7-8: Circular structure configured by generating the Maya arch into circular vault. Author's image.

Temple Structures and Roof Combs

Temples were located on the summit of tall pyramids or solid platforms rising above the plaza level (Figure C-16). Temples were relatively small structures with one or two interior vaults creating a sanctuary within the building. The exterior of the temple was adorned with multi-colored sculptural art and murals that presented a dramatic scene. The roof of the temple supported a tall superstructure or framework known as a roof comb. The roof comb was adorned with decorative sculptural elements that enhanced the heaven-reaching goals of the rulers. It has been postulated by archaeologists that certain roof combs featured special sound and light effects created to enhanced the wonderment of the temple structure. Special effects were produced through environmentally driven devices such as wind chimes and mirrors.

The roof comb atop the elevated temple was analogous to a modern billboard. Intended to promote propaganda and incite awe in the populace, it was also an excellent example of creative Maya engineering. The Maya engineers designed the structure of the roof comb as a three-dimensional space frame with an open matrix of vertical and horizontal concrete members. The vertical plane of the roof comb had a surface that has more open space than solid structure. Maya technology understood the advantage of open, lightweight roof comb structures to minimize lateral and vertical loadings. This geometry was intended to reduce wind forces, to lower the weight of gravity loading, and to minimize seismic forces on the temple structure.

The temple and roof comb were constructed of structural members with high-strength materials that were designed to resist extreme environmental forces in the Maya regions. Many temples and roof combs are intact after 1,500 years of resisting numerous earthquakes and thousands of hurricanes. The location of the temples at the top of the tallest structures in the Maya world resisted the magnified forces from seismic event acceleration, and they were required to resist the highest loads from hurricanes forces due to their unsheltered height above the ground surface.

The structural stability and strength of the roof comb and the temple were dependent on the inherent stability of the roof comb structure. Roof combs were constructed with different architectural configurations based on the style of the region. The similarity of the roof combs in different sites lay in the open framework of the structure and its integration with the strength of the cast-in-place concrete materials of the temple construction. The geometry varied with the regional style of the art and architecture of the edifice.

The roof combs at Palenque are constructed of cast-in-place concrete in a vertical configuration space frame. The majority of the Palenque roof combs are open to reduce lateral loads and gravity loads. The front and rear facade of roof comb members align with vertical members in the temple structures. The lateral and vertical loads from the roof comb are resisted by the temple structure.

The roof comb at Temple 33 at Yaxchilan features a structural system construction of a cast-in-place concrete A-frame configuration. The roof comb has openings in the north and south facades. However, the object of reducing weight and surface area was for reducing seismic and lateral forces. The structural resistance of the roof comb is achieved by a combination of the action of the angular A-frame and bending about the horizontal axis of the large vertical members. The front and rear facades align with the interior vertical walls of the temple.

The architectural and structural configurations of roof combs at the city of Tikal are of a different architectural and structural design than other Maya sites. These roof combs are high vertical structures that do not have openings in the facades. Rather than utilize the facades as armatures for sculpture placement, the facades themselves appear to have been carved with monumental sculptures. The roof combs have a larger base then other examples of Maya roof combs. The interiors of the Tikal roof combs seem to be open volumes. The front and rear walls of the structure vary from approximately 4 meters thickness at the base to thinner wall thickness at the top. The interior spaces between the roof comb walls are transected at intervals with horizontal diaphragms, which are connected to the outer walls.

The Tikal engineers took a different approach to resisting lateral and vertical forces generated by the large roof comb. The completely enclosed roof comb offered a strong structural system. The thick walls at the front, rear, and sides developed a tube-like structure for resisting lateral loadings. The interior diaphragms proportioned lateral loads between the walls that, in turn, transferred the roof comb loads down to the temple structure, and then into the pyramid structure.

Pyramid Structures

As travelers stood at the entrance of a great Maya city, they would be awed by the beauty and towering heights of its monumental structures. The single Maya structure that caused shock and awe to the observers was the grandiose soaring pyramid topped with a gorgeous temple and a towering art-festooned roof. This trio of structural elements was elevated high above the rainforest canopy and proclaimed the power of the city and the wealth of the ruler.

Maya pyramid structures rose to heights of more than 230 feet, a height that was not exceeded for a millennium. They were taller than the Leaning Tower of Pisa, which topped out in 1319 at 183.27 feet, and the world's first sky scraper, constructed in Chicago in 1885 with a height of 185 feet. Maya pyramid builders were ahead of their time in the construction of tall structures.

The structure of the basic construction of a pyramid did not apply innovative structural mechanisms devised by Maya engineers, but was a mass structure that applied the sum of Maya technology, including cast-in-place concrete, cut stone, carved art, the tools of surveying, and accurate measurements in the construction. The exterior skin or facade was constructed of composite stone and concrete that encapsulated the structural mass comprising the interior core of the pyramid. The interior of the pyramids, with few exceptions, did not contain functional spaces such as vaulted chambers or passageways. One exception would be the Temple of the Inscriptions pyramid at Palenque, which held the tomb of Pakal.

In many cities, pyramids were constructed in stages and grew in size as the city expanded. Buried beneath the tall pyramids were the remains of earlier pyramids (Figure 7-9). The encapsulation of one or more earlier pyramids was driven by the desire for display of power by the rulers, who wanted to outdo their predecessors with a grander show of the art, architecture, and soaring height of the temple. Examples of multiple phases of pyramid construction include the Pyramid of the Magician at Uxmal and El Castillo at Chichen Itza (Figure C-16).

Whether the pyramid was a stand-alone project or staged efforts over several centuries, the implementation of the core was constructed by a series of compartmentalized retaining structures. The core of the pyramid was contained by retaining structures built just inside the perimeter of the new exterior (Figure 7-9).

The exterior of the four-sided triangular was often stepped upward in a ziggurat of nine levels, terminating at a temple platform. Many pyramids have steep, smooth, curved corners with up to four grand staircases on the various faces of the pyramid leading from the ground to the temple atop the looming structure. The designers of the pyramids often used structural geometry and the movement of the sun to create illusions of shadows and light during festival days. Many pyramids have the tendency to reflect sound that appears to be falling rain or bird calls.

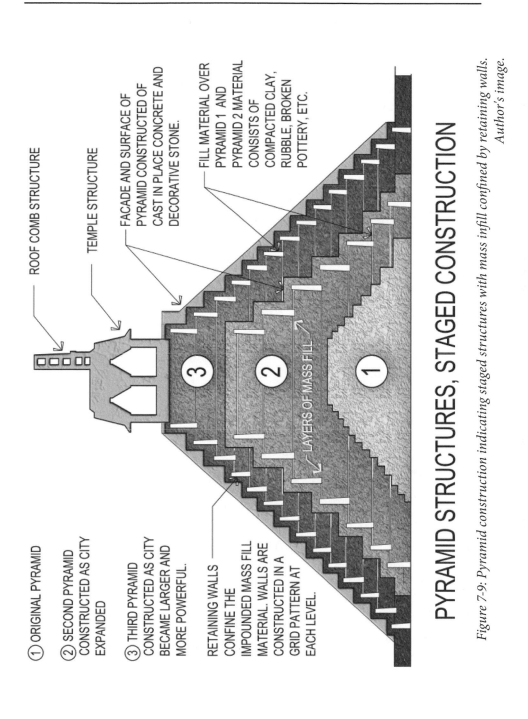

ROOF COMB STRUCTURE

TEMPLE STRUCTURE

FACADE AND SURFACE OF PYRAMID CONSTRUCTED OF CAST IN PLACE CONCRETE AND DECORATIVE STONE.

FILL MATERIAL OVER PYRAMID 1 AND PYRAMID 2 MATERIAL CONSISTS OF COMPACTED CLAY, RUBBLE, BROKEN POTTERY, ETC.

LAYERS OF MASS FILL

① ORIGINAL PYRAMID

② SECOND PYRAMID CONSTRUCTED AS CITY EXPANDED

③ THIRD PYRAMID CONSTRUCTED AS CITY BECAME LARGER AND MORE POWERFUL.

RETAINING WALLS CONFINE THE IMPOUNDED MASS FILL MATERIAL. WALLS ARE CONSTRUCTED IN A GRID PATTERN AT EACH LEVEL.

PYRAMID STRUCTURES, STAGED CONSTRUCTION

Figure 7-9: Pyramid construction indicating staged structures with mass infill confined by retaining walls. Author's image.

Tower Structures

Maya towers rose above the central plaza of many city centers. It is possible that some towers had astronomical functions with markers for changes in the seasons. The structure could have been used as watch towers for earthly matters or erected to elevate the status of a ruler. Towers were sometimes stand alone structures or were part of a larger building.

The tower rising above the palace in Palenque is unique. This structure is built as a functional edifice and was erected of cast-in-place concrete beams at various levels supported by a cast-in-place concrete wall. The interior stairway leads to the top of the tower. The tower is assumed to have been an observatory for viewing the stars. However, the hilly terrain and the height of the towering rainforest surrounding the tower blocks the nighttime sky from a view from the top platform, casting doubt on its effective use as an observatory.

The two cast-in-place concrete towers supporting the long-span suspension bridge over the Usumacinta River at Yaxchilan (Figure C-22) were 25 meters in height. The tower structure was topped with a Maya vault structure. The vault was part of the bridge support system and included connections for the suspension cables.

The Rio Bec style of architecture featured tall towers rising out of an elongated base structure. The number of towers at specific sites varied in height and number. Xpuhil, with three towers of great height, has the most impressive structural and architectural design of the Rio Bec style. Becán has two towers, and Chicanná and Rio Bec have single towers. The towers constructed in the Rio Bec style are unique in the Maya world. Their purpose is unclear to archaeologists. The towers are built with tapering cross-sections as they rise from the base. They were tapered upward to create a vertical perspective and to appear taller. The exterior stairways were nonfunctional and were carved from the facing stone. The temples and their accoutrement, including the doors, were carved from stone.

The facades of many Maya towers were carved with magnificent art and were painted with colors that reflected the regional style of art and architecture. The structural systems employed for the tower construction consisted of an outer shell of cut limestone block and an interior structure of mass cast-in-place concrete. The interior of towers usually had stairways in order to reach upper levels.

Palaces

The power elite lived in large palatial residences that were adorned in brilliantly colored sculpture and paintings in the regional style. Palaces were large buildings with numerous rooms. They were constructed as single story and multistory structures. Palaces varied in size and height of living levels, as well as in size, from 200 rooms at Cancuén, Guatemala, to five stories in height at Edzná, Mexico.

The vaulted exterior chambers of palaces were aligned with the facades to maximize wall openings for natural ventilation. The Maya vault structural system was the major element for the construction of palaces. In multistory palaces, the second and third levels were set back to align their outer walls with the inner wall of the lower story (Figure 7-7 and Figure C-13). In some cities, palaces were designed and constructed with ventilation, running water for plumbing and fountains, and interior stairs.

8

Survival in the Seasonal Desert

Northern European cultural lore endorses the notion that technical innovation is stimulated by the need to survive and prosper in a frigid climate. They argue that organized civilization is not possible without the technical innovations required to overcome the negative effects of the natural environment. Their concepts hold that technological development is unnecessary in tropical environments where resources and manpower are not required for the collection and storage of food and fuel for warmth during cold weather. They endorse the notion that the enchanted tropical climate creates a blissful lifestyle where life is easy and scantily clad natives prance about as they pick ripe fruit off the trees.

The domain of the Maya is sited completely in the tropics in a location more than 750 miles (1,800 km) south of the Tropic of Cancer. Maya engineers proved that their feats of tropical technology were, in fact, more sophisticated than the technology of their Northern European counterparts at similar stages of cultural development. The tranquil climate of the Yucatán Peninsula released the Maya from the necessity of cutting firewood for warmth, manufacturing warm clothing for the cold, storing food for winter, and constructing weather-tight residences. However, they faced a fickle environment that demanded engineering measures beyond the ken of Northern European technology. The natural environment deprived them of a dependable supply of water from rainfall or the aquifer. The verdant and torrid environment of the Yucatán manifested serious natural liabilities that challenged the survival of the Maya; they faced the constant specter of thirst. Maya water-management technology solved the dilemma and provided a dependable water supply that enabled the civilization to survive and prosper.

The skill and technology of the ancient Maya enabled them to dominate their environment for more than 3,000 years. They developed methodologies to overcome the foibles of the environment and enabled the survival of the world's largest cities—cities that supported some of the densest populations in history. (The population density at Tikal, Guatemala was on a par with the density of modern Los Angeles.) Maya engineers developed efficient projects that sustained the civilization by providing potable water systems, irrigation for agriculture, aquaculture techniques, and water storage systems.

The search for Maya water-management technology, once the exclusive realm of archaeology, has been joined by archaeo-engineers, NASA satellite mapping scientists, and other crossover researchers. The success of the new disciplines of archaeo-engineers has advanced the known body of knowledge of the lost technology of Maya water-management engineering. These experts are using digital tools, including remote sensing and computer simulations, to raise the veil of secrecy hiding the lost treasures of Maya water-management engineering.

Maya engineers were faced with a double whammy that had to be overcome: six months of heavy precipitation, from roughly May to October, followed by a dry season between November and April. In addition, voluminous amounts of storm water fell on the porous limestone landscape, which drew in the water directly down into the deep aquifer. The end result was a seasonal desert and a lack of natural surface water that would, if it existed, have provided year-round water supplies for the populace. These natural characteristics of the environment would have daunted the most ambitious of Northern European technologists. The unique character of the Maya environment was significant to astute observers of the area. The famed Diego de Landa, bishop of the Yucatán, wrote in his 1566 book, *Relacion de las cosas de Yucatán*, of the character of the land and water supply in the Yucatán, "In this respect, nature has acted differently in this country from the rest of the world, where the rivers and springs flow above the ground whereas here all run in the secret channels underground."

The solution involved the capture of the massive volume of storm water that fell during the rainy season, then the collection and storage of that water to provide an ample supply for the needs of the cities and irrigation for agriculture. Maya civil engineers faced Mother Nature's challenge and applied their ingenuity to develop different solutions for locations that had different water source issues. These solutions involved optimization of aquifer-fed well water supplies, collection of water into underground storage reservoirs and surface water reservoirs, and an aqueduct water-supply systems.

The Seasonal Desert

The Yucatán Peninsula encompasses a varied landscape and a wide range of climatic conditions. It extends from the mountains of the Sierra Madre, to the dense canopied rainforests of the interior, to the extensive wetlands, mangroves, and coral lagoons that constitute the Caribbean coastal area. The Yucatán lies within the Atlantic hurricane belt, directly in the path of powerful hurricanes and tropical storms that traverse the Atlantic from the coast of Africa and travel westward into the Caribbean. The damaging winds and torrential rains from tropical storms and hurricanes were a threat to life, and a challenge to the hydraulic and structural engineering capabilities of Maya technology.

The world of the Maya lies well below the Tropic of Cancer. The Yucatán is cloaked in a hot, humid, tropical climate with some of the heaviest annual rainfall in the tropics. The rainfall ranges from 40 inches (1,000 mm) in the Northeast to 200 inches (5,000 mm) on the East Coast. As much as 90 percent of storm water falls during the rainy season. The average percentage of days per month with rainfall varies from 25 percent during the rainy season to only 7 percent of the days in the dry season. The average temperature in the Yucatán is 92 degrees F (32.3 degrees C). The highest average temperatures occur in July and August, when the highest daily temperature may reach 100 degrees F (38 degrees C), and low temperatures rarely extend below 65 degrees F (18 degrees C).

The common image of the Yucatán conjures up lost cities slumbering under a canopy of tangled rainforest vegetation. The placid images of this lush and verdant environment are misleading. The heavy tropical vegetation depends on the torrential precipitation during the rainy season. During the dry season, the rainforest depends on moisture from its tap roots, which extend deep down into the aquifer. This phenomenon of alternating periods of heavy rain and drought-like conditions turns the Yucatán Peninsula into a seasonal desert. The lack of surface water leaves the area totally without a source of water during the dry season. A seasoned explorer knows that one can easily die of thirst during the dry season while wandering in the lush, humid rainforest.

The cyclic wet/dry contrast of the seasons is the result of a meteorological phenomenon stemming from the seasonal migration of precipitation associated with the inter-tropical convergence zone. This inter-tropical convergence zone migrates to the South during the winters, leaving the Yucatán in drought-like conditions for six months. This atmospheric condition, known as the meteorological equator, results in a northern shift of the zone during the summer, and with this shift, heavy rains come to the Yucatán.

Unlike other great civilizations that selected riverine sites for their cities, the Maya did not have the luxury of establishing major cities along natural water sources. The exceptions were a handful of cities that were fortunate enough to found their cities on the few natural water sources in the Yucatán. The majority of important Maya city-states developed in locations without permanent water sources. Great cities such as Tikal, Caracol, and Calakmul selected locations with natural terrain that offered advantageous defensive characteristics for their city and features that enhanced the potential to collect, store, transport, and distribute life-giving water for the population of the cities and for agricultural irrigation.

The heuristic technology of the Maya civilization triumphed over the fickleness of nature. Maya engineers optimized their technology and overcame the lack of water that characterized the seasonal desert. The innovative solutions included the diverse technologies of civil, hydraulic, and structural engineering. The solutions assumed many roles, including shaping the slopes of the roofs of the buildings, landscapes, and hardscapes to structured storage systems and enhancement of natural sources of water.

Geological Features of the Yucatán

Hundreds of millions of years in the past, an ancient ocean deposited the skeletal remains of marine micro-organisms and coral that became the sedimentary rock that forms the karstic limestone foundation of the Yucatán. Karstic limestone has a characteristic physical feature that includes small-scale fissures and voids. Despite its extraordinary biological richness and some of the heaviest rainfalls in the tropics, with very few exceptions, there are no lakes and virtually no surface streams on the Yucatán Peninsula. The heavy flow of storm water rapidly percolates downward through the shallow soil layer and into the permeable limestone, and is deposited into a network of caves, subterranean rivers, and channels that form the aquifer. The complex underground system of conduits swiftly transports water through the aquifer away from the central area of the peninsula and into the Caribbean Sea. The aquifer manifests itself as freshwater surface springs along the coast of the Caribbean Sea.

An extraterrestrial visited the Yucatán 65,000,000 years ago and changed the course of earth's history. It is unknown if the extraterrestrial was a meteor, asteroid, or a comet. Its impact with the northern coast of the Yucatán generated a cataclysm that circled the planet: a 2-kilometer-high tsunami sped across the oceans and inundated shorelines, fire storms raged across the earth, and dust blotted out the sun, casting the planet into darkness. A sudden cooling of the atmosphere and an increase in sulfur content snuffed out life on the earth's surface.

The impact triggered the K-T (Cretaceous/Tertiary) extinction of the majority of the planet's animal life, most notably the dinosaur. Burrowing mammals, which were fairly small, furry creatures, survived and evolved into biological niches formerly occupied by reptiles and replaced the dinosaurs as the dominant land animal. These little guys became our ancestors.

The linking of the extinction of the dinosaurs with a catastrophic extraterrestrial impact gained international acceptance with the 1980 Nobel Prize–winning theory by Louis and Walter Alvarez. The giant Chicxulub Crater in the northern Yucatán is considered the best candidate for ground zero for the catastrophe and causing the K-T layer (Figure 8-1).

Geologists have concluded that a 10-kilometer-wide bolide, or exploding meteor, collided with the earth on the northern edge of the Yucatán near the present-day town of Chicxulub. This event closed the Cretaceous period. The famous ring of cenotes outlines the shock waves of the impact, and it was discovered that the K-T boundary contains higher concentrations of iridium than normally occur in the earth's crust. The earth was covered with this "ejecta blanket" from the Chicxulub blast.

The outer perimeter of the 183.3-kilometer-wide crater was fractured by the blast of the impact (Figure 8-1). As time passed, the limestone covering the fractured limestone dissolved, reducing the surface thickness and the affected surface area collapsed. The surface openings in these natural

Figure 8-1: NASA image of Chicxulub Crater indicating cenotes in white.
Courtesy of NASA.

wells exposed the waters of the deep Yucatán aquifer and created the complex of natural wells called cenotes. The pattern of natural wells formed the famous ring of cenotes, which became the sources of life-giving water for the Maya in the Northern Yucatán. It is ironic that the extraterrestrial that destroyed so much of life on earth would re-emerge as part of the history of Mesoamerica. The 65,000,000-year-old alien intruder that formed the cenotes would partner with Maya technology to provide water for the Maya civilization.

Maya Technology to the Rescue

It was a rarity for Maya cities to be located on a permanent source of running water. However, ancient Maya cities located near the ring of cenotes in the northern Yucatán had a choice of hundreds of permanent, natural wells when siting their cities. The city of Cobá was founded on a series of lakes fed by a shallow aquifer that assured the city a dependable supply of water. The ancient cities of Yaxchilan, Copán, and Piedras Negras were sited on rivers that supplied water and provided transportation resources. The city of Palenque was fortunate to be located on a site with a surfeit of free-flowing water from natural springs. These cities were, however, the exception to the rule and had other water-management issues, but a lack of a reliable water supply was not one of them. The vast majority of Maya cities required engineering solutions to assure a dependable source of fresh water.

As the population of the Maya civilization grew, its technological capabilities evolved into a positive force that overcame the daunting natural obstacles that impeded the survival, health, prosperity, and growth of Maya city-states. Early Maya technicians recognized the threat of the hostile environmental and the fragility of the water supply. Water-management technology, driven by the demands of the expanding population, overcame the obstacles of the environment. Maya technicians were charged with developing means to deliver and maintain a constant supply of clean water. However, when engineers pondered the development of water resource systems, they had two strikes against them. They had to face the dual challenge of a capricious rainfall creating a seasonal desert in the Maya domain, exacerbated by the porous karstic landscape that intercepted their collection efforts by drawing down storm water directly into the aquifer. Maya engineers respected the powerful impact of their fickle environment and the sponge-like characteristics of their geology. They understood the foibles of the environment, and configured their cityscapes and civil works to optimize the collection, storage, and distribution of storm water.

Maya engineers delivered innovative water-management systems integrated with advanced agriculture systems to develop increased crop production. Advances in agriculture yield were developed through a variety of intensive technologies including raised fields, terraces, and irrigation systems. The pressure on developing sustainable sources of water peaked during the late Classic Period, when the Maya population reached its maximum. In AD 750, the population of the Maya world may have peaked at 15,000,000 people. The majority of the population resided in urban centers. Dr. Tom Sever, NASA archaeologist, has opined that the Maya population was one of the densest populations in human history. Using satellite data and climate models, Dr. Sever determined that population levels reached an all-time high after AD 800. Population density ranged from 500 to 700 people per square mile in the hinterlands and up to 1,800 to 2,600 persons per square mile in the urban center of city states. By comparison, modern-day Los Angeles County averaged 2,345 people per square mile.

Maya technology developed innovative water-management techniques and structures to satisfy the year-round demand for fresh water, which included systems for collection, storage, and distribution. The solutions for water acquisition and distribution assumed multiple technical configurations based on the variation in the dispositions of water sources. Water sources included deep natural wells called cenotes, underground storage structures called chultunes, large scale open reservoirs, and underground aqueduct structures.

Cenotes: The Path to the Sacred Water of the Underworld

A cenote is a natural well extending down to the swift-flowing fresh water of the aquifer coursing below the surface of the Yucatán Peninsula. Clusters of these deep, natural wells are known as the Chicxulub ring of cenotes, first observed on NASA satellite images (Figure 8-1). The cenotes brought life-sustaining water to Maya cities built around the natural wells and enabled the northern Yucatán cities to survive longer during the Classic collapse. Cenote is a word derived from the Yucatán Maya word *dzonot*, which means "sacred well." This word was construed by Spanish conquistadors into the word *cenote*.

The technological challenge of engineering systems to provide a safe and comfortable lifestyle was not completely solved with a perennial supply of fresh water. The deep cenotes required engineering solutions to access the groundwater located deep below the surface. Engineering solutions ranged from steps carved into the walls of rock to wood bridging scaffolds leading down to the water level.

The requirements of irrigation for agriculture and protection from floods due to torrential storm water from hurricanes and rainy season storms were challenges that were overcome by Maya engineers. Even in cities with cenotes as a permanent water source, water-management technology stepped up to prevent flooding, an essential measure to ensure the survival of the city. Water-management systems included sloping the roofs of buildings, patios, and the surfaces of other hardscapes in order to transport storm water away from residential areas. Storm water was then directed into agricultural fields, underground reservoirs, or natural depressions to serve as a reserve of water during drought. The roads in the city were designed to be part of flood control. Elevated roads diverted flood waters away from the occupied areas of the cities as well as offered pedestrians a dry walkway.

Cenotes in the northern Yucatán come in a variety of sizes and geometries of the wells. Some cenotes are still being used today as potable water sources, and some have been turned into tourist attractions both for the pleasure of swimming in the beautiful waters (Figure C-18) and the opportunity to scuba dive into the water and explore the underground rivers coursing through the aquifer. Others have caved in and are filled with debris.

Chultunes: Water Collection and Underground Storage Systems

The majority of Maya lowland cities were located in areas without access to permanent water sources. Maya engineers resolved water-management issues with water collection and storage systems that went well beyond the construction of simple capture and containment systems. These complex systems were integrated into the planning and construction of the entire built cityscape. The cityscape was designed to utilize all exposed horizontal surfaces to optimize storm water acquisition and direct it into storage systems called chultunes. Chultune is a word combining *chul*, meaning "wet" or "becoming wet," with *tun*, which means "rock" or "stone." Combined, the words can be defined as "rock place that becomes wet." The chultune-based hydrological system for a city was designed and constructed to capture storm water and direct the flow into the orifices of underground structural reservoirs for storage and use during the dry season.

The water capture system included the design of urban structures with sloped roofs that diverted water into plazas and canals designed to transmit water toward the collection system of chultunes (Figure 8-2). The use of chultune-based water-management systems extended from Uxmal in the Puuc Hills to Uaxactún, located in the southern lowlands of the Petén. The concept of chultune water catchment and storage systems spread

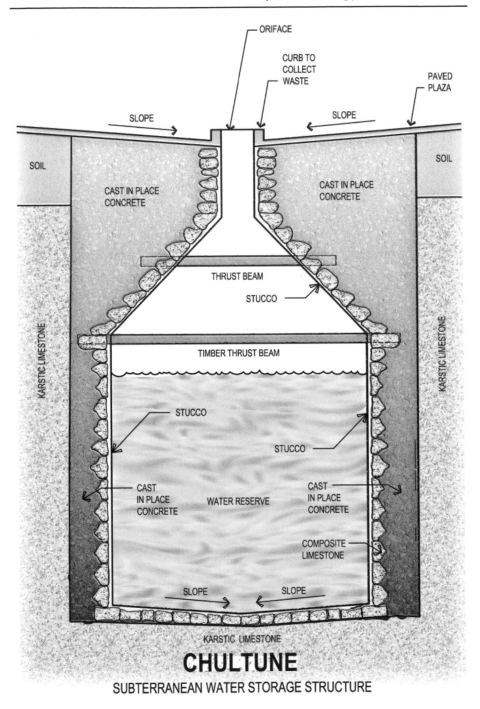

ORIFACE

CURB TO
COLLECT
WASTE

PAVED
PLAZA

SLOPE   SLOPE

SOIL   SOIL

CAST IN PLACE
CONCRETE

CAST IN PLACE
CONCRETE

KARSTIC LIMESTONE   KARSTIC LIMESTONE

THRUST BEAM

STUCCO

TIMBER THRUST BEAM

STUCCO

STUCCO

CAST
IN PLACE
CONCRETE

WATER RESERVE

CAST
IN PLACE
CONCRETE

COMPOSITE
LIMESTONE

SLOPE   SLOPE

KARSTIC LIMESTONE

CHULTUNE
SUBTERRANEAN WATER STORAGE STRUCTURE

Figure 8-2: Structural section and construction of typical chultun.
Author's image.

throughout the entire Maya zone. The chultune water capture system was designed to optimize the collection of water during the rainy season and store the captured water for an 18-month supply (Figure 8-3). Chultunes were excavated in the limestone stratum in many locations throughout an urban area. In some cities, more than 100 chultunes served the needs of the city. They were located under plazas, integrated into building designs, and situated in sloped collection terraces.

The geometrical configuration of chultunes and their number and location were optimized to collect, store, preserve, and retrieve stored water. These reservoirs varied in size, but a typical chultune structure would include an underground containment chamber with a base dimension of 3 m × 3 m. The height of the walls of the reservoir from the base to the spring line is 4 m. The dome structure enclosing the top of the chultune is a truncated Maya vault structure encompassing the containment vessel. The access opening at the top of the reservoir is a cylindrical orifice constructed of concrete. This opening of the orifice is 1 m in height and .5 m in diameter (Figure 8-2).

The ingenious engineering and construction of the chultunes structure is described in Figure 8-2 and Figure 8-3. The initial step in constructing a chultune was the evacuation of its structure. Excavation would extend through the shallow soil layer and into the limestone substrate. Excavation of the firm limestone created the desired rectangular volume that defined the containment structure. The construction of the containment vessel consisted of paving the floor with stone blocks and erecting cut stone walls with cast in place concrete placed between the stone and the excavation around the perimeter walls. The walls extended up to the spring line of the encapsulation dome. The roof was constructed of composite stone and concrete using Maya structural engineering techniques for a vault structure. The dome extended upward to the apex, where the cylindrical shaft of the orifice was constructed. The orifice shaft provided a minimum opening to reduce evaporation but permitted access for water vessels. The interior of the stone structure was covered with a waterproof stucco surface to prevent leaking.

The number of chultunes varied with the population of the city, and their volume was designed to provide a sufficient quantity of water for the target demand. This demand required a city water supply for the six-month dry season, plus a factor of safety equal to a volume of 18 months of water

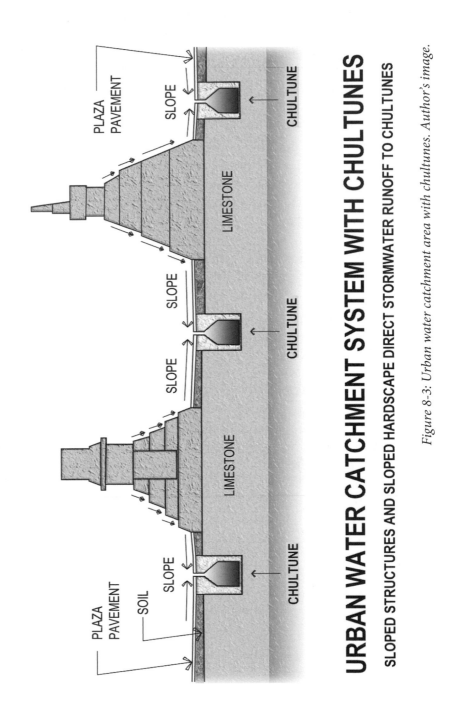

URBAN WATER CATCHMENT SYSTEM WITH CHULTUNES

SLOPED STRUCTURES AND SLOPED HARDSCAPE DIRECT STORMWATER RUNOFF TO CHULTUNES

Figure 8-3: Urban water catchment area with chultunes. Author's image.

supply to account for unexpected periods of droughts. This encapsulation structure for water supply was a brilliant design, and modern technology has not improved on the basic concept. In fact, modern fiberglass cisterns used in contemporary applications have a design similar to Maya chultunes. The volume of a typical chultune was 44,000 liters at full capacity. At the consumption rate of 3.3 liters per person per day, this satisfies the requirement of 36 persons for 365 days, or 72 persons for 183 days.

Field observations and forensic engineering investigation of existing chultunes have been performed at several Maya cities, including Uxmal, Oxkintok, Labná, Chicanná, and Xtampak. Measurements of exterior structural portions were taken, and the exterior portions, including collection structures and the interior walls of the chultune, were photographed. Photographs and video of the interior of the chultunes indicated that the geometry and construction of these examples is quite similar to the classic design described. The dimensions of the orifices satisfied the classic standards and were similar; however, the depth of orifices varied with the site. The interior photos of the chultunes indicate smooth stucco coatings. Figure C-19 illustrates the masonry structure of the access orifice in a chultune at Xtampak.

The Open Reservoir: Shaping the Cityscape to Optimize Water Capture

The absence of a perennial water supply for the largest of Maya cities required an engineering effort on a grand scale. During the Classic Period, the world's largest cities, like Tikal, Calakmul, and Edzná, employed similar hydrological solutions to satisfy the water-supply needs of their burgeoning populations. The large populations in the city, as well as in the hinterlands, required creative solutions to create a water-management system that supplied potable water for the city and irrigation water for agriculture. Their answer was to integrate the design and construction of all urban components, including the topography of the cityscape, the shape of the terrain, and the configuration of monumental structures and hardscape, into an efficient collection, storage, and distribution system required to produce a dependable water supply. Their concept was brilliant: locating the city on high ground, modifying the gradient of the topography, and optimizing roof structures to collect water, a process and implementation that evolved over a period of centuries (Figure 8-4).

The large-scale, monumental architectural complexes were located on the summit of the hills and ridges. The buildings, the landscape, hardscapes of patios and plazas, and the elevated roads were designed as a system to collect storm water and divert the flow toward collection points. Reservoirs were constructed on the height of the topography of the central city, and along the sloped hillsides. In addition to the excavation of new open reservoirs, engineers took advantage of depressions in the topography that were once the quarries that supplied the stone for building the city. These recycled depressions and new reservoir sites were lined with clay, concrete, or stone walls, and stuccoed faces to prevent leakage.

The water-management system controlled the flow of water using complex hydraulic engineering systems including dams, sluice gates, flood gates, and water-diversion systems, including elevated roadways and dikes. The engineering technology used in this system was based on the same principles as modern hydrological systems. Water-control mechanisms of the Maya system were enabled when the reservoirs were at full capacity during the rainy season. Water flow was diverted from the reservoirs and flowed past the full reservoirs into the agriculture fields and into low-lying wetlands. During the dry season, this ingenious system applied gravity to induce the flow of water to the agriculture fields lying at lower elevations below the reservoirs. Water could be supplied to the agricultural areas by opening sluice gates in the perimeter of the reservoirs, permitting water to flow downward into the cultivated fields.

The water-management system at Tikal had a series of 13 reservoirs with a total capacity of 147,631,068 liters. Calculations indicate that this total volume would sustain the city for 18 months. This provided a six-month supply for typical rainfall and an 12-month supply for water shortage situations. The creation of this hydrology-based cityscape was a centuries-long endeavor using a large, well-organized workforce. Massive amounts of earth and rock were moved to shape the terrain that created this water-supply system. The efficiency of an integrated cityscape watershed system is determined by the volume of storm water captured, mitigation of seepage loss in the transport of the storm water, the size of the storage structures, and loss of water volume due to evaporation and seepage.

Unlike the chultune system, the open-surface reservoir system was highly susceptible to evaporation due to the large area of water surface. Maya engineers minimized surface evaporation by planting water lilies in

Figure 8-4: Design of urban watershed and collection system for reservoirs. Author's image.

the reservoirs. The broad leaf of the prolific water plant covered the water surface in the reservoir and reduced evaporation. Additional advantage of the water lily plant included purification and filtering of the water supply.

Aqueducts: Maya Engineers Control Water and Create Public Space

Maya innovation was at its best when resolving solutions for populations that required dependable sources of water and was equally innovative in solving issues of urban places with an excess of water. The ancient Maya city of Palenque is situated in the hilly rainforest of Chiapas. The city was founded on a plateau with natural features of the terrain marked by hills, deep gullies, and sheer cliffs. The site had a surfeit of natural water courses flowing across the center of the city. The natural water sources included nine waterways fed by 56 springs. The city of Palenque is named after a nearby town; however, the original name was Lakamba, meaning "big water," because of its numerous water courses.

The natural sources of water, although providing an adequate supply of water for the population, had a negative downside. The rainy season storm water combined with the natural flow resulted in the flooding of the city. During the rainy season, 47 percent of the annual rainfall, amounting to a total of approximately 1 meter of rain, fell during a four-month period. The massive rainfalls caused the streams to overflow, as storm water rushed down the steep slopes from the hills and combined with heavy storm water falling on the level cityscape. The expanding city required extensive flood control measures. In addition, the open-channel water courses traversing the city center created impediments to the construction of buildings and expansion of the urban center of Palenque.

Maya technology solved the multi-faceted urban water issues with the construction of an underground aqueduct system designed to collect water upstream of the city center, and transfer the water under the city center and into the Otulum River downstream of the city. This ingenious underground hydraulic system controlled water flow and created a flood-free urban space. The channels of water that flowed through the city center were captured, controlled, and buried in vaulted, structural concrete conduits. This engineering application allowed the expansion of plazas where none could have been built before. This hydraulic system combined urban planning, hydrology, hydraulics, vaulted structures, and technical innovations to achieve the solution (Figure 8-5).

The goals of the engineering effort were to control the flood water by constructing subterranean cast-in-place concrete aqueducts to control flooding of the cityscape and to create public space for growth of the urban center. Maya engineers created new urban space on the level plateau; the new flood-free area was then paved for plaza space. Additionally, the steep slopes of the hillsides were terraced to create level building platforms for urban structures. The terracing of the hillsides slowed and controlled the flow of rainwater into the plazas.

It is apparent that Palenque engineers understood the principles of hydraulic engineering. They used the aqueduct system to generate positive water pressures in the palace (Figure 8-6). The aqueduct line buried adjacent to the palace extends in a north-south direction and is parallel to the east side of the palace. The aqueduct was constructed with a steeper grade when approaching the palace in order to increase the speed of water flow. The shape and area of the aqueduct was reduced at a point underneath the palace. The reduction of area in a conduit will increase the velocity and pressure of the water in the smaller conduit downstream. The increased pressure creates what is termed a "head of water." Hydraulic analysis of the water flow and geometry of the aqueducts indicate that a head of water equal to 6 meters was generated. This pressure indicates that water can be raised to 6 meters in height above the aqueduct producing sufficient positive water pressure to induce water flow into the palace. This pressure would permit the flow of potable water for drinking, domestic uses, toilets, and fountains in the palace. As can be imagined, running water was a luxury, and locating a hydraulically engineered system adjacent to the palace would be an appropriate location. Ceramic tubes, suitable for piping, have been encountered at other Maya cities, including Edzná. Though the systems for increasing water pressures are evident at Palenque and toilet spaces have been identified in the palace, the piping system at Palenque has not been found.

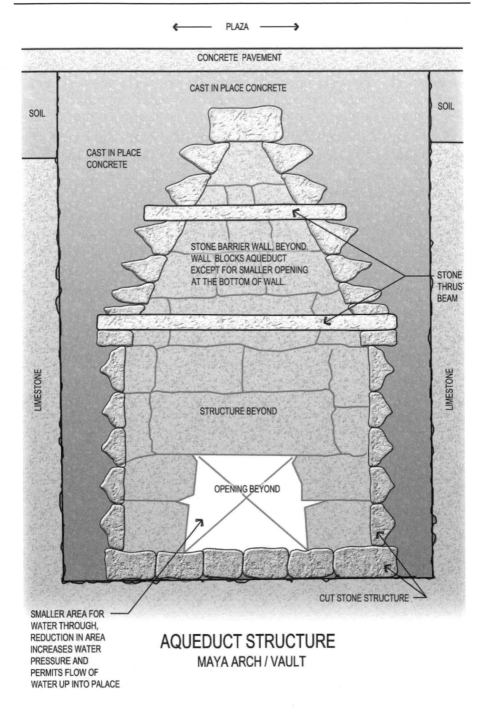

Figure 8-5: Diagram of structural, hydrological, and construction details of typical Maya aqueduct. Author's image.

C-14: The astrological observatory at Cobá is a solid, cone-shaped building unlike other observatories.

C-15: Maya pyramid at Mayapán in the Yucatán, Mexico.

C-16: El Castillo pyramid at Chichen Itza, constructed in various stages through time.

§-17: Recently discovered walls at Chichen Itza, dated to 100 years earlier than the pyramid

C-18: Natural wells, or cenotes, formed by the impact of Chicxulub Meteor in the Yucatán.

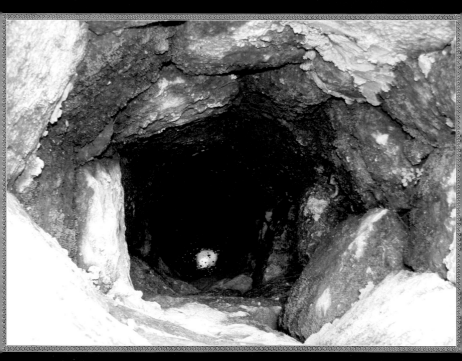

C-19: View into a working chultun at Xtampak, showing cut stone walls

C-20: The Cobá terminus of the Cobá-Yaxuná sacbe. C-21 (inset):
Aerial view of the Cobá-Yaxuná sacbe, flying to the west toward Yaxuná.

C-22: Computer rendering of Maya suspension bridge across the Usumacinta River

C-23 (above): Maya tools and gouges made from jadeite.
C-24 (below): A hand working Maya chisel made from jadeite.

C-25: Hafted Maya jadeite chisel.

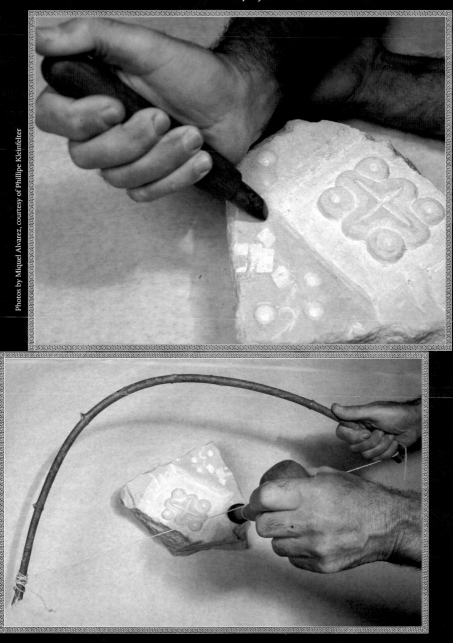

C-26: Handheld bow drill using jadeite drill bit.

C-27 (left): Images of ancient Maya royalty look much like the Maya of today (above, C-28), who still respect their customs, beliefs, and native dress.

Figure 8-6: Photograph of interior of existing Palenque aqueduct.
Photo by Kirk French.

Maya Technology Increases
Agriculture Yields

As the Maya population, grew the demand for increased agriculture yields became a constant challenge that had to be satisfied. Higher crop yields meant a demand for more water. Maya water-management technology met the challenge of that demand with a multidiscipline effort to generate abundant agriculture for the needs of the Maya population, plus a surplus for trade. Their interdisciplinary approach to solutions included combining the principals of hydrology with agronomy to increase agricultural output. The Maya had practiced agronomy for millennia. Those innovative agriculture technicians developed maize from a native grass more than 8,000 years ago. The type and variety of cultivars increased as the Maya agronomists entered their Classic Period. Technological innovations enabled the population to expand at a rate that outstripped capabilities for feeding the populace using traditional agriculture methods. Agriculture technology made a significant contribution to their ability to produce larger quantities of food. They developed sustainable long-term growth strategies for agriculture systems including replenishment of soil, irrigation and fertilization, cultivation of hillside terraces, canals, raised fields, wetland agriculture, irrigation dams, and a diverse aquaculture.

The only solution was to depart from tradition and develop new methods to increase the agriculture yield. Traditional farming methods included cultivation of plots using the slash and burn technique. This method of cultivation produced a low crop yield because of the thin soils of the Yucatán and the long-term cycle of reclaiming depleted agricultural plots. Slash and burn, or swidden agriculture, requires cutting down a section of forest and burning the cut vegetation. The ashes provided nutrients for the soil. However, the soil becomes depleted two to five years after the initiation of the cycle. The land is then planted as an orchard and allowed to return to its natural growth. This may take a period of five to 15 years. In the meantime, new land is cleared and burned, and another cycle begins. Maya engineers combined technology and proven cultivars to increase food supply by creating new fertile land areas including the use of reclaimed wetlands, terraces, raised fields, and new irrigation methodologies.

Terraced Fields

Regions teeming with large populations turned to the integration of civil engineering and agriculture technology. The use of sustainable agriculture terraces was introduced to areas that had hilly terrain with a minimum of flat terrain for agriculture use. Terraces were hydrological structures that were constructed on a sloped hillside. Initially the level or bottom land areas were cultivated. As the demand for additional food supplies increased, additional arable land was required for farming. Agriculture terraces were then planned, designed, and constructed on the hillsides above the bottom land. The use of agriculture terraces served multiple purposes, including increased area for cultivation, reduction of soil erosion, and capture of water for use in the dry season.

They significantly increased the area of available cultivated fields by altering the geometry of the hillside topography from its natural slope to the stepped configuration of the terraces. The terraces reduced erosion. Prior to altering the hillsides, the land was naturally sloped downward, permitting storm water to rush down the slopes, which caused erosion and flooding of the agricultural areas at the bottom of the slopes. The storm water slowed as it flowed across the level section of the terraces. This water was absorbed and stored by the deep soil fill retained by the terrace walls and used to irrigate cultivars during the dry season.

The terraces were planned to optimize the development of level, arable land as they stepped down the slope. The vertical stone retaining wall structures that created the stepped terraces on hillsides were founded on limestone bedrock. The walls, known as gravity retaining structures, are constructed of cut stone masonry and are wider at the base than the top of the wall (Figure 8-7). The width of the base is one-third of the height of the wall. The walls are backfilled with soil that extended to the top of the retaining wall and is level with the base of the uphill retaining wall. This geometry developed a triangular volume of fertile soil backfill. The terrace system had a great advantage over typical level ground agriculture. The Maya farmers used innovative soil re-building methodologies on the terraces, including growing cycles interspersed with carbon and nitrogen deposition via cyclic burning and flooding.

Flooding of the terraces was accomplished by two methods: The most common was the yearly deluge during the rainy season. The second, in areas that supported up-hill reservoirs and canals with water-regulation gates for controlling irrigation water, was the opening of the gates to permit water to pour down to the terrace structures. The stored water flowed down the terraces and recharged the moisture in the soil.

Raised Field and Wetland Agriculture

Wetland agriculture was extensively practiced by Maya agronomists. Bountiful crops were grown in marshes and wetland regions where food production was otherwise impossible due to the presence of standing water. Maya agriculture technicians constructed and managed a wetland-based agro-ecosystem throughout the realm. In some areas, 40 percent of the land is based in wetlands. Taking advantage of this swampy land provided the Maya with an expanded food supply. The agro-ecosystem included the design and construction of canals, raised field platforms, and aqua-farming. The canals and raised fields were one of the concepts developed to cultivate crops in conditions of low-lying marsh land and water accumulation caused by the heavy rainfall. The canal and soil platform systems were techniques developed by Maya engineers that increased agriculture production in conditions that prohibited the use of traditional farming.

The efficient canal and raised field systems were laid out and constructed in a Cartesian grid pattern. The canals followed the grid pattern

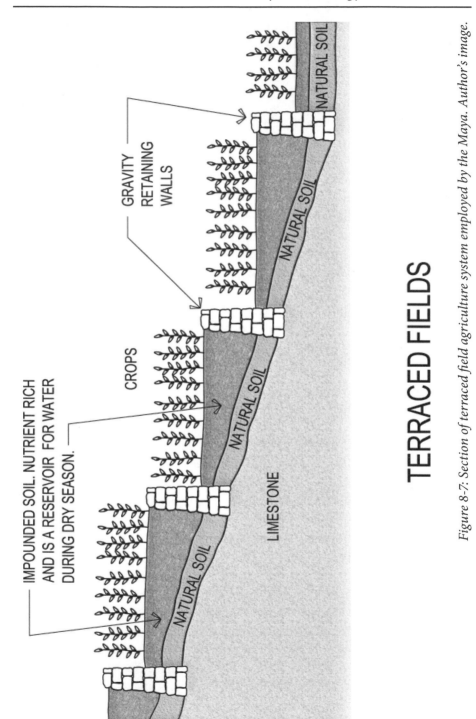

GRAVITY
RETAINING
WALLS

CROPS

IMPOUNDED SOIL. NUTRIENT RICH
AND IS A RESERVOIR FOR WATER
DURING DRY SEASON.

NATURAL SOIL

NATURAL SOIL

NATURAL SOIL

NATURAL SOIL

LIMESTONE

TERRACED FIELDS

Figure 8-7: Section of terraced field agriculture system employed by the Maya. Author's image.

and transcribed the limits of the rectangular raised fields. The canals were excavated down to the bottom of soil levels, and the soil was placed within the grid of the canals to elevate the surface of the interior into platforms by mounding the excavated soil to create a planting surface between the canals. Additional, borrowed soil was added to the raised fields to an appropriate level that kept the roots of the crops above the water level. The bottom of the canals was often sealed with clay to prevent the loss of water (Figure 8-8).

The plots developed by the platform were planted, and cultivars were produced and harvested. As the cycle of crop growing progressed, soil eroded from the raised fields and flowed into the canals. This eroded soil became mixed with organic matter from the spoilage of animal, plant, and aquatic life living in the canals. Maya farmers maintained the canals and fertilized the soil by removing the rich sediment from the bottom of the canal and then placing this enriched nutrient on the surface of the raised field structure to rebuild the soil. This sediment increased the nitrogen level, which produced high yields of crops four times that of fields farmed using contemporary methodologies. The raised fields were further enriched by creating a compost of the crops, which remained on the soil surface after the harvest.

The agro-ecosystem of canals and raised fields proved to be a long-term strategy for feeding the population and enabled an added advantage of producing two crops per year. The increased yield would be raised with one crop planted on the surface of the raised fields during the rainy season, and another crop would be grown in the muddy and nutrient-rich bottom of the canal during the dry season. Canals or artificial water courses had other purposes as transportation routes for canoes or defensive moats. Canals supplying the water were also used as aquaculture systems: growing turtles, fish, amphibians, and vegetation that supplemented the diet of the Maya.

This great source of fertile land and ample water supply was exploited by the Maya culture and became the most productive agricultural source in the lowlands. With the aid of satellite imagery and remote sensing, researchers from George Mason University and the Geological Society of America have discovered a vast area of raised fields in northern Belize. The satellite images indicate a massive grid of raised fields more than 100 kilometers in width. Research has indicated that raised field agriculture was widespread, with 40 square kilometers identified in Quintana Roo.

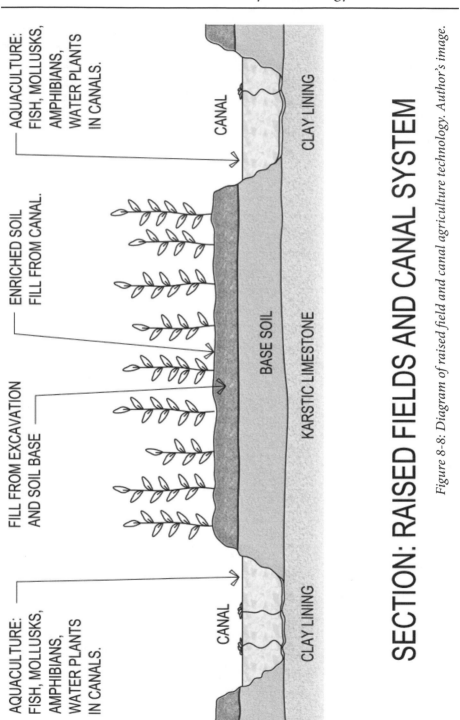

Figure 8-8: Diagram of raised field and canal agriculture technology. Author's image.

Maya Water-Treatment Systems

One can easily envision the condition of rainwater stored for six months in the static and closed underground reservoir of a chultune. The water has not only lost its freshness and has become vapid, but the lack of oxygen in the closed chamber creates a state of turbidity and becomes the perfect incubator for the growth of pathogens. The storm water collected in the reservoir had flowed across open surfaces, and there was always a high probability of bird feces being flushed into the containment structure. The stored water would have become aerobatic due to the lack of oxygen. In short, the water was distasteful and unhealthy.

Maya technology developed filter techniques to provide clean, potable water from stored water for cities that depended on chultunes and reservoirs. Water-treatment technology utilized two methods to provide clean water, based on the type of storage. These include the application of organic methodologies for water stored in open reservoirs, and microfiltration for water stored underground in chultunes or other storage systems that required filtering to clean the water.

Biological Water Treatment Systems

The natural, biological treatment processes utilized water lilies planted in the large open reservoirs. This decorative plant contributed to both the preservation and filter treatment of stored water. The wide leaves of the plant floating on the surface reduced evaporation by providing a surface cover and shade to prevent algae growth. The stem and root system of the water lily recycled organic waste; these plants produce and enrich dissolved oxygen into the stored water. They provide a microenvironment for numerous invertebrates that ensure extensive natural purification. The plants are suited for absorbing nutrients through their roots and storing these nutrients in their leaves. The stem and leaves in the water plants prevent sedimentation and provide a substrate for the growth of beneficial microorganisms. Frogs, dragonflies, and salamanders that controlled mosquito larvae will multiply naturally. The animals, insects, and water lilies integrate to form the natural biological treatment center engineered by Maya technology. Water lily plants could be also harvested and used as natural fertilizer in agriculture. This natural biological process produced a source of potable water for large populations.

The use of water plants in natural, biological water treatment centers has been introduced into contemporary water-treatment centers. The concept is now being used for cities with populations of 100,000. Modern water-treatment plants use aquatic plants for their ability to absorb pathogens, metals, and other contaminants from water. It appears that Maya technology applied a system that contemporary environmental engineers have discovered is economical and environmentally suitable.

Microfiltration Process For Clean Water

The majority of Maya cities did not enjoy the opportunity of using natural biological treatment processes in open reservoir systems to provide a dependable source of clean water. The majority of large Maya cities in the northern and southern highlands depended on chultunes for water storage during the dry season. Water stored in the underground structured reservoirs was subject to turbidity and the growth of pathogens. When water was distributed from chultunes, it was clouded with sediment and pathogens. This water was not safe to drink. Again, Maya engineers turned to the most abundant materials available to the culture, the same material that absorbed their rainwater and was used for fabricating cement and masonry for building these grand cities. They used the karstic limestone underlying the Yucatán shelf and exploited the porosity of this multi-purpose material to fabricate high-quality water filters.

The limestone could be shaped into various geometries to serve the purpose as a water filter. Karstic limestone has up to 40 percent porosity in its mass, with pre-sizing from 0.20 micron to 6 micron. This material qualifies as a microfilter using modern water filter standards. Water collected from a chultune would be processed using a limestone filter. Two types of limestone water filters fabricated from limestone by Maya technicians have been identified as part of the water-treatment system:

1. A limestone cylinder with a cone-shaped, truncated end that is used with an exterior reservoir of turbid water (Figure 8-9 and Figure 8-11). Turbid water entering the filter at the top was processed in the limestone and clean water flowed from bottom.

2. A cone-shaped vessel of limestone with an interior reservoir for turbid water. The interior reservoir permeates turbid water through the porous limestone shell. This process converted turbid water into clean water that flowed from the bottom of the filter vessel (Figure 8-10).

Figure 8-9: Cone water filters at Chichen Itza in 2004. Author's image.

Figure 8-10: Maya water treatment filter with internal reservoir.
Author's image.

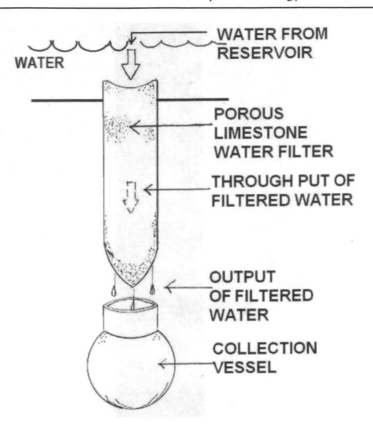

Figure 8-11: Diagram of cone filter filtration process.
Author's image.

Tests of the limestone water filters indicate that 1 to 2 liters per hour can be processed by a single filter. Each filter would yield 24 to 48 liters per 24-hour period.

Artifacts of Maya Water Filter Technology

Examples of Maya limestone water filters have been encountered at various sites and in collections. Examples include the solid limestone filter and the hollow water filter vessel. The solid limestone filter has been encountered at Maya archaeological sites. The elongated, cylindrical-shaped filter has the characteristic truncated cone configuration. Figure 8-11 indicates this shaped solid limestone filter. The hollow water filter vessel has been observed in museums and on historic sites. At Chichen Itza, the solid

Figure 8-12: Excavation of Platform of Venus with cone water filters.
Image in public domain.

cone filter stands as an architectural mystery. However, it is possible that the role of the solid cone-shaped filter once played an important role in the life of the city. The subject structure is located to the north of the plaza between the Castillo and the Sacred Cenote. John Lloyd Stephens and Frederick Catherwood first related their observations of Chichen Itza and this structure in their 1842 volumes, *Incidents of Travel in the Yucatán*. The structure is noted as a "ruined mound." Later records indicate that Doctor and Mrs. Le Plongeon excavated the "ruined mound" and uncovered a platform with stairways on each facade. Their excavation trench exposed more than 100 cone-shaped limestone artifacts. The Le Plongeons had the cones unearthed and laid on the ground outside the mound. These cone-shaped artifacts gave the platform its initial name, "the platform of the cones."

In 1889, while working at Chichen Itza, Alfred Maudslay photographed "mound 14" with the platform in the background (Figure 8-12). In the foreground, the limestone cones have been arranged in a line at the east side of the platform. Maudslay reported that the cones were unearthed by the Le Plongeons. It is unknown when the name of the structure changed from "mound 14" to the "platform of the cones," but it held that title until it was changed to the "Platform of Venus."

Today, at Chichen Itza, the cones are stacked like artillery shells in a fenced enclosure adjacent to the Venus platform. They are mysteriously aligned with the main axis of the platform, biding their time to reveal their true role in Maya technology. The facade of the Venus platform displays bas-relief carvings of the diving god "Venus," as well as a number of water-related motifs including the water lily, turtles, and fish. It would appear that the platform had a strong relationship to water and possibly represented the power of the water lily lords.

The mysterious cone-shaped artifacts are obviously limestone water filters. A field sketch by the Le Plongeons indicates an organized stacking of numerous limestone cones buried in the core of the platform. It is arguable that this structure was once used as a water-processing facility to filter turbid water from cenotes. The water in the Sacred Cenote is notorious for its turbidity and the location of the platform is suited for water transfer. The facility had been decommissioned as a water-treatment center, and the cones were buried below the platform prior to the modifications to be used as ceremonial platform. The "orphan" limestone cones are now positioned a few feet from the platform structure. They are near their Maya burial site, as if waiting for a visionary archaeologist to identify their true function, which may have been filtering water to preserve the health of the population of Chichen Itza.

9

The Maya Interstate Highway System

The commercial and political success of Maya city-states was dependent on their ability to efficiently maintain the flow of communication, commercial trade, and the movement of traffic between city-states. Their ability to travel between strategic destinations was dependent on the condition of overland routes. These routes, once limited to winding jungle trails, left travel conditions at the mercy of the capricious natural environment.

The vast majority of the 125,000-square-mile Maya realm consisted of rough natural terrain, overshadowed by the dark rainforest canopy, overgrown with tangled roots and covered with slick, green moss, making travel difficult in any weather condition. During the long rainy season, copious amounts of tropical rainfall made travel on the rutted soil tracks difficult for the typical traveler and nearly impossible for the cargo porters straining under back-breaking loads.

Maya technology was challenged to develop a creative solution that would overcome the reliance on rough jungle trails. These routes retarded travel in the best of weather conditions and became a quagmire of torturous proportions during the rainy season. Maya creativity rose to the challenge of travel routes that restrained commerce and hindered the power base of the city-states. The solution was an all-weather road system that facilitated the flow of goods, communications, and the swift movement of military traffic, while enhancing political and economic relations between polities.

This innovative roadway system was developed around 300 BC and spread throughout the realm. Maya call these roads *sacbe* (plural, *sacbeob*), which means "white road," referring to the white color of the road pavement. The road systems were constructed well into the late Classic Period and used for centuries in the Post-Classic Period with little maintenance. Examples of these roads have been observed throughout the Maya world, and they represent a significant investment in capital resources and human labor. Their construction and application were an important element in the Maya system of politics and commerce.

The Design Criteria for the All-Weather Roadway System

The Maya power elite, when faced with a transportation dilemma threatening the growth of their wealthy and powerful city-states, began the search for a technological solution. The transportation of commercial goods, military movements, communication, and other travel purposes could not operate on the treacherous jungle trails. The requirements set down by elite management became the engineering criteria for an efficient ground transportation system that would be adopted throughout the Maya world.

Maya engineers approached the challenge by focusing their creativity on the use of proven technical innovations to develop solutions for an all-weather highway. Their solution was one that would support a variety of two-way traffic and was constructible in a variety of environmental conditions, including jungle terrain, savannahs, and marshlands, using locally available materials. To develop the optimal design for a multi-functional, all-weather roadway, Maya engineers applied their proven technology, materials of construction, and engineering skills to develop the innovative prototype. They combined design and construction materials, including structural engineering, linear surveying, cast-in-place concrete, composite masonry and concrete systems, and construction management.

The design methodology for implementation of the engineered routes included a variable criterion that enabled construction of the roads in diverse terrains. The specifications allowed the use of local materials available along the route. The basic geometric profile of the sacbe required a 10-meter-wide, paved, concrete surface elevated a minimum of 1 meter above the ground surface by stone sidewalls and a cast-in-place concrete base. The smooth, white, concrete pavement of the road enabled a solid non-slip footing for travelers while resisting the growth of invasive jungle vegetation. To maintain a dry pavement, the surface of the concrete paving was shaped with a convex crown to facilitate the drainage of storm water from the road surface. The sidewalls elevated the roadway above the jungle floor to prevent flooding during the rainy season and deterred jungle growth. Maya engineers relied on the elevated surface of their roads to keep their pavement clear of mud, storm water, and the attack of the encroaching jungle. The geometry, construction details, and composition of the typical sacbe is shown in Figure 9-1 and Figure 9-2.

Alignment Criteria of Roadway Systems

The construction of a sacbe began with the selection of the route and the engineering design of the roadway. Maya roads were designed as straight alignments between two points, no matter what the distance. The alignment followed the vertical geometry of the surface terrain, rather than using cut-and-fills to change the vertical contours of the roadway. Maya engineers preferred road routes to pass over the crest of a hill or follow the contours of a natural depression. This method of alignment also reduced the opportunity for ambush by invaders by eliminating potential hiding positions.

The field engineering for the construction of a Maya roadway used a few simple surveying instruments. The basic engineering tools have not changed in contemporary road construction. The basic tools for establishing horizontal lines and right angles were based on the plumb bob, string lines, and water levels. Curved roads were just not in the Maya repertoire. The basic surveying tool used by the Maya was based on gravity, whereas contemporary surveying instruments are based on digital technology that use laser beams for leveling and distance. The results are the same, but digital tools are 99 percent accurate. The overall alignment of Maya roads was based on celestial navigation.

The route of the sacbe cut an open swath through the forest, enabling sunlight to penetrate the shadows and dry the surface of the roadway after a rain. The same open slot permitted the surface of the white roads to be illuminated by moonlight and starlight. This celestial light enabled travel during the night, making the sacbe a true year-round transit route.

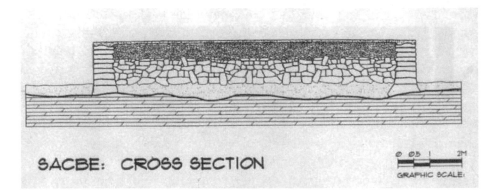

Figure 9-1: Cross section of structural detail and geometry of typical sacbe. Author's image.

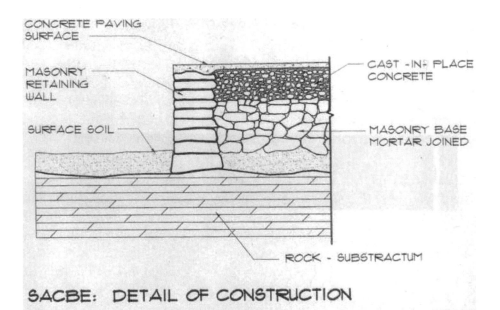

Figure 9-2: Detail of Maya sacbe with materials of construction shown. Author's image.

The 10-meter-wide sacbe had sufficient width to offer the opportunity for two lanes of travel in each direction. Lacking the advantages of beasts of burden, the Maya relied on manpower for transportation. It is apparent that heavily laden bearers would keep to the outside or "slow lane" in each direction. Fast movers, such as messengers, travelers without burdens, and military traffic, would have the right of way in the inside fast lanes. These four lanes of traffic would require the entire 10-meter-wide pavement, with 2.5 meters for each of the four lanes. Modern roads have lanes that are 3 meters wide for highway traffic, a very similar lane width to that used by the Maya.

The sacbe system, in many cases, extended for long distances. To provide aid and support for travelers, the sacbe system included rest stations with water and provisions. Military garrisons were positioned along the routes to maintain order and carry out administrative duties, such as the collection of tolls. The sacbe system extended throughout the peninsula, interconnecting the major city-states. The concept, purpose, and geographic distribution of the sacbe system was similar to the interstate highway system in the United States, the Autobahn system in Germany, and the Roman road system in the Roman Empire. It served to enable military forces to move swiftly to a trouble spot. The hard surface of the sacbe provided a firm footing for marching warriors. The paved roadways also became a major economic factor and grew the wealth and culture of the Maya. In a similar manner, the modern interstate highway and the Autobahn have changed the primary purposes of the highways from a military role to the lifeline for economic transport.

Comparison Between Maya Road Technology and the Roman Road System

Historically, Roman road construction has been considered the ultimate in well-constructed, all-weather roads. These roads outlasted the sturdy building constructions of the Roman Empire for a millennium and a half. The Roman roads were well constructed all throughout the empire, but were at their optimum in Italy, where cast-in-place concrete was available to the road builder. However, the Roman roads north of the Rubicon River were also well constructed of locally available material.

The comparisons of these famous Roman roads with the Maya sacbe system indicate similarly sound structures that have also lasted for well over 1,000 years. In addition, the construction techniques used by both technologies are quite similar. The major difference is the elevated geometry of the Maya road surface. The Romans based their design on the natural environment of Europe and North Africa versus the tropical jungles and rainstorms in the Maya criteria. Maya roads were elevated a meter above the adjacent terrain, whereas Roman roads were built just above grade level. Roman roads were 6 meters in width, and the Maya roads were 10 meters in width. Like Maya engineers, the Roman civil engineers constructed their roads to follow the natural terrain. The quality of the construction of the roads depended on the strategic importance of the road and the availability of local materials. Major, fully paved Roman roads were constructed of four to five layers of structural-grade materials installed in a foundation excavation of approximately 1 meter in depth.

The depth of the foundation depended on the quality of the supporting soil. Roman engineers used innovation in order to select appropriate local materials for road construction. Construction initiated with the survey of the road's centerline, using survey tools similar to the Maya, based on the plumb bob and the water level. The foundation excavation down to bearing soil proceeded along the centerline. The strata of construction materials included a base course of sand and mortar, followed by a layer of flat, worked stones that were set in mortar, and then a layer of gravel set in clay or concrete. The final structural layer was the installation of large, worked, hard stones set in concrete. The top level of hard rock was the travel surface; this stone pavement was laid to produce a crown for drainage. Large curb stones were set at the perimeter, and the lateral drainage gutters completed the construction.

The Roman engineers and their contemporary Maya counterparts followed the theory that a well-constructed road would require minimum maintenance. The Maya road-builders had the luxury of an ample supply of cement for producing cast-in-place concrete, concrete paving, and stucco. Roman road-builders were required to rely on a source of natural volcanic cement found only in Italy. Transport of this valuable construction material had a limited range. It has been only in recent years that road-builders have returned to quality road construction similar to the Maya and Roman roads.

Many Maya roads have been covered by the encroaching jungle and alluvial material, and have been degraded by the roots and lack of maintenance. However, some Maya roads have been paved over and serve as the base for contemporary highways. Thousands of miles of sacbeob stretched across the Yucatán Peninsula during the Classic Period. By comparison, only 114 miles of paved road had been built in the United States before 1914.

Incidents of Encounters With Ancient Sacbe

When the conquistadors invaded the Yucatán in 1542, the Maya sacbeob had fallen into a state of dilapidation, due to the 600 years that had passed since the decline of the Classic Maya civilization. Maintenance and construction of the roads had ceased and the jungle environment engulfed the marvelous road systems. Although some roads were reported to be in a state of usable quality, the majority of the sacbeob were in a state of deterioration, covered by jungle tendrils and alluvial deposits.

The first reports of the Maya roads were recorded in the 16th century by colonial historians; later accounts of observations in the 19th and 20th centuries were noted by explorers, archaeologists, and travel writers. Archaeologists did not carry out formal studies of the sacbe system until 1934, when the Cobá to Yaxuná sacbe was surveyed by the Carnegie Institution of Washington. After Alfonso Villa's report, "The Yaxuná–Cobá Causeway," on the 1934 survey was published in *Contributions to American Archaeology*, many archaeologists doubted the actual existence of the Maya roadway system. Archaeologists, when judging the existence of the roadway system, considered the raised highways to be unique to the eastern Yucatán. However, research of historical chronicles, journals, and reports by observers indicated that sightings of the sacbeob have been reported for centuries at various locations across the breadth of the Maya domain.

Maya strongholds in the southern lowlands and the Petén were not conquered by the Spanish until the dawn of the 18th century, some 150 years later. Reports of sacbe sightings from that area of the Maya world came later in history. After the conquest and during the colonial period, the 300 years of Spanish rule discouraged exploration of the Yucatán, which only began in earnest after the Mexican Revolution in 1821, when travelers and archaeologists began to explore the technological and artistic works of the Maya. Written accounts of the reports by historians and soldiers, though mostly a footnote to history, indicated that a technologically advanced highway system had been observed throughout the domain of the Maya city-states and were not solely confined to the eastern Yucatán.

The reports of an advanced roadway system constructed by the ancient Maya were considered by archaeologists to be a mythological feat remembered as a folk memory by the native culture. The reports of these roads were solely based on Spanish historical chronicles recorded by conquistadors until the mid-19th century. Moreover, actual Maya roadways had not been identified and studied until the 20th century. Archaeologists did not investigate the fabled roadways until the 1934 Carnegie survey of the Cobá to Yaxuná sacbe.

Although the majority of early reports of Maya roads were from the Northern Yucatán, exploration, archaeological investigation, eyewitness observations, and Spanish colonial accounts have described encounters with the ancient roads in diverse locations throughout the realm of the Maya. It has become apparent that the standard design of the engineered roadway was adopted and constructed through the Maya world. The sacbe system was a common denominator for transportation and communication adapted to suit local political and environmental conditions.

Research has indicated that parts of the sacbe system were in use by 300 BC and were still in use well after the collapse. Early records of observations of the Maya roadway system were recorded in 1562 when Bishop Diego de Landa, in *Relación de las cosas de Yucatán*, reporting on the architecture of the city of T'hó (Mérida), wrote, "There are signs nowadays of there having been a very beautiful causeway from some to others." De Landa also described a 62 km paved road extending from T'hó to Izamal. In 1610, Bernardo de Lizana made reference to ancient roadways in his *Devocionario de Nuestra Señora de Izamal y Conquista Espiritual de Yucatán* (*Prayer Book of Our Lady of Izamal and Spiritual Conquest of the Yucatán*). When describing the Maya religious center of Izamal, he wrote, "They...made pilgrimages from all parts, for which they had made four roads or causeways to the four cardinal points, which reached to the ends of the land and passed to Tabasco, Guatemala, and Chiapas...so that today in many parts may be seen pieces and vestiges of them." In 1688, Diego Lopez de Cogolludo observed there were paved highways that traverse and ended on the east on the seashore so that pilgrims might arrive in Cozumel for the fulfillment of their vows.

It would be 233 years before another historical note relative to observations of sacbeob was recorded. John Lloyd Stephens describes reports of the sacbe from Cobá to Yaxuná. He describes the architecture of Cobá with a *calzada* or paved road, of 10 or 12 yards in width, running to the southeast to a limit that has not been discovered with certainty, though some agree that it goes in the direction of Chichen Itza.

In 1883, Désiré Charnay, the French archaeologist and explorer, reported that on his explorations he encountered an ancient paved roadway in the eastern Yucatán from Izamal to the sea, facing the island of Cozumel. Charney was reporting on a portion of the sacbe that extended from T'hó to the Caribbean coast at the town of Ppole (Puerto Morelos). Reports of sections of this fabled sacbe have been reported by de Landa and Diego Lopez de Cogolludo. This route has been referenced in Colonial and modern studies, and would have extended in an east–west direction from Mérida to Puerto Morelos.

It would be the 20th century before Victor Pinto verified the nature and route of the 20-kilometer sacbe from Kabah to Labná in the Yucatán. In 1912, Dr. Sylvanus Morley reported that when construction crews from the United Fruit Company were constructing a company railroad in Honduras, the excavations carried out on the outskirts of Quiriguá encountered a "magnificent causeway of cut stone." It was reported that the sacbe extended from Quiriguá to the northeast traversing toward an unknown destination.

In 1966, Lawrence Roy and Dr. Edward Shook investigated the sacbe extending from Izamal to Aké. They walked the route, taking compass readings and measuring its width. This east–west route may be part of the fabled 300-kilometer Ppole to T'hó road. In 1959, geologist A.E. Weidie reported that a railroad formerly used by *chicleros* extended to a point 20 km west of Puerto Morelos, and that the railroad had been built on the raised structure of an ancient roadway extending in an east–west direction. From 1995 to 2002, archaeologist Jennifer Mathews of Foundation for the Advancement of Mesoamerican Studies, Inc. (FAMSI) carried out surveys on that same sacbe. Her studies extended 48 kilometers to the west from Highway 360 at Puerto Morelos. Her reports detail surveys and photographs of a broad sacbe with a prototypical design configuration. The numerous inter-site sacbeob at the ancient city of Cobá, surveyed and recorded by Dr. William Folan and Dr. George Stuart in the early 1970s, indicate the role of the roadway system in a city's development. Dr. William Folan also investigated sacbeob extending from Calakmul to El Mirador. The sacbeob were observed crossing marshland as they extend toward El Mirador. These sacbeob, a modified prototypical design using earth fill to suit the marshland conditions, were studied by Folan in the 1990s. Archaeologist Richard Hanson, in conjunction with NASA, is investigating sacbeob extending from El Mirador to other sites. Archaeologists Arlen and Diane Chase have surveyed sacbeob extending from the site of El Caracol in Belize. The historical and contemporary reports of engineered roadways by the ancient Maya have presented sufficient evidence that indicates not only their very existence, but their wide distribution throughout the Maya domain. David Bollen, in a paper submitted to FAMSI, stated that a few years ago it was thought that sacbeob did not exist in Campeche, the Petén of Guatemala, or in Belize. Now that there is valid reporting of the wide range of sacbeob, it would seem that the discoveries of them crossing the great Maya domain have just begun.

Archaeo-Engineering Surveys of the Sacbeob

The traces of sacbeob were often difficult to visually locate due to shrouding by the rainforest environment. In some cases, the ancient roads were covered by jungle detritus and alluvial fill, and degraded by prying roots. Man has also contributed to the destruction of the ancient roads. They were dismantled by local builders who used the stonework of the road structure as a quarry. They have been destroyed by modern developmental activities and agricultural expansion. However, the low vertical profile of these roads is another reason for the difficulty in locating evidence of their presence. The sacbe, which is barely a meter in height, does not present a noticeable mound or high vertical profile. The majority of encounters have been by chance and are usually the product of other archaeological or construction activities. Aerial photography and remote sensing by satellite have increased the incidents of detection of the linear telltale traces of these roadways. These roads can be also viewed by an observer on the Internet. Vestiges of the roads can be visually located on Google Earth, which has become a valuable tool for archaeological research, and for viewing sacbeob and other artifacts. The length and remoteness of these roads have not attracted the archaeological investigations that have been lavished on the

Classic cities. The cost of searching for and consolidation of the roads on the ground would be prohibitive.

The 100-kilometer sacbe extending from Cobá to Yaxuná exhibits the classic criteria of the Maya road system. This route is the only long-range sacbe system that has been surveyed by an archaeological institution. The original survey, carried out in 1934 by Alfonso Villa, ascertained the route of the road and encountered unique archaeological artifacts along the route. The published report included a map, photographs, and a detailed narrative of the survey and historical background on sacbeob.

From 1995 to 2002, a comprehensive, digitally based ground and aerial survey of the Yaxuná to Cobá sacbe was carried out by an archaeo-engineering team led by me. A survey had not been carried out on this route since Villa's work in 1934. Extensive archaeological surveys of sacbeob were carried out in the 1970s in the area of Cobá, a sacbe-rich site. However, the surveys did not include the route of the 100-kilometer sacbe to Yaxuná. The goal of our contemporary survey was to assess and confirm the civil and structural engineering technology used in the construction of the roadway, and establish the route using ground-based GPS positioning instruments, photography, satellite images, and aerial surveys. Furthermore, our investigation carried out observations and took photographs of the ruined sacbe at each terminus, intersections at Sacbe No. 3, and at intermediate crossings of modern roads.

The 1934 survey was a work of a brave and intelligent man. With his crew of 12 men, he hacked his way through the 100-kilometer route and provided archaeology with an overview of the complexity and efficiency of the sacbe system. Our contemporary survey was not required to carve a path through the jungle, but used digital tools, computers, aerial survey, and remote sensing by NASA satellites to observe, measure, survey, and collect data from high above the ancient roadway. We did not attempt and cannot match Mr. Villa's courage and fortitude. However, the comparison of Villas traditional jungle survey and O'Kon digital surveying combined to provide a new insight to the ingenious Maya road system.

The 1934 Carnegie Institution Survey of the Route

The original survey was the brain child of Villa, a member of the Carnegie Institution of Washington archaeological team working at Chichen Itza. Villa had previously explored portions of the Cobá to Yaxuná sacbe, but had not yet traveled the entire 100-kilometer route. At this time archaeologists were unsure if the road connected Cobá to Chichen Itza or to Yaxuná. Villa discussed his knowledge and experience of this paved road with Dr. Sylvanus Morley, then in charge of the Chichen Itza project. Morley charged Villa, a surveyor, with the mission of exploring and surveying the route from Yaxuná to Cobá.

The survey team was composed of Villa and 12 men; 10 men were assigned to cut a path through the thick vegetation engulfing the route of the sacbe; one man led the horses transporting the provisions, equipment, and water; and another man assisted Villa with surveying measurements and photography. Villa's survey tools consisted solely of a handheld Brunton compass, a tripod, a 100-meter-long chain or measuring tape, and a range pole for back sighting. The Bruton compass is a precision instrument and can be leveled to increase accuracy. It is an adequate surveying device for surveying compact archaeological sites, but is challenged when required to accurately survey over long distances.

The survey team began its work on February 27, 1934, and proceeded from Yaxuná toward Cobá. The beginning of the sacbe at Yaxuná was marked by a ruined mound located in the center of the city. A stairway, located on the east side of the mound, served as a survey benchmark. At this point, the sacbe was measured to be 10.3 meters wide and 60 centimeters in height. The actual height was probably greater, but the debris of a millennium reduced the wall measurement. The structure of the sacbe at Yaxuná had been badly deteriorated, mostly due to locals using the structure as a quarry. The survey continued over the entire route of the road. As the Villa expedition cut its way over the roadway, Villa noted locations of the villages of Sisal, Sacal, Ekal, San Francisco, and Xcahumil. Villa recorded and photographed stone mile markers, culverts, ramparts, and archaeological structures. One of the interesting discoveries was a cylinder of solid stone that Villa referred to as a "road roller." The stone was 4 meters in length and 70 centimeters in diameter, with a weight of 5 tons. There are various opinions that have been made about its usage, including a phallus symbol and a method of transport for large stone material.

The sacbe maintained a height of average 75 centimeters as the survey moved eastward. However, at a deep depression, the wall height increased to 2.5 meters. Overturned trees along the route exposed the interior and confirmed the construction of the sacbe: it has vertical sides of roughly dressed stones, large undressed stones laid in a mixture of cast-in-place concrete, smaller stones form the bed, and the roadway surface is paved with cast-in-place concrete.

For the majority of the route, the sacbe travels in a straight alignment following the topography of the terrain (Figure 9-3), only varying a few degrees from the easterly bearing for a few kilometers, then re-adjusting back to eastward. As the route neared the ancient city of Cobá, the route of the survey turned southeast before entering the city, where the sacbe intersects a north–south Sacbe No. 3. An octagonal plaza is located at this intersection. The plaza and sacbeob form geometry similar to a traffic circle. With a 4-meter-tall, truncated pyramid in the center, the sacbe then enters Cobá and ends at the eastern terminus, in the plaza of Nohoch Mul, the tallest pyramid in the Yucatán. A distance of 100 kilometers and 385 meters had been measured from the benchmark at Yaxuná. The dimensions of the road at the terminus were 9.80 meters in width and 60 centimeters in height. Villa produced a drawn survey map of the route. The map includes a cross-section of the sacbe structure and villages along the route.

It is of interest to note that Villa recorded legends relative to the building of the sacbes. The tall tales were in fashion during the time of his survey. Maya, while marveling at the monumental works of their forefathers, believed them to be the work of magic. They believed that these great engineering works were raised by men with supernatural powers. These men were lords of the elements, who, by means of a special whistle, brought life to stones that arranged themselves into marvelous and beautiful buildings and roads without the aid of human labor. These men were eventually turned to stone by divine punishment

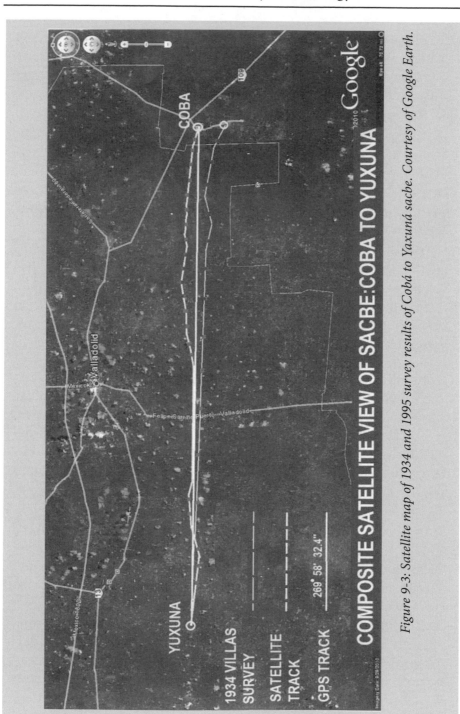

Figure 9-3: Satellite map of 1934 and 1995 survey results of Cobá to Yuxuná sacbe. Courtesy of Google Earth.

and are now the stele with human effigies that are admired in Cobá today.

The sacbe from Cobá to Yaxuná was said to be built by a magician named Ez. He performed his work in the dark, and by his magic arts, he caused the 100-kilometer road to be constructed in one night. He was so absorbed in his work that when he arrived in Cobá, he was surprised by the dawn and was turned into a stone statue. For the Maya, Cobá is a mythical place where one encounters many dangers. The terrible Hacmatz is a ghastly creature who waits patiently in the jungle by the dark of night; this animal consumes the bodies of men. The unaware who venture in Cobá after dark are devoured, as the Hacmatz entraps them by sticking out its tongue and snaring its prey.

The 1995 O'Kon Expedition to Explore the Cobá to Yaxuná Sacbe

Solving the mystery of the Maya sacbe system has been the keystone to understanding the relationship of Maya road technology with the wealth and power of the Maya city-states. The existence and extent of the sacbe system has been doubted by archaeology for more than a century. In 1995, I assembled an archaeo-engineering team to investigate the Cobá–Yaxuná sacbe and verify its character and existence. The study included the evaluation of the sacbe alignment using global positional coordinates at various locations along the route, including the termini at Cobá and Yaxuná and at intermediate points in the route.

The team consisted of three professionals who traversed portions of the sacbe at each end and at the midpoint. We were not required to suffer 20 days of hacking our way through the jungle undergrowth using a hand-held compass, tripod, and 100-meter measuring chain. We did not use our machetes and did not require a horizontal line of sight for surveying, but used a Trimble global positioning system (GPS) navigation receiver, as well as state-of-the-art (film) cameras. I was accompanied by archaeologists Dr. Nicholas Hellmuth and Carl Stimmel. We had worked together previously on deep jungle archaeological expeditions and had a proven track record. The scope of work that would verify and expand the work of Villa included the use of GPS positioning equipment at the Cobá terminus, the crossing of the Cobá–Yaxuná sacbe and Sacbe No. 3, and GPS readings at the intersection of Modern Highway 195 south of Valladolid and at the benchmark at Yaxuná. The four locations for the survey were selected for their critical locations on the sacbe route and their accessibility. Following are the locations and their characteristics.

1. **Survey Location No. 1: The terminus at Cobá.** The sacbe is consolidated and the road terminates at a position at the south front of Nohuch Mul. This is the highest pyramid in the Yucatán. This location was obviously the central plaza in Cobá. Four other sacbe from the cardinal directions terminate at this large plaza. GPS readings and photographs were recorded.

2. **Survey Location No. 2: The intersection with Sacbe No. 3.** The Yaxuná sacbe extends westward from the plaza for approximately 700 meters to the intersection with the north–south Sacbe No. 3. A unique traffic control system was constructed at this intersection. The traffic at this intersection should have been significant. The flow of traffic on the major Yaxuná Sacbe No. 1 and the long-range Sacbe No. 3 merged and crossed at this intersection. The sacbeob ramped up 5 meters to the center of the intersection and formed a level platform. A 4-meter-tall, truncated pyramid is located at the center of the intersection; a tunnel sized for the passage of one person traverses the pyramid in an east–west direction. This passage could have been part of a defense system. The platform extends outward from the perimeter of the pyramid, forming a basic traffic circle. This configuration of road intersection enabled the four lanes of two-way traffic to be controlled by the rules of the road, such as maintaining one-way traffic around the circle and requiring entering traffic to keep to the outside lanes. Without this clever traffic rotary mechanism, the swift movers and heavy-loaded porters would cause a traffic jam. GPS readings, sketches, and photographs were recorded at this intersection.

3. **Survey Location No. 3: The intersection of the Yaxuná Sacbe and modern Highway 195.** Approximately 57 kilometers to the west of Cobá, the Yaxuná–Cobá sacbe is intersected by modern highway No. 195. This north–south highway cuts through the ancient road, leaving a neat cross section at each shoulder that reveals the technical composition of the road. The 1,400-year-old concrete pavement, stone side walls, and cast-in-place concrete base are clearly visible. GPS readings, sketches, and photographs were recorded at this location.

4. **Survey Location No. 4: The terminus at Yaxuná.** During this survey the ruined mound that served as the western terminus of the sacbe was investigated. The structure was degraded; however, the ramp of the sacbe up onto the structure was apparent. The sacbe extending to the east was clearly visible for a substantial distance. The site of Yaxuná is a flat plain with elevated temperatures. During the hour-long wait for the Trimble Navigation to acquire three signals, the heat became unbearable. The temperature rose to well over 110 degrees F; there was no shade on the sacbe. We took turns sitting in the shade of the van and studying the ancient city. Across the site, the recently discovered pyramid rose above the plain. Climbing to the summit one can see Chichen Itza 18 kilometer to the north. It was a great spot for Cobá to spy on Chichen Itza or to signal from the promontory. Finally, we acquired the three satellite signals, packed up, and turned the vehicle northward, enjoying the cool 4-70 air conditioner—that's four windows open while driving 70 kilometers an hour. GPS readings and photographs were recorded at the site.

The results of the survey were assessed and analyzed, and delivered at an architectural conference. However, we knew more work must be carried out to further define the route of the sacbe.

The 2000 Ground Survey of the Cobá to Yaxuná Sacbe

During the period of 1995 to 2000, the site of Yaxuná was consolidated, and archeological work was ongoing at Cobá. It was determined we should verify the 1995 GPS readings in relation to the consolidated structures. In addition, photographs of the newly consolidated structures are important to the history of the sacbe and the ancient cities. The GPS receiver used for this survey was a Magellan eXplorist, and the cameras were now digital. The second archaeo-engineering survey was carried out by a team of two professionals: me and anthropologist Carol Smith. The goal was to take GPS readings and photograph the recently consolidated sacbe and structures at Yaxuná. The observation tour initiated at Cobá and followed the same pattern as the 1995 survey.

1. **Survey Location No. 1: The terminus at Cobá.** The condition of the terminus sacbe had been altered. The end of the road had been consolidated. All other elements at the terminus were the same. GPS readings and photographs were recorded.

2. **Survey location No. 2: The intersection with Sacbe No. 3.** The condition of the intersection and pyramid had not changed since 1995. GPS readings and photos were recorded at this location.

3. **Survey location No. 3: The intersection of Yaxuná–Cobá sacbe and Highway 195.** The sacbe cross-section was overgrown with vegetation, but the condition of the structure had not changed.

4. **Survey location No. 4: The terminus at Yaxuná.** The appearance of the site had changed dramatically since 1995. The majority of the site structures had been consolidated, including the use of painted stucco on the surface of the structures. The quadratic terminus building had been restored; the sacbe had been reconstructed and paved as it ramps up onto the structure. GPS readings and photos were recorded at this location.

The results of the GPS readings at all points were identical to the readings taken with the Trimble in 1995. It appeared that while the technology had changed, the results were the same.

The 2001 Aerial Survey of the Cobá to Yaxuná Sacbe

The 1995 and 2000 surveys were ground-based and traversed critical sections of the sacbe to verify the alignment, positioning, and technological constructions. After the year 2000, remote sensing by satellite photos for the area between Cobá and Yaxuná was commercially available. However, cloud cover on the mosaic satellite images obscured much of the route and did not permit sufficient clarity to detect the alignment of the road beneath the cloud covered expanse.

The remote-sensing photographs were not an option, due to their obscurity in order to visually trace the route. It was determined to fly an aircraft at low levels along the route of the sacbe from Cobá toward Yaxuná. The goal was to photograph the alignment and structure along the 100-kilometer route. Though I hold a private pilot license, it was decided to lease a chartered twin Cessna from Cancun International Airport. Flying an aircraft with your knees while photographing is a young man's game.

The flight took off from Cancun International and turned southwest toward Cobá. As we neared Cobá and the tall pyramid of Nohuch Mul approached, the pilot punched Yaxuná's global coordinates into his avionic system and set the Cessna on autopilot. As the aircraft slowly banked to the west, we flew over the terminus of Sacbe No. 1 and set a westerly course for Yaxuná. The sleek Cessna followed the course established by signals beamed from the manmade celestial bodies orbiting the earth. It was ironic that our pathway would be led by the same philosophy that guided the ancient Maya. However, ours was a digital signal and not cosmic.

I was surprised how the sacbe revealed its course in various ways. The rainforest had been cut for agricultural purposes along lengths of the sacbe. Grass-covered fields prepared for cattle ranches extended to a line of tall trees that were approximately 10 meters in width on the south side the grassy glades. The pathway of the sacbe was clearly marked by the line of trees that extended to the horizon (Figure C-21).

Beneath the trees lay a 10-meter-wide and 1-meter-tall mass of stone and concrete, more trouble to remove than to leave in place. This left the concrete structure and the trees on the sacbe. The tall trees were the markers for the ancient roadway traversing the terrain. The aerial photograph Figure C-21 clearly indicates the alignment of the road from Cobá to Yaxuná.

The sun glinted from the white stucco on the monumental structures as we neared Yaxuná. The ancient road and its elevated terminus clearly marked the restored sacbe climbing up the terminus structure. The aircraft orbited the site several times, photographing the sacbe, and then turned due east toward Cobá. Returning along the ancient sacbe route, the pattern of the ancient road replicated itself. Soon Nohuch Mul appeared on the horizon and we crossed over Cobá's lakes. Our aircraft then turned toward Cancun International Airport and home base.

Comparison of the Technologies of Survey Equipment

It is interesting to note the great difference in technology achieved between the dates of each survey date. It was assumed that the leap in technology between 1934 and 1995 would make a vast difference in capabilities, and so it was. No longer did we labor with a line of sight survey and machetes; the GPS freed us from the tortuous trek. However, the difference in technology during the short period between 1995 and 2000 was surprising not only because of the advances in survey equipment, but also of that in cameras and cell phones. Our GPS receiver in 1995 was a relatively large, handheld device with an antenna consisting of a long wire lead. It required acquiring signals from a minimum of three satellites to receive a reading of a two-dimensional global position, and signals from four satellites to receive the ground elevation. In 1995, the wait time to receive signals from three coincidental satellites in the Yucatán was lengthy. During that time period, not many satellites were over passing the Yucatán. We'd receive one signal, then two, then zero, then one—and so on until an hour had passed and the screen indicated acquisition of three signals. Success! We hooted and hollered, "We got three!" There on the screen was our global positioning reading. This lengthy sequence took place at all four locations of the survey.

Our cameras used high-speed-film and our cell phones were attached to our cars back home.

The GPS readings in 2000 verified the readings recorded in 1995 with similar coordinates relative to the alignment of the road. It is here that we note the advances in technology that occurred in the five-year period. The GPS receiver used in 2000 was a Magellan eXplorer. In addition to providing global positioning coordinates, this small, handheld device had many other features of significance to the archaeo-engineer in the acquisition of signals. In 2000, we acquired the signals from six satellites in five minutes rather than the hour-long wait in 1995. In addition, technology advances enabled our use of digital cameras and laptop computers, versus the celluloid-based cameras used in 1995. Our telephones were in our pockets rather than patiently waiting for us at home.

The loop had been closed. Villa's courageous and legendary survey trail in 1934 and the O'Kon surveys of 1995, 2000, and 2001 had confirmed and verified that the sacbe was a monumental engineering effort. Our intentions had been the same while the available technology had changed. We relied on celestial orientation for positioning our strategic points, and celestial navigation to fly the route. It is interesting to note that Maya engineers used the fixed points of the cosmos for celestial positioning, and we relied on celestial guidance of the digital kind.

The Analysis of the Surveys

The 1934 survey was greatly penalized by the lack of appropriate survey equipment. Villa was equipped with a handheld compass that was dependent on the variable magnetic north. The magnetic declination in the Yucatán is approximately 5 degrees. Villa could not take global coordinates. His survey, when plotted on a Google Earth satellite image, actually places Cobá some 5 kilometers south of its actual position. However, Villa is a true hero of archaeology. He and his team hacked their way though the 100.33-kilometer route of the sacbe. He substantiated without a doubt the true goal of his mission: to prove that the sacbe did exist and that it terminated at Cobá. He reported on the nature of the construction of the road and artifacts along the way. He prepared a report that, even in the 21st century, is unparalleled in the narrative, graphics, and photographs of a survey for a sacbe. His drawing of the survey indicates the complete route with stations of the road and villages along the way. He exceeded the goals of his mission and stands today historically as the sole author of a complete visual, graphic, and narrative published document relating to *in situ* sacbeob. The accuracy of the measurements is not of great importance. The real achievement of Villa's expedition was the proof of Maya technology.

The graphic results of the 1995 survey using the GPS positioning data are indicated in Figure 9-3. The 2000 survey verified the readings at all four points indicated a bearing of 269° 58' 32.4" between Yaxuná and the intersection of the Yaxuná–Cobá sacbe and Sacbe No.3. This is 99.992 percent accuracy for an east–west line between Yaxuná and the entrance to Cobá. If a true east–west line were extended from Yaxuná to Cobá, it would miss the target of the terminus by only 87 meters. It is noted that the sacbe on the Carnegie Institution survey deviated at several points from a straight alignment. However, the alignment of the start and finish of the road is unique. The length of the route was calculated to be 98.45 kilometers using global coordinates, versus the 100.336 kilometers surveyed by Villa. The global-coordinated calculations used a straight line to determine the length between points. The Villa measurements indicated slight turns in the route of the road, which would require a longer distance between points. Villas measurements of the exact road may be more accurate, but it would take a ground survey to verify the actual distance. Our aerial survey in 2001 verified the actual route of the sacbe. This alignment is indicated on the satellite image (Figure 9-3); the actual alignment was based on the tracking study carried out on the Google Earth image.

In summary, the 1934 survey verified the route and characteristics of the route. O'Kon surveys verified the unique east–west alignment of Cobá and Yaxuná, and the course of the road as it traversed between the two ancient cities. It sometimes deviated from a true east–west course, but always returned to the east–west line of the route. The route between Cobá and Yaxuná did exist and connected the two cities on a true east–west direction.

The Legendary Sacbe:
The Pilgrims' Path to the Sea

The existence of various forms of sacbeob in the Maya world has remained in folk memory and includes mythological roadways, celestial skyways, and subterranean routes. This search, however, seeks the lost road from Mérida to Cozumel, and is confined to observable and measureable terrestrial roadways that are the result of technological achievements of Maya engineers. This most intriguing of the mystic terrestrial sacbeob is the legendary path of pilgrims that extends from the city of T'hó, today's Mérida, in the Yucatán, to the east coast and on to the Island of Cozumel. This sacbe presents more tantalizing clues of its existence than any other example of Maya roadway. This fabled road extended 285 kilometers from T'hó eastward to the Caribbean coast and the city of Puerto Morelos. From this port, pilgrims would embark on seagoing vessels for the sacred crossing to the Island of Cozumel and the opportunity to worship at the temple of Ixchel. She was the goddess of the moon, fertility, midwifery, medicine, and magic. Ixchel was a woman's goddess. The temple of Ixchel had a long history; it has been determined that her temple was an active and popular shrine from 100 BC until the conquest during the 16th century. Millions of the faithful traversed the sacbe and made the sea passage. Maya women visited the shrine at least once during their lives, coming from distant points in the Yucatán, Guatemala, and Honduras.

In modern transportation planning, a "desire line analysis" is a study that plots the desired destinations of travelers and the volume of traffic to certain points. The analysis is used to plot and plan the routes of proposed highways. If one was to plot the desire lines of Maya pilgrims from the major cities in the Yucatán to the port of departure for the sacred voyage to Cozumel, the route of the pilgrims would extend from major Maya population centers directly to the coast of the Caribbean.

The legendary highway was more mystical than mythical, but it had many real and practical applications in addition to the travel of pilgrims over the 285-kilometer roadway, not only to the shrine of Ixchel, but to the holy city of Izamal, where faithful visited the birthplace of Itzamna, the Maya God of wisdom, art, and languages. The passage of pilgrims, plus the commercial and administrative traffic between the largest cities in the Yucatán, made this a very popular route.

The existence of the long mystical sacbe has been reported since the 16th century by Spanish chronicles, and traces of the route have been investigated by explorers and archaeologists into the 21st century. In the 16th century Bishop Diego de Landa observed that a sacbe extended from T'hó to the ruins at Izamal. In 1688, Diego Lopez de Cogolludo reported his finds on this fabled road in *Historia de Yucatán* (*History of the Yucatán*): "There are remains of paved highways which traverse all this kingdom and they say they are ending in the east on the seashore...so they might arrive at Cozumel for fulfillment of their vows, to offer their sacrifices and to ask for help in adoration of their false Gods."

In 1966, archaeologists Dr. Edwin Shook and Lawrence Roys investigated the 32-kilometer sacbe from Aké to Izamal, 200 kilometers to the east along the same alignment. Geologist A.E. Weidie reported, in 1962, the discovery of a raised bed of an ancient roadway that extended 20 kilometers from Puerto Morelos on an east–west line along the same alignment as the Aké to Izamal route. From 1995 to 2002, archaeologist Jennifer Mathews of FAMSI confirmed evidence of that same east–west elevated sacbe extending more than 20 km to the west from modern Highway 180 at Puerto Morales.

The legend of the sacbe of the pilgrimage route traversing the northern Yucatán persists in folklore, historical accounts, and archaeological investigations. Segments of the route have been mapped and investigated, but the entire 285-kilometer route has not been assembled and assessed in a logical study using global positioning, remote sensing, and satellite imagery until the O'Kon survey of 2010.

The O'Kon Investigation of the Pilgrims' Sacbe

The route of the sacbe from T'hó to the Caribbean coast has been the subject of historical conjecture since the Spanish conquest. Segments of the legendary route have been investigated, but the complete 285-kilometer route has not been surveyed as a complete road running from Mérida to Puerto Morelos. To physically trek over the entire route using ground-based survey equipment would be daunting for any explorer, in any era. However, with Global Information Systems

(GIS) the feat can be accomplished with a minimum of boots on the ground. The GIS system integrates information from digital data received from satellites feeding geographical information into ground-based software and hardware.

The object of the O'Kon survey was to register global positioning data at critical locations along the route of the pilgrims from Mérida to the Caribbean coast. Then the global positioning data was introduced into the GIS software using the system to develop vectors along the path of the road. The vectors will basically map the route. Furthermore, to verify ground features of the route, the vectors will guide the way to the extant vestiges of the ancient road and develop a ground track, and confirm the GIS vector studies and develop a virtual route of the road. The plan for acquiring ground-based GPS readings along the route included strategic points at known positions along the road. These include positions at the salient cities including Mérida, Aké, and Izamal, and points along the road terminus at Puerto Morelos. Traveling by automobile, our team started the ground survey and acquisition of GPS positions in Mérida and traveled east toward the Caribbean coast. GPS readings were taken at the following points:

- **Mérida:** A GPS reading was recorded in the zócalo or central plaza of Mérida.
- **Aké:** A GPS positioning reading was taken at the center of the site.
- **Izamal:** A GPS positioning reading was taken at the zócalo.
- **Puerto Morelos:** GPS positioning was taken at two locations on the terminus of the road. Readings were recorded at the east and west ends of the 16-kilometer stretch of road.

Google Earth was used to plot the GPS positions derived from the survey, enabling the plotting of the route from Mérida to Puerto Morelos. Close observation of the satellite imagery along the projected route indicated clear traces of the degraded sacbe at several locations. Evidence of the road was clearly indicated between Mérida and Aké, and between Aké and Izamal. Images of the sacbe were obscured by dense forest for an approximate distance of 100 kilometers. The clear configuration of the sacbe again was revealed 21 kilometers from the Caribbean. The route extends along the road and into Puerto Morelos. Puerto Morelos appears to be the departure point for countless Maya pilgrims to Cozumel.

Analysis has indicated that the weight of evidence from eyewitnesses, historical accounts, survey investigation, and GIS analysis makes its highly likely that the pilgrim road from Mérida to the coast actually existed. Furthermore, the alignment of three ancient cities and the port city exactly along an east–west azimuth and the route of the road is more than coincidental. The bearing of 269.87° 53' 42" is 98.94 percent accurate compared with an east–west line of 270 degrees. The strong evidence indicates that an east–west alignment along the major pilgrim route begs the question, Which came first—the cities or the road? The parts have been proven to exist; now research must be carried to prove that the sum of the parts is equal to the whole. Though the investigation of the road started in the mid-20th century, this legendary road still requires more investigation to verify the exact path of Ixchel's sacbe.

10

Bridging the Gaps in the Forest

The Yucatán Peninsula has an abundance of natural characteristics that presented challenges to the survival of the Maya civilization. However, natural barriers to overland travel did not present a challenge. The Maya lowlands had a flat terrain with minor differences in elevation. There are few surface features or geologic gaps that offered impediments for travel between Maya city-states. The absence of natural obstacles to land travel minimized the requirement for Maya engineers to erect bridge structures.

There is an obvious linear relationship between the need to span a natural impediment and the number of bridge structures that were constructed by Maya engineers. Considering the minimal requirements for construction of bridge structures in the Maya domain, it is no surprise that few examples of Maya bridge structures have been encountered by archaeologists. Furthermore, the location of bridges near large cities would attract more attention and would be more likely to be discovered than a bridge located in an isolated area. An urban-based bridge would surely have been discovered and investigated early in the annals of Maya archaeology.

The majority of the Maya bridges that have been documented are of short and medium spans. These bridges spanned canals, moats, and small streams, and engineered urban structures within the precinct of the ancient cities. The range of span lengths and the type of engineered materials used in the bridge structures varied widely. Techniques for construction of bridges by Maya engineers became embedded in their culture and have become a part of the technological patrimony that extended from the Classic

Period, through the conquest and the colonial period, and continues on in contemporary Maya building skills.

Examples of Maya bridge engineering include short-span, cast-in-place concrete structures over streams or canals, medium-span timber bridges over rivers, and long-span rope-cable suspension structures over broad rivers. Maya technology had an engineering solution for each type of spanning requirement. The remains of some bridges exist today, though others that were constructed with degradable construction materials have faded into the past. However, many structures have left tantalizing clues to their existence.

Historical Perspectives of Pre-Columbian Bridge Technology

The Americas had a technological advantage over much of the world in the construction of long-span suspension bridges. The Inca Empire, which ruled South America from the 12th to the 15th century AD, developed suspension bridge systems as part of their long-range road system. Suspension bridges spanned the numerous canyons and gaps in the mountainous terrain. The saga of legendary Inca bridge-building technology has become a popular part of American and world history books, the chronicles of the King under Spanish Colonial rule, and best-selling novels, all of which brought the romantic story of the Inca and their bridges to the attention of the world. This was not the case for the Maya, whose civilization had collapsed 600 years before the conquest and did not have Spanish chronicles describing examples of their lost technology.

"On Friday noon, July the twentieth, 1714, the finest bridge in all Peru broke and precipitated five travelers into the Gulf below...it had been woven of osier by the Inca more than a century before." With these opening words, famed novelist Thornton Wilder begins his novel *The Bridge at San Luis Rey*, one of the towering achievements in American fiction and a best-selling work that has become popular throughout the world.

"To make one of their bridges, a great quantity of osiers is collected. They make three single osiers into a long rope according to the length needed for the bridge. In this way, they increase and thicken the ropes until they are thicker than a man's body or thicker. They mount them on two high supports...three of the great ropes are used for the floor of the bridge and two as handrails on each side." This description of Inca bridge construction was written by Peruvian Garcilaso de la Vega, the son of an aristocratic Spanish conquistador and an Inca princess. Garcilaso traveled to Spain in 1561. His writings include *Comentarios Reals de los Incas* (*Royal Commentaries of the Incas*). This work, published in 1609, has enormous literary value, and is not merely historical chronicles. The work includes Spanish history of the conquest, as well as accounts of daily Inca life learned at the feet of his maternal relatives, and provides firsthand details of the methodology for constructing Inca bridges.

The two works, one by the son of an American diplomat and the other the scion of Spanish aristocracy, are separated by four centuries in time, but are bound by the political intrigues of their time; each chose to write a monumental work that involved Inca suspension bridge technology. Their works and the writings of archaeologists brought the Inca engineering of long-span suspension bridges to the attention of the world. Suspension bridges were not the only bridge in the Inca engineer's repertoire. The Inca built pontoon rafts, wood beam bridges, and stone slab bridges. However, the suspension bridge was the most spectacular of their construction feats. It is estimated that more than 200 rope-cable suspension bridges constructed by the Inca were detailed in the Spanish chronicles. These bridges used thick cables crafted of grass, maguey fiber, and osier. Osier is the flexible branch or rod-like twig of the willow tree, similar to that used in wickerwork.

The Inca are still constructing suspension bridges during the 21st century. The yearly rebuilding of each bridge is carried out by the Inca as a tribute to their creative ancestors. Inca suspension bridges have been constructed by students in modern engineering classes. However, in lieu of willow and ichu grass, the students use henequen rope from the Yucatán. The Maya used this type of rope for their suspension bridges more than 700 years prior to Inca bridge-builders.

Because of the records left by the Spanish chronicles, the Inca had a historic advantage over other pre-Columbian cultures, with the exception of the Aztecs. The Maya did not have this advantage. The Maya civilization and its technology had collapsed 600 years before the conquest. There were no technological accounts to record.

Chronology of Maya Bridge Technology

The majority of documented Maya bridges were erected at the height of the construction efforts during the Classic Period. These structures mostly fit the category of short-span bridges and are related to the construction of Maya cities and their close environs. These bridges include spans over canals, moats, streams, and urban architectural features. The Classic Period also saw construction of longer bridges, including medium-span bridges over rivers and long-span suspension bridges, including the longest bridge in the ancient world, which extended across the Usumacinta River. During the conquest, historic chronicles of the Spanish scribes recount bridge construction activities by the Maya to a single account of bridge building. The tales relate that a long bridge was built over a wide river crossing to assist the conquistadors in traversing a route across the Yucatán toward Guatemala.

After the 1810 Mexican revolution, the opening of the boarders of Mexico and Central America to foreigners enabled discoveries that were previously closely guarded secrets by the xenophobic Spanish colonial government. The new policy of permitting explorers and scholars to traverse the jungles enabled the discovery of the technological achievements of the Maya civilization. Discoveries included techniques for using rope cables for construction of suspension bridges. Although archaeology has accepted the use of short-span structures in urban context or crossing water courses, it has not accepted the advanced technology applied for long-span suspension bridges. What follows is an examination of Maya bridges, using a reverse time line that starts with 19th-century rope-cable suspension bridges and travels back in time to bridge construction during the conquest, and further back to the Classic Period, when bridge construction reached its apex and became the lifeline of Classic Maya cities.

Bridge Construction in the 19th Century

Research in Maya construction techniques indicates that technological knowledge generated during the Classic Period became a part of the cultural patrimony that has extended to the 21st century. In his landmark volumes *Incidents of Travel in Central American, Chiapas, and Yucatán*, published in 1841, John Lloyd Stephens describes his travels in the highlands of Guatemala and his encounters with a Maya suspension bridge spanning over a river:

Riding along the river, we reached a suspension bridge of most primitive appearance and construction called by the natives "la hammaca," which had existed there from time immemorial. It was made of osiers twisted into cords, about three feet apart and stretching across the river with a hanging network of vines, the ends fastened to trunks of two opposite trees it hung about 25 feet above the river, which was here some eighty feet wide and was supported in different places by vines tied to the branches. The access was by a crude ladder to a platform in the crotch of the tree. In the bottom of the hammaca were 2 or 3 poles to walk on. It waved in the wind and was an unsteady and rather insecure means of transportation. From the center of the Vista of the river both ways under the arches of the trees was beautiful and in every direction the hammaca was a most picturesque-looking object.

The detailed observations by Stephens's keen eye provided a clear overview of the structural mechanisms of a Maya suspension bridge. This type of lightweight structure was used for foot traffic over the river. He described the material and composition of the suspension rope cables and their anchorage attached to immense trees on opposite sides of the river. He describes the bridge walkway platform of laterally oriented poles for supporting foot traffic. He states that suspension ropes were made of osiers, which are willow branches, twisted into cords. Considering the height of the bridge above the ground, it might be difficult to identify the composition of the ropes. His referencing long willow branches braided into length is interesting. The willow native to Guatemala is the bonpland willow (*salix bonplandiana*). This variety of willow does not have the "weeping willow" or drooping willow branches that were used by the Inca in making rope. The ropes in the bridge described by Stephens were obviously made of henequen to develop a sufficient length for the 80-foot-long suspension cables. The geometry and composition of this basic suspension bridge follows the technical formula for suspension bridge structures developed in the Classic Period and used throughout the Yucatán for centuries, until the 20th century when steel and concrete bridges were substituted for the locally constructed suspension structures. Stephens describes the construction of the bridge as "primitive in appearance." The bridge may have been primitive in geometry, but not in technology. The bridge owes its irregular geometry to the random geometry of the branches in the anchorage trees. Stephens's use of the term *suspension bridge* is interesting; the first suspension bridge built by those of European descent was the Brooklyn Bridge, completed in 1883. This was 42 years after the volumes were published. When he observed the Maya rope bridge, the term *suspension bridge* was not yet in general use.

Visual evidence of Maya suspension bridge construction to cross rivers in the latter part of the 19th century is shown in Figure 10-1. The 1875 photo is by the famous British photographer Eadweard Muybridge. This is the same area of Guatemala where Stephens encountered the rope bridge described in his book. A close review of the photograph indicates that the bridge is apparently under construction or is undergoing retro-fitting for maintenance purposes. Note the coils of henequen rope laying on the river bank, at the bottom right-hand corner of the photo, in readiness for installation. The *braceros* are still posed in position during their repair operations in order for the ancient camera to capture that magic moment in time. The suspension rope cables are being attached to substantial trees that will serve as anchorage for the bridge suspension ropes. The tree anchors will resist lateral and vertical forces in the suspension rope system. It appears the upper set of cables on the nearside have been secured to the anchorage, while the far side cables have not been placed with a similar parabolic "sag" in the catenary of the near side cables, nor has it yet been anchored to the large tree to the right of the photo. The bridge is strong and technically correct, but is geometrically asymmetrical due to the irregularity of the randomly placed anchorage trees.

The diameter of the individual suspension rope appears to be approximately 1 inch, and the assembled cables are 2 inches in diameter, compared with the suspension cables on Inca spans that are the "size of a man's body," as described by de la Vega. The difference is that henequen rope used by the Maya bridge contractors has a tensile strength of 18,000 psi, whereas willow twigs are substantially weaker and would require a greater area of resistant material and increased diameter of cables. The suspension bridge described by John Stephens in 1841 and the 1875 photographs are obviously structures constructed by small political units for their own use and local access over the river. The bridges do not serve as roadways or support traffic from beasts of burden. The term *osier* described as the bridge cable material was probably a misnomer; the cables were surely fabricated of henequen. This high-strength rope was used for millennia by Maya for construction. The finished product may not be attractive, but its strength properties and geometry serve the purpose of crossing a natural obstacle and verify the levels of Maya bridge-building technology.

Figure 10-1: Photo of Maya hemp rope suspension bridge (1875). Photo courtesy of Carnegie Institution for Science.

One can be sure that numerous examples of these suspension bridges were constructed in the Yucatán during the Classic Period, and their use continued through the colonial period and into the current era. The design of the bridge includes efficient catenary geometry for foot traffic and can be made with local products by *braceros* (laborers). The use of henequen fibers was a logical application of high-strength rope invented by the Maya.

Bridge Technology During the Maya Classic Period

The golden age of construction peaked at the height of the Classic Period. Maya technical achievement grew with the expansion of cities, the construction of monumental buildings, the installation of infrastructure, and the extension of the sacbe system to connect the flow of communications and commerce between city-states. Maya engineers linked the whole system of intra-city and intercity communications with a technologically based road and bridge network. Bridges were constructed in a variety of short, medium, and long spans using technological, advanced structural systems, and materials and geometry that included cast-in-place concrete, strong tropical hardwood, and high-strength cable-rope suspension structures. Maya bridges completed the missing link in a diverse variety of intra-site and inter-site transportation systems, including bridges in the internal street systems of cities, bridges over flowing rivers, bridges crossing agricultural canals, bridges for sacbeob, and long-span bridges over broad rivers. The representative examples of Maya bridge construction are identified by the standard engineering designations based on the length of their spans. A short-span bridge is less than 3 meters long; a medium-span bridge is 3 meters to 24 meters, and a long-span bridge is one that is more than 24 meters.

Maya Short-Span Bridges

Explorations of Maya cities have uncovered a large number of short-span bridge structures that constituted an integral part of the internal pedestrian flow and entrance routes to the cities. These short-span structures, many of them parts of a monumental structure, are frequently overlooked by archaeologists. They are structural bridges even though they are considered to be part of the architecture. Bridge structures in numerous Maya cities have been investigated by the author. The structures in the city and the entrance ways to the city offered a diverse variety of bridge structures.

Stairway Bridge Spanning Walkway at Hormiguero

The ancient city of Hormiguero is located in the present-day Mexican state of Campeche. The city flourished during its peak period of AD 650–850. Only a minor part of the 84 buildings at the site have been consolidated. Structure 5 is part of the central group, which is a complex of large temples of the Rio Bec style of architecture. Structure 5 is a towering pyramid with an artistically dramatic facade at its top-level temple. A wide stairway dominates its main facade. Maya engineers enhanced pedestrian pathways of the cities by spanning the broad staircase over a ground-level walkway. They developed a passageway, under the broad staircase, using a Maya arch to span the gap in the supports.

Palace Stairway Bridges at Edzná

The ancient city of Edzná is located in the east of the state of Campeche. This dramatic city with monumental architecture has an extensive network of engineered canals and raised agricultural fields. The acropolis looms high over the site. The tallest and most dramatic structure on the acropolis is the multi-level palace (Figure C-8). The structure rises to a height of five levels, and each level features a network of vaulted rooms. The front of the main facade has a wide stairway that ascends from ground level to the fifth level. The stair has access landings for each of the five levels. The broad monumental stair would bisect the activity on each level without a technological solution for bridging over that level. The second and third levels feature Maya bridging structures for the stairs. The second level uses a flat slab concrete structure to span across the open area way (Figure C-10), and the third level uses a Maya vault to create the bridge spanning mechanism for the stair (Figure C-9).

The Bridge Over the Otulum River at Palenque

Palenque is one of the star attractions in the galaxy of Maya architecture. The city has a surfeit of natural springs, and features aqueduct tunnels built by Maya engineers and formed by the Maya arch. The tunnels form conduits for the springs that flow into the Otulum River to the south of the city center. The sacbe crossing over the river has a Maya bridge structure that spans over the river. The bridge is constructed of cast-in-place concrete and cut-stone masonry, and applies the structural geometry of the Maya arch. This bridge has been in place since the Classic Period.

Medium-Span Bridges

The medium-span Maya bridge structures were constructed of a variety of engineered materials, including cast-in-place concrete and high-strength timber. The medium span structures spanned small rivers and canals.

Bridge Over Defensive Moat at Becán

The city of Becán is a unique Maya city. The city is surrounded by a water-filled moat. The moat has five entrance portals spanning over the waterway and entering the city walls. At each portal a causeway/bridge structure crosses the moat (Figure 10-2). The bridge does not have openings in its superstructure, because it also serves as a check dam to control water management in a sector in the moat. The moat also serves as a dry-season water reservoir for the city. The causeways control access into the city for defense while controlling the water quantities in each sector of the moat. This dual-purpose structure has been in place since the Classic Period.

Figure 10-2: Bridge and causeway over moat around Becán. Author's image.

Timber Bridge Structure Over Pusilha River

The Maya city of Pusilha is located in Belize on the river of the same name. The location of the city places the city-state on either side along the river. The river bifurcates the city as it flows eastward between the acropolis and the main part of the city. The acropolis is sited on a steep hill to the south of the river and rises to a height of 79 meters above the river. The north portion of the city is located on level plane. The width of the river at the bridge was reduced to 10 meters by large cast-in-place concrete abutments requiring a span of approximately 10 meters in length. If the concrete bridge abutments had not been built in a manner that reduced the span, the bridge would have required a span longer than 24 meters. The greater span would have placed the beam in the long-span category. A much longer and deeper timber beam would be required. Maya engineering creativity was able to design a shorter-span bridge, which greatly reduced the construction issues, material acquisition, and logistics.

Investigation of the site indicated that the bridge abutements (Figure 10-3) were constructed of composite, cast-in-place concrete and cut stone in the same configuration as large Maya structures. The forensic engineering analysis of the bridge indicated that configuration of the bridge superstructure and buttresses were shown as on the section. A high-strength timber beam of 1 meter in depth and 10 meters in length was required to span the river. The walking surface of the bridge was composed of small-diameter timber members spanning in a traverse direction over the main beams. The surface of the deck was paved with concrete over the timber structure. The advantage of this structural system is that the cast-in-place concrete and high-strength timber beams form a composite structure, increasing the strength. The structural system provides the required strength and the concrete surface waterproofs the timber and resists degradation. The bridge was necessary to connect the bifurcated sections of the city. The spans were elevated some 7 meters above the low water line. This height maintained the spans above the high water level during flood season.

Stairs were used to access the bridge deck level. Other methods of gaining access up to the span elevation would impede the flow of water during the rainy season when the river rose to flood levels. South of the bridge, the terrain rose 79 meters to the level of the acropolis. However, the north buttress was on a more level terrain, and the water could overflow the flat terrain and continue downstream. However if a 10-percent ramp was constructed

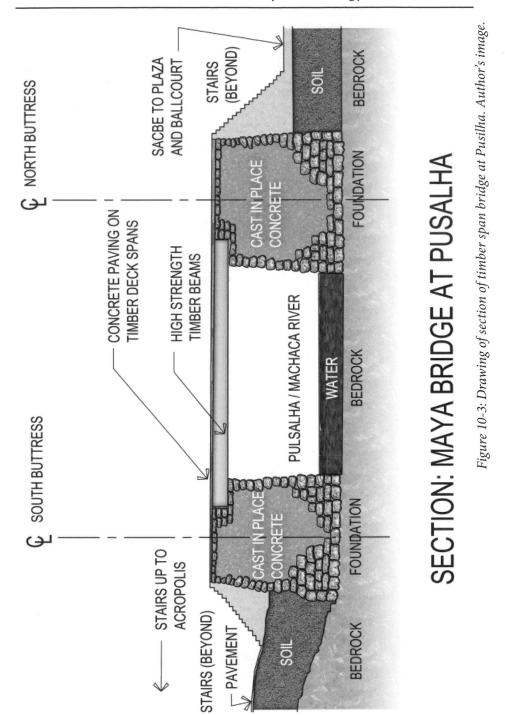

SECTION: MAYA BRIDGE AT PUSALHA

Figure 10-3: Drawing of section of timber span bridge at Pusilha. Author's image.

from the top of the south buttress to a level point on the flat terrain, the length of the ramp would be approximately 61 meters. This length of ramp would result in a virtual dam that would impound the flood water and force the water into the north city-scape. Therefore, the only logical solution was the use of stairways at each end of the bridge that allowed access to the deck and minimized the profile of the bridge, thus reducing the chance of floods while permitting river crossings during the flood season.

Maya Long-Span Bridges

Maya engineers used standard technology and the necessary high-strength materials to construct short- and medium-span bridges. However, bridges more than 24 meters in length are considered long spans and require a higher degree of technology. Medium-span bridges used heavy structural members that support loads in bending, but long-span bridges require structures of lightweight tension members. Long-span structures were required to utilize higher strength materials and a structural system applying parabolic geometry acting in pure tension. It is certain that 19th-century Maya knowledge of the methods of construction of suspension bridges was in the folk memory and extrapolated the techniques of building suspension structures developed during the Classic Period. No traces remain of these 19th-century, cable suspension bridges spanning small rivers. These structures have completed degraded. In a similar manner, the degradable rope and timber materials of Classic Period long-span suspension bridges have totally disintegrated, while their tall concrete and stone support towers had been reduced to ruins. The ingenious Maya engineers of the Classic Period knew the secrets of constructing multi-span rope cable suspension bridges across rivers. These bridges were supported on concrete and stone towers high above the river flood waters. The most significant of the great long-span suspension bridges was constructed across the mighty Usumacinta River at the ancient city of Yaxchilan. This bridge was the lifeline for the city and assured a year-round method of traversing the broad river. The accounts of the construction of the bridge and procedures used in the computer-based virtual reconstruction of this marvel of Maya technology are a prime example of the creativity of archaeo-engineering.

Maya Engineers Construct a Lifeline for a Grand City

The ancient Maya city of Yaxchilan is situated within an omega-shaped oxbow formed by the powerful Usumacinta River. The bend in the river is so severe that only a narrow strip of land stands between the two banks of the wide river at the narrow neck (Figure 10-4). For six months a year, the river is in a wildly surging flood stage, creating a 200-meter-wide turbulent barrier around the city. The broad, swirling river embraces the oxbow and converts this magnificent city into an isolated "island" with its perimeter almost entirely bounded by water. Archaeologists have studied this unique city since 1882. However, during that period of study, no one had posed or answered the obvious question: How did this prosperous city survive the six-month cycle of flooding and isolation without the ability to cross the broad river while maintaining their political power and acquiring the necessary sustenance for survival?

The answer was not in the use of *cayucos* (dugout canoes), for crossing the swirling water of the broad and swiftly flowing river would seize the small craft as it attempted to traverse the river, carry it downstream, and sweep it around the bend. A great distance would be traveled with the *cayuco* trapped in the swift centrifugal flow of the outside curve of the oxbow. After furious paddling during the crossing, landing the *cayuco* on the opposite bank would be as perilous as traversing the river—that is, if the *cayuco* managed to avoid a collision with the giant trees and other debris being swept along the curve. The answer to a safe crossing of the river had to be a Maya engineering solution.

It was a fortuitous combination of timing, serendipity, and experience in forensic engineering that enabled the author's recognition of the configuration of the ruined structures in the river and those on the Yaxchilan's Grand Plaza. These events initiated the archaeo-engineering investigations for reconstructing Yaxchilan's lifeline over the Usumacinta River. This was an ingenious feat of Maya technology that may prove to be their most creative engineering project. Their solution for the river crossing was the construction of a long-span suspension bridge—a structure that was destined to be recognized as the longest bridge in the ancient world.

Today, little remains of this unique achievement in civil engineering. However, by analyzing and recognizing clues scattered throughout archaeological records, combined with contemporary evidence generated by field surveys, aerial photography, remote sensing, and computer applications, the collected data was synthesized and used to develop topographic data and three-dimensional computer simulations that led to the virtual reconstruction of the bridge. Forensic engineering techniques were used to

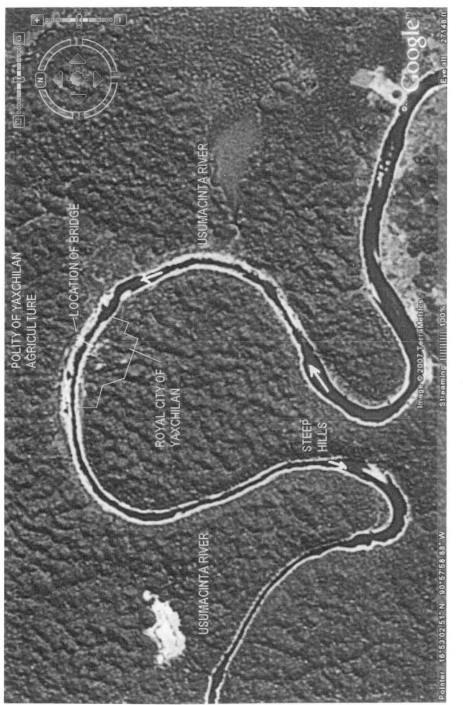

Figure10-4: Satellite map of omega in Usumacinta River at Yaxchilan. Courtesy of Google Earth.

conceptualize the geometry of the bridge structure, identify the construction materials, and postulate engineering techniques used to construct the bridge, as well as determine the critical role the bridge played in the political and economic activities of the city-state of Yaxchilan.

Close Encounters With Maya Technology

In February 1989, I was part of an archaeological expedition traveling deep into the Usumacinta River basin lying between Mexico and Guatemala. Our goal was to traverse the Pasión and Usumacinta rivers in native cayucos. That portion of the rivers that could be navigated by boats, while Avon rafts were required traversing the section of rapids in the lower Usumacinta River. The itinerary included visits to Ceibal, Altar de Sacrificios, Yaxchilan, Piedras Negras, and Palenque. Our group was a mixed bag of Mayanists: an archaeologist, an artist, a London School of Economics professor, eco-tourists, a civil engineer, and our leader, who was a nurse, in addition to the river men who were the crew on the boats, cooked our meals, and watched our backs. The 10-day odyssey consisted of river travel, overnight camps on the river banks, and self-guided explorations at each of the sites.

We had jumped off at the river port of Sayaxché, Guatemala, located on the shores of the Pasión River. On the third day of travel, after visiting several sites, we were on the downriver segment of the trip, drawing close to our next destination, the ancient city of Yaxchilan. The brown, swirling waters of the Usumacinta swept past as we made our way downstream through the tropical wilderness. It was a scene out of a fantasy. We were surrounded by the dense rainforest. Spider monkeys were swinging from vines while toucans and macaws flitted through the towering tropical hardwoods. I was reclining in the bow of the 75-foot-long boat, anticipating my first glimpse of the ancient city of Yaxchilan. My forward position in the *cayuco* placed me in the shelter of the thatched roof of our native craft. This spot on the bow afforded relief from the searing tropical sun for me and my cold can of Gallo *cervesa*.

The afternoon sun was reflecting from the glimmering water, and the glare made it difficult to see even with the maximum UV protection on my sunglasses. The captain steered right as we entered the nearly 360-degree omega in the Usumacinta. "Look sharp," said Tammy Ridnour, the leader of the outfitters of the expedition. "Yaxchilan is on the south bank." The captain steered to port. My first glimpse of the unique riverine city was the tall palace structures located high on the green hills overlooking the river. As we prepared to land on the north river bank, I noted a large cylindrical ruin of worked stones rising 3 meters above the water on the left side of the river. The configuration of the ruins seemed familiar to me. I looked to the right and observed a similar but less-defined structure that aligned with the south ruins. "Hey!" I blurted out. "These ruins look like the structural piers for a bridge!"

"Impossible," said a voice behind me. The archaeologist had spoken. "That is impossible. The Maya were a Stone Age culture, and they did not have the capabilities to build complex structures." I turned and pointed to the tall structures on the hill and asked, "Then who built those buildings?" His response was "They are simple stone and mortar construction, typical of a Stone Age culture." That ended the archaeological discussion. I was sure that a bridge had spanned this river, and I was determined to search for the answer.

The *cayuco* slid onto the edge of the river bank. The beach-like river bank extended inward for 10 meters then upward to a vertical bank rising 8 meters to the level of the Grand Plaza. It was time to disembark, unload our gear, climb the steep path to the top of the river bank, and set up camp. We pitched our tent, toured part of the site, and were then served an excellent dinner prepared by Jose, the *capitano*, and his crew. Bedtime always came early for me and Vernon Harris, my long-time friend and tentmate, and I zipped up our tent and we slipped off into dreams of Maya glories.

The next day I returned to the beach and observed the ruins on the south side of the river. Close observation confirmed my first-glance analysis. The cylindrical shaped structure was approximately 10 meters in diameter and was elevated 3 meters above the waterline (Figure 10-5). The ruin was constructed of worked stone. It was difficult to see much of the pier structure on the north side because of the high water level. I took photos of the south structure and sketched the ruin. I vowed to carry out further investigation relative to the nature and characteristics

Figure 10-5: Photo of bridge ruins in Usumacinta River in 1989.
Author's image.

of this important pre-Columbian structure. To initiate the investigation and analysis of the structure, I would require a comprehensive review of the archaeological studies of the site, three-dimensional surveys of the bridge support structures, and topographical mapping of the site. After two days, our group surrendered our boats at Yaxchilan and boarded Avon rafts to traverse the river rapids down to Piedras Negras and then to Palenque.

Our new crew of riverboat men was a talented group of expatriate Americans. They included a college professor, once teaching at the University of the Yucatán, whose life had been set adrift by Hurricane Gilbert; a California surfer dude; and our experienced expedition leader, Tammy. I thought we were ready for anything—well, almost anything—until we were "captured" by Guatemala guerillas at Piedras Negras.

Piedras Negras is a magnificent Maya city down river from Yaxchilan. The site is located in Guatemala, and during the late 1980s, the site was a refuge for guerrillas fighting against the establishment. Piedras Negras is situated in some of the densest tropical rainforest in the Yucatán. The structures at the site had been consolidated by archaeologists, studied, and then left to the vagaries of the rainforest. The site did not have the advantage of live-in guardians provided by the government that are present at Mexican sites. In short, the site was unoccupied, or so we thought.

I did not notice the first guerrilla until he stepped out of the underbrush with his AK-47 at chest level. He did not have to speak, as I immediately stopped; he was silently joined by two more comrades armed with M-16s. My Spanish was very basic, and I felt we needed a diplomatic native speaker who also knew the territory. Enter Jim Dion, the down-on-his-luck college professor, who had been active with the rebel movement and assisting villages in developing potable water systems. Jim was familiar with the leaders of the movement; he had to be "the man." I raised my right hand to the warriors while tuning and requesting Jim Dion to come forward. Jim stepped up and saved the day.

I could ramble on with a long dialogue of the encounter between the lambs and the guerrillas. The guerillas did not believe that we were archaeological tourists; they said we did not look like mild-mannered tourists and were convinced we were agents of the CIA. They were not, of course, happy with the CIA. Jim casually took a seat on a fallen log and chatted with the leader. The other two armed men stood vigilantly by his side. All three were hard-bitten veterans of the long war and were born killers. It sounds silly in retrospect, but white plastic caps were in place over the ends of their weapons. I had the fanciful illusion that we were safe unless they removed the caps. Jim charmed the leader with his excellent Spanish and intimate knowledge of their cause and its leaders. The conversation and Jim's revelation as a friend of the cause was welcomed.

Matters lightened up, they apparently were glad to meet a sympathizer of their movement. They spoke of their fight for freedom and how they had won the war, but the army leaders would not grant amnesty. They lived there in the ruins of Piedras Negras, where the precious Maya ruins afforded protection from air force attacks. They asked us not to mention this encounter when we reached Guatemala City, or they would make trouble. If pressed, we were to say we had encountered the guardians of the orphans and widows. We parted ways in the ruins. They said they would keep watch on us overnight and decide our fate, and their instructions were to stay near our tents, which were set up on the shore of the river. Sundown came and we bedded down, taking turns standing watch during the night. We were nervous. Dawn broke with a torrential rainstorm and heavy fog. We quickly and silently packed up and slid our rafts into the water, not knowing what to expect from the line of rainforest trees. We launched our rafts downriver in the misty downpour, never looking back toward the guardians of the orphans and widows.

The archaeological tour was very enlightening, and on my return to Atlanta, the thought of the Maya bridge at Yaxchilan kept playing out in my mind. I was fascinated by the riddle of the "rocks." I began to research archaeological studies that had taken place at the site. I knew that someone during those studies had left clues to the riddle. If so, the clues would be in plain sight. Archaeological research, analysis, and engineering hypotheses were carried out in my engineering firm during the period from 1989 to 1994, with several return visits to the city of Yaxchilan to gather site data, confirm alignment of structural components, and survey critical elements of the structure. My first priority was to develop graphical and analytical data relative to the site, including aerial photography and remote sensing. Furthermore, research into the archaeological records of studies of the site would provide an overview of the graphic history of the site and initiate the archaeo-engineering research.

History of the Yaxchilan Site

The city of Yaxchilan is situated along the banks of the Usumacinta River and was the power base of a city-state that included a vast domain located south of the river. The majority of the temples and palaces of the city were located on the terraced hillsides, as well on sites that bordered its Grand Plaza. Maya city planners developed the Grand Plaza along the banks of the river, and it served as the focus of daily activity of this rich and powerful city-state. This navigable river served as a transportation conduit for the city. The riverfront and the Grand Plaza was parallel to the river and was the focus of activity for river travel, land transport, political activities, commercial trading, and everyday domestic life.

The area around Yaxchilan receives one of the heaviest yearly rainfalls in the Yucatán Peninsula. During the rainy season this excessive precipitation promoted an abundance of agricultural products that contributed to the wealth of Yaxchilan but elevated the water of the Usumacinta to flood levels for as long as six months of the year.

Yaxchilan became one of the most powerful city-states during the Maya Classic Period. The warrior-king, Yat-Balam, founded the city in the fourth century AD. This powerful king and his descendants ruled Yaxchilan until its decline five centuries later. During their reign, they built gleaming temples atop the terraced hills and luxurious palaces along the Grand Plaza. Magnificent structures were constructed on massive terraces carved into the surrounding hills.

The steep hills and broad river provided a natural defensive barrier for the city. The river formed an omega-shaped meander encompassing the city on the west, east, and north, and the steep hills protected the narrow south side. These barriers created a natural fortress that protected the city from military invasion. The hills formed a palisade and the river formed a moat. However, in order to efficiently operate this city of 50,000 people, it was necessary to have an all-weather passage across the treacherous Usumacinta River to connect this vibrant urban place to their assets in the villages and hinterlands across the river (Figure 10-4).

Archaeological Data of Yaxchilan

Due to its remote access, the art and architecture of the site at Yaxchilan have suffered minimal looting, and a solid chronological and historical background has been established through studies and interpretations of hieroglyphic inscriptions. Research has indicated that the Maya carefully recorded the history of this city during a period of 500 years. Modern archaeologists have studied Yaxchilan for more than 130 years. Numerous photos, site maps, renderings, drawings, narrative observations of the site, the buildings, and hieroglyphic art are included in the corpus of archaeological studies, but these academic studies totally overlooked the need for the lost landmark of bridge engineering that was critical to the survival and success of this "island" city.

It was Alfred Maudslay who made the first archaeological visit to the site in 1882. He references the ruins of the stone and concrete bridge piers located in the river in *Biologia Centrali-Americana*. He writes that the "pile of stones" was situated in the river was used as a landmark for the site. This landmark ruin appears in a photograph, taken by Maudslay, and is located on his map of the site depicted in this publication. Maudslay apparently felt that the "pile of stones" had special significance to the site.

A review of the extensive archaeological studies for the site shows that most written texts reveal a piece of the puzzle that indicates the need for an all-weather bridge. However, archaeologists could not conceive that this "Stone Age" culture had created such an amazing engineering feat. Before archaeologists could be convinced that the bridge and the sophisticated technology required for its construction had once existed, they had to be convinced of the need for a long-span river crossing. Archaeo-engineering studies were needed to point out that, in order to survive and operate efficiently, the seat of power in Yaxchilan required a dependable and safe passageway to cross over the river. The swift water levels of the river rise to a height of more than 15 meters during the rainy season; therefore, a river crossing was mandatory to maintain the political and economic power of Yaxchilan.

Archaeo-Engineering Investigation of 1989 Field Data

In March 1989, during our initial visit to the ancient city of Yaxchilan, we first observed the ruins of the pier structures in the river (Figure 10-5). The position and configuration of the pier structures in the river supported evidence that a bridge had once connected the city of Yaxchilan with the north side of the river. This initial observation and the concept of a potential bridge structure created enthusiastic response from my engineering colleagues, but was met with negative responses from the archaeological community. Detailed surveys of the bridge piers were impossible during the initial site visit, because the necessary equipment was not available. The need to carry out a topographical survey and to locate additional structural elements related to the bridge was required for the analysis. Furthermore, observations of the flow characteristics of the river water indicated that the speed of the water on the outer curve was more rapid and forceful than the water movement in the inner curve, due to the action of centrifugal force. It was possible that other, more degraded elements of the bridge structure were secreted beneath the surface on the north side.

In order to establish the existence of bridge ruins below the water surface, aerial photography of the site would be commissioned to provide a comprehensive, high-angle overview of the plaza and the bridge ruins in the river. The aerial investigation was intended to establish and identify a spatial relationship between the visible structure and the submerged ruins of the bridge.

Aerial Photography of Yaxchilan

Low-level aerial survey flights were flown over the site in March 1991. The Cessna 172 aircraft was flown by Canadian bush pilot Rick Muyres. Maya tool expert Philippe Klinefelter photographed the ruined structures in the river, as well as the structures on the site. The aerial survey effort was successful and my hypothesis of an additional submerged bridge pier structure was verified. The structure of the northern pier has suffered severely from the lateral forces generated by the fast-flowing water on the outside curve of the river. Waterborne debris was thrust against the northern pier by the swift centrifugal flow along the outside edge of the curve in the river. The impacts of large trees transported in the swiftly flowing water have imparted great damage to the northern bridge pier. The south bridge pier maintained a 3-meter height above the river water level. The slower water flow on the inside curve tended to reduce the damage to the south pier.

In the aerial photograph, it is seen that the majority of the masonry structure of the north pier has been degraded, and its stone block work is visible below the water surface arrayed in a spiral debris field extending downstream. The geometry of the remaining south pier and the foundation of the submerged north pier are clearly visible. The planar shape of the submerged north pier is similar in size and geometry to the south pier. This similarity in plan size and distance from the river bank reinforced the evidence of the existence two bridge piers. The Grand Plaza and its tall structures are clearly in view in the aerial photograph.

The 1993 Site Visit Survey of Bridge Components

The collected site data, aerial photography, satellite mosaics, and structural concept of the bridge configuration were assembled and integrated into the hypothesis. The critical data collected since the 1989 site visit were very promising. The aerial photos and site topographical surveys were digitized and resolved at the same scale. We developed a digital composite map of the area of the bridge including the plaza, the river, and the Guatemala side of the river. However, the geometry of the ruined piers had to be verified by field dimensions. Furthermore, a search for other bridge components had to be carried out on the ground. A second site exploration was launched to verify the digital information garnered from aerial photos and topographical maps and to physically carry out ground exploration for additional bridge components.

The second exploration of the site was carried out in March 1993, working under the auspices of a film permit from the Mexican Instituto National de Anthropologia y Historia (INAH). The engineering team was accompanied by a public broadcasting film crew under the direction of archaeologist Dr. Nicholas Hellmuth. The mission of the film crew was to photograph the engineering investigation related to the hypothesis of the Maya bridge. The crew set out from the Mexican river

Figure 10-6: Photo of bridge suspension rope mechanism. Note "wear grooves" in circular support. Author's image.

port of Fonterra. Professional outfitters transported the team in large pontoon boats. We traveled down to the city of Yaxchilan and set up our camp in the same location used during the first visit.

The procedures for surveying the river and the bridge structure were planned in advance of the visit. The area of the river adjacent to the bridge location was visually surveyed and photographed above and below the water level. Field sketches were developed of the alignment and geometrical configuration of the salient elements of the bridge structure adjacent to the river. Additional bridge mechanisms were encountered, investigated, and photographed (Figure 10-6). When the survey was completed and analyzed, the overall configuration of the bridge, its method of construction, and its operating mechanisms became apparent. Field sketches were developed detailing the geometry of the structure and the nature of the materials of constructions of the bridge.

Maya engineers had constructed a long-span bridge using the optimum high-strength materials available for construction. They configured masonry and composite, cast-in-place concrete, high-strength henequen rope cables, and timbers into the construction of a three-span suspension bridge. The following is a summary of our structural hypothesis that was developed and sketched in the field.

The Structural Concept of the Bridge

The bridge was hypothesized to be a three-span, rope cable suspension structure. The bridge spanned from the south bank of the river to the south pier; the long middle span was supported by the two intermediate composite stone and concrete piers (south and north pier) located in the river; the bridge spanned from the north pier to the north embankment. The bridge terminated at the north embankment anchorage. The bridge walkway was located at the elevation of the Grand Plaza.

South Bridge Pier

The south bridge pier is located 25 meters from the river's edge. The remains of this pier extended 3 meters above the water level and have a base dimension of approximately 10 meters. The structure is constructed of a facade of worked stone with an interior in-fill of cast-in-place concrete.

North Bridge Pier

The center of the north bridge pier is 63 meters in distance from the center of the south bridge pier. This distance of 63 meters equaled the length of the center span of the suspension bridge The remnants of the superstructure, which were located by aerial photography and verified by divers at the time of the 1993 survey, were almost completely under water at the time of the survey (Figure 10-5). The foundation for the tower was formed by large, flat stones, which were laid directly on bedrock. The diameter of the pier was measured to be 10 meters, the same dimension as the south pier.

Bridge Abutments

Bridge abutments that terminated at each end of the bridge were located at the south and north ends of the bridge. The abutments provided anchorage for the rope cables and support for the walkway. The force of the water flow has degraded and displaced the bridge abutments. The embankments founded on the soil of the riverbank were undermined, collapsed, and then dispersed downstream by the scouring effect of the swiftly flowing water.

Bridge Mechanisms

Several uniquely carved stone mechanisms were observed downstream from the piers (Figure 10-6). The mechanisms consist of two large, parallel, carved-stone surfaces connected at midpoint by a rounded concave element. Observations indicated smooth, circular grooves in the mechanism apparently caused by wear due to the friction from the rope cable suspension system; the rope cables were supported by this mechanism. This device is similar to rope cable guideways used in modern bridge construction and would have been used as the suspension rope keepers for the bridge piers and anchorage guides at the abutments.

The Grand Stairway

Observations along the riverbank indicated the ruins of a 10-meter-wide stairway that led up from the south riverbank to the Grand Plaza. The stair was sited directly to the west of the bridge.

Archaeo-Engineering Synthesis and Analysis of Data

The site visit of 1993 yielded a plethora of critical information that contributed to the data for reconstructing a virtual, computer-based bridge structure and a three-dimensional fly-through of Yaxchilan, the Usumacinta River, and the Maya bridge. Field data from the expeditions, aerial photography, remote sensing, and the historical evidence were assessed in my office in Atlanta, Georgia. The research efforts were synthesized, and the bridge was reconstructed using forensic engineering techniques and digital tools. Computer modeling and simulation techniques verified the centerline location of the bridge, the geometry of the bridge structure, and the topography of the Grand Plaza.

The 1993 site visit, which was primarily dedicated to structures at the level of the river, did not survey structures on the plaza level. However, chance encounters led to vital information that we had totally overlooked. It was logical that a grand bridge would have a significant entrance structure located on the Grand Plaza, and we had not searched the plaza level for a structure that would fit the description of a monumental bridge approach structure aligned with the centerline.

In her book, *Yaxchilan: The Design of a Maya Ceremonial City*, archaeologist Dr. Caroline Tate describes each individual structure along the river side of the plaza and includes a reference to the ruins of the bridge pier, which she considered to be the remains of a flood-ravaged structure lost to the river. However, she actually identified the bridge approach structure on the Grand Plaza in her description of Structure 5. This long stone platform is parallel to the river and plaza. It has a hieroglyphic stairway facing the Grand Plaza and is described by Dr. Tate as "a long low platform paralleling the axis of the main plaza." She notes that no trace of masonry superstructure has been found on the top. To the rear of the building is a narrow soil esplanade with a steep descent into the river. It was obvious; she was describing the configuration of a classic bridge approach structure.

The entrance facade of Structure 5 consists of a stairway made of six risers constructed of 188 individual stone blocks carved with hieroglyphics. Dr. Tate also describes the ruins of a stairway down to the riverbank adjacent to Structure 5. She writes that "in ancient times someone entering there would have passed between the structures as a gateway to the city." Dr. Tate provides a clear description of an elevated platform, which served as a grand entrance to the city. Structure 5 combined the flow of travelers arriving by boat and gaining access to the plaza via the broad river stairway with the pedestrians crossing the bridge to develop a monumental entrance to the Grand Plaza.

The description of Structure 5 on the Grand Plaza was presented in Dr. Tate's book, which was published in 1993. The publication date of Dr. Tate's fine work was after the forensic engineering studies of the bridge were well advanced. The connection between the ruined structures in the river and Structure 5 on the Grand Plaza changed the character of the bridge and expanded the focus of our engineering research to include the dramatic effect of the bridge structure on the Grand Plaza. A review of the digitized site map indicated that Structure 5 appeared to be in alignment with the bridge structures. This alignment enhanced the engineering hypothesis for the geometry of the bridge structure: a three-span suspension bridge once spanned the river and terminated its approach structure on an elevated esplanade that also served as the top platform for a grand stairway extending up from the riverfront. This exciting concept had to be proven by additional field investigation and computer-based bridge design applications in order to verify the altered hypothesis. The research and investigation for the bridge structure had to be thoroughly researched and developed properly, or the archaeological community could not be convinced of the existence of the bridge.

The archaeological maps were scanned and the geometry of the structures on the Grand Plaza was integrated into the comprehensive plan exactly as surveyed. The scanned site graphics were introduced into the digital analysis and the bridge geometry from field surveys. Then aerial photos were integrated with the historical site maps to develop a composite plan. Field survey measurements taken at the site were used to confirm the distance between the edge of the riverbanks and the center alignment of the bridge pier structures.

This comprehensive computer site analysis indicated that the river was approximately 20 percent greater in width on the historical maps than was measured during the field surveys. The geometry of the river banks and pier structure locations in the river were digitally adjusted on the archaeological map of the site. This combination of historic mapping and digitally corrected data generated an accurate dimensional and geometrical image of the angular centerline of the bridge with the Grand Plaza.

Introducing data from the aerial photographs, the angle of incidence between the centerline of the two bridge pier structures and the edge of the south riverbank was established from the aerial photographs. Using the known location of the south bridge pier as a fixed point, the angle of incidence between the bridge centerline and the river edge was introduced into the computer model in order to extrapolate the centerline onto the Grand Plaza.

The resulting computer graphic indicated that the centerline of the bridge extended southward over the riverbank and intersected with the eastern end of Structure 5 on the Grand Plaza. It was quickly recognized that Structure 5 possessed the logical design configuration and artistic dignity to serve as the terminus of the bridge on the Grand Plaza. The centerline of the bridge aligning with the two pier structures and intersecting Structure 5 confirmed the discovery of a rare find in engineering history. The conclusions of Dr. Tate in her book were confirmed: Structure 5 was the bridge approach structure and served, along with the stairway, as the impressive gateway to Yaxchilan.

With the planar locations of the bridge and its structures identified, it was important to verify the capabilities of the bridge to span the river at a safe elevation above the high water level during flooding. The topographical maps indicated that the top surface of Structure 5 is approximately 22 meters above the riverbank at low water level. Historical records indicated that the flood levels of the river have occurred at a height of 15 meters above the low water mark. The elevation of Structure 5 at 22 meters above the low water mark placed the top surface of Structure 5 at 7 meters above the high water mark. This geometric arrangement fulfilled another engineering requirement: flood safety. The key elements of the bridge, including the top of Structure 5, the causeway to the southern abutment, the surface of the suspended timber bridge decking, and the northern abutment, were placed well above normal seasonal flood levels.

The discovery of the intersection of the bridge centerline with Structure 5 was an exciting development. The synthesis of the collected data and computer modeling developed a logical basis for the existence of this lost landmark of ancient engineering.

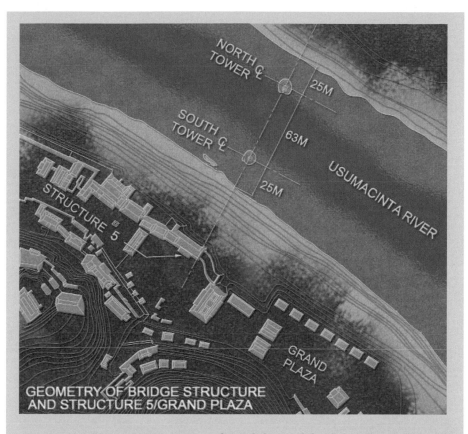

Figure 10-7: Site map of Yaxchilan with bridge structures located. Author's image.

The 1994 Site Visit to Confirm the Bridge Structure

Prior to finalizing the computer simulations and modeling efforts, a further field expedition was launched to verify, on the ground, the alignment of the bridge structures and the plaza structures through actual site observations and surveys. In April 1994, the ceremonial city of Yaxchilan was again visited to investigate and verify the geometrical relationships developed during the forensic engineering analysis and computer applications that reconstructed this unique bridge structure. Again there were surprises; the road to Yaxchilan included an unexpected adventure.

During 1994, the Zapatista Army of National Liberation under the control of the mysterious Subcomandante Marcos declared war against the Mexican State. Dr. Nicholas Hellmuth and I were traveling to Yaxchilan, and we came prepared to cross the battle lines in Chiapas. We were shorthanded because of concern for the unstable political situation and the requirement for crossing the active battle lines in Chiapas on the way to the river and to Yaxchilan. We were working under the auspices of a permit issued by INAH and a letter of safe conduct issued by Theodoro Maus, the Consul General of Mexico in Atlanta and a personal friend. These official documents, I thought, should work. But to guarantee our safe passage through the lines, we also packed bottles of tequila and cartons of Marlboro cigarettes in our backpacks.

The single road from Palenque to the town of Fonterra on the Usumacinta and our *cuyuco* to Yaxchilan had a series of roadblocks and checkpoints manned by the Mexican Army and the opposing Zapatista rebels. Passing through the Mexican Army checkpoints with their neat revetments was formal. They inspected our INAH papers and safe-conduct letter, and approved of our archaeological mission. They searched the car and then passed us through. The Zapatistas were much less formal. A single felled tree blocked the road, marking their lines. We did not see the first ski-masked sentinel until he stepped out of the bush and barked, "Who are you and where are you going?" Just as in the movie *The Treasure of the Sierra Madre,* they were not interested in our "stinking papers." Once they found we were on an archaeological mission, they were actually quite friendly and really cheered up when we gave them our gifts: a carton of Marlboro cigarettes and a bottle of tequila. We were then given permission to pass on. I thought I would really impress them when I told them that Emilio Zapata and I shared the same birth date. Not so. They did not hear my qualifications that I was sure would make me an honorary Zapatista. Instead they were busy laughing with each other and happily sharing the carton of cigarettes. I don't know about the tequila, but we continued on our way to the Usumacinta River and our awaiting *cayuco.*

During this visit to Yaxchilan, the alignment of the centerline of the salient bridge components (the bridge piers, the river stairway, and the mysterious Structure 5) were observed, surveyed, photographed, videotaped, and mapped. The topographical survey and the field evidence clearly indicated that the mystery of Structure 5 was solved. The survey instruments showed that the centerline of the bridge intersected with the southeast part of Structure 5. The engineering hypothesis of the long-span suspension bridge at Yaxchilan was verified. The monumental platform of Structure 5, with its grand hieroglyphic stairway, was the terminus of the grand suspension bridge over the river as well as the Grand Stairway leading up from the riverfront. The confluence of the bridge and the stairway at the Plaza level verified the theory that Structure 5 was the grand entrance to the great city of Yaxchilan.

Computer Simulation and Virtual Reconstruction of the Bridge

Based on the confirmed data from the 1994 expedition, an updated computer simulation and a structural engineering analysis for the bridge were developed. The research and analysis confirmed that seventh century Maya engineers constructed a long-span, rope cable suspension bridge across the Usumacinta River. The rope-cable support system was supported from tall composite stone and cast-in-place concrete bridge towers and anchored by stone mechanisms at the north and south abutments. The rope cable suspension system was connected to a series of suspender ropes that supported the timber bridge-deck system.

The geometry and design were integrated into computer graphics. The geometry of the structural towers and centerline dimensions of the towers are based on the measured field survey (Figure 10-8). The walkway height was established by the elevation of Structure 5. A vaulted Maya arch at the top of the bridge piers served as a three-dimensional structural support for the rope cable guide ways (Figure 10-9). The bridge pier and the vaulted arch were constructed of a stone exterior with a cast-in-place concrete interior. It was important that the rope cable guideways be connected into the mass of the concrete wall of the tower arch to optimize the stabilizing effect of the vaulted arch. Large forces were generated by the rope cable support system, and the supports required substantial resistance.

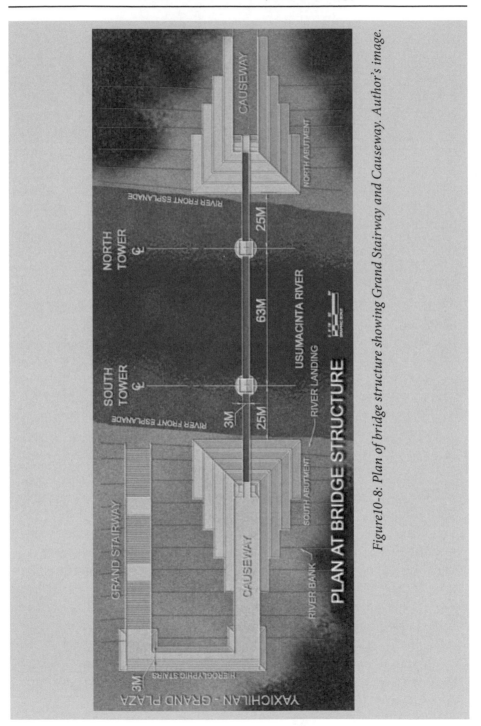

Figure10-8: Plan of bridge structure showing Grand Stairway and Causeway. Author's image.

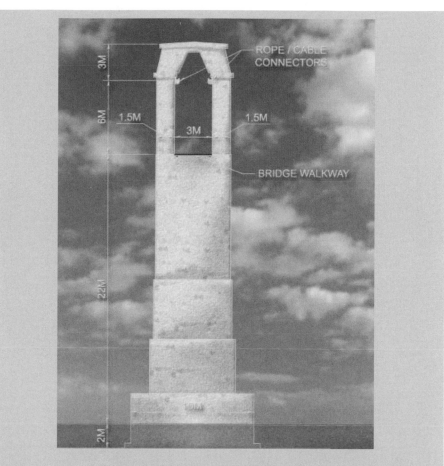

*Figure 10-9: Elevation of bridge tower pier showing
lowest water level and overall dimensions.
Author's image.*

The rope cable suspension system assumed a catenary shape typical of cable-supported bridge systems (Figure 10-10). The center-to-center span between the bridge support piers in the river, based on field surveys, is 63 meters. A vertical dimension of 5 meters was selected for the sag in the rope cable system. This amount of sag was selected to carry out engineering calculations for the forces generated in the rope cable. The weight to be supported by the bridge cables was calculated using the maximum number of people assumed to be walking in a ceremonial procession while crossing the bridge, plus the dead load of the bridge

Figure 10-10: Elevation of bridge structure with Yaxchilan Grand Plaza and river structures. Author's image.

deck. Beasts of burden did not exist in Mesoamerica, so rolling loads from carts were not included.

The bridge deck was assumed to be 3 meters wide and made of wooden planks spanning between cross beams supported by suspender ropes connected to the cable support system. Using the known strength of hemp rope, calculations indicated that the rope cable system would require a bundle of 5-centimeter diameter ropes on each side of the bridge walkway. I commissioned an architectural rendering of the bridge (Figure 10-11) and a three-dimensional computer fly-through (Figure C-22).

The techniques utilized in the construction of the structure were applications of known Maya technology. The use of composite stone and cast-in-place concrete for tall structures was common in Maya engineering. The use of high-strength henequen rope by the Maya has been well documented by archaeologists, and the application of the Maya arch is found in the majority of Maya structures. This lone example of a long-span bridge in the Maya world can be explained by the lack of rivers and surface waters in the northern Yucatán. However, suspension bridges of shorter spans, as we have seen, have degraded and are gone forever. The concept of this landmark bridge structure provides a logical solution to the question of how this lively urban center could operate on a year-round basis.

Digital Tools and Proof of Reconstruction of Maya Technology

The initial computer applications for the reconstruction of the Maya suspension bridge were initiated in 1992. Advances in digital tools have increased exponentially since that time. The original analysis was reviewed using high-speed digital computers in 2006 by the international engineering firm of Ove Arup. The analysis was part of a television presentation for the History Channel. The structural design passed all the requisite tests of engineering stability. Furthermore, a rigorous computer analysis of the bridge structure was carried out by Dr. Horacio Ramirez de Alba from the University of Mexico and was published in the technical journal *CIENCIA ergo sum*.

Figure 10-11: Rendering of Maya bridge at Yaxchilan. Author's image.

The discovery and reconstruction of the Maya Bridge was published in *Civil Engineering Magazine* in April. 1995 and *National Geographic Magazine* in October 1995. After the publishing of the discovery, interest increased in the scientific community. In 2006, the History Channel produced an episode relating to the Maya bridge. In preparation for this production, new computer-generated graphics were prepared. The original computer graphics of the structure had become outmoded, and new computer software technology was used to regenerate high-definition graphics for the reconstruction of the bridge and develop a three-dimensional computer fly-through of the city of Yaxchilan and its bridge.

This reconstruction of Maya innovation would not have been possible without the use of digital tools and computer simulation, and the modeling of engineering creativity. This expansion of the capabilities of digital tools has enabled practitioners to leap forward in the investigation and analysis of archaeo-engineering issues.

The Longest Bridge in the Ancient World

The first civil engineers in the Americas archived a historical technological feat by combining advanced materials of construction with proven structural design skills and creative construction techniques. The breathtaking structure spanning the Usumacinta River solved the critical need for a lifeline for the city of Yaxchilan. This engineering project may have been the most creative and dramatic project ever carried out by Maya technology. This bridge has been awarded its rightful place in world engineering history.

Engineering historian Dr. Neal FitzSimons researched and developed a chronological record reflecting the construction of bridges throughout history. Dr. FitzSimons developed a chart of the longest known bridges in the world, starting in 600 BC with a 69-foot-long bridge built by the Etruscans and extending to the completion of the Brooklyn Bridge in 1883. The list includes the Maya suspension bridge over the Usumacinta River. A review of Dr. FitzSimons's records indicates that the Maya bridge at Yaxchilan, constructed in the seventh century, was the longest bridge in the world until 1377, when Italians built a fortified stone bridge with a span of 72 meters over the Adda River at Trezzo, Italy.

The Maya solved a critical transportation issue for a city and found a place in world engineering history. The bridge at Yaxchilan was the longest bridge in the world from AD 700 to 1377, a period of 677 years. Though the superstructure of the bridge at Yaxchilan has crumbled during the last millennium and the remaining piers are a ghost of their past, this bridge has secured its place in history.

11

Maya on the Move

Through the jungle and over the seas, Maya transportation technology systems enabled the movement of trade goods and materials over the roads of the Maya domain and to distant ports in the seas engulfing the Yucatán Peninsula. The transport systems of the Maya operated on raw manpower for transporting material between cities, building construction projects, and powering their seagoing cargo vessels. The lack of indigenous working animals in the Americas was overcome by Maya creativity. They innovatively applied manpower as an efficient substitute for animal power. Ingenious methods of manpowered transport systems on land and at sea enabled the Maya civilization to succeed and prosper during the Classic Period and beyond the conquest.

Death in the Pleistocene:
Mother Nature's Practical Joke

At the end of the Pleistocene Era (2,000,000 to 10,000 years ago), North and South America were populated with a wide variety of animals that have now gone extinct. The majority of the now-vanished species were large mammals, known as megafauna. The extinct animals were massive beasts, including the 20,000-pound mastodon, 6-foot-tall giant ground sloths, sabre-tooth tigers, 10-foot-tall short faced bear, and a range of other exotic animals. They included creatures that originally evolved in North America including *equus*, the modern horse, and *camelops*, the modern camel. The herds of these species had split into two groups. The Northern band migrated west across the Bering land bridge and the other traveled south into North America. The northern bands of horses and camels migrated to Siberia and then across Asia. These animals became domesticated and supplied the power and transportation for all the great civilizations of Asia, Africa, and Europe. The southern herds remained in North America and were victims of mass extinction at the end of the last Ice Age. Their demise deprived the Americas of beasts of burden. The majority of this extinction had occurred when man migrated to the continent. After the extinction, a great number of megafauna, defined as any animal more than 100 pounds in weight, survived to the 21st century. These include deer, bears, cougars, moose, alligators, and humans. The largest extant American land animal is the bison, which can weigh up to 2,200 pounds.

Humans migrating to the American continent found poor candidates for beasts of burden. It is interesting to point out the irony in the humor of Mother Nature. She sent herds of indigenous horses and camels from the Americas into Asia, where they served as the power source for the great conquering empires, and then, in the Americas, she extinguished the life of these same animals. When next seen in the Americas, the horse had a Spanish conquistador on its back.

The Classic Maya never became aware of Mother Nature's practical joke played on the Americas. The Holocene extinction had erased all of the animals that could potentially be domesticated and used as beasts of burden. The Maya were not aware of the very existence of such an animal. Wild animals lack the traits of trustworthiness and mild temper that characterize the true domesticated working animal, and they cannot be tamed. However, the Maya were successful in the domestication of certain animals, including the dog, and animals with agriculture applications such as turkeys, ducks, and stingless bee.

In South America, llamas and alpacas were domesticated, in addition to guinea pigs. The llama used as a pack animal can carry up to 65 pounds. A Maya porter could transport more than 120 pounds. Feeding the llama requires a total of 8.8 pounds of corn a day whereas a Maya porter only requires 2 pounds per day of corn. The Maya used their creativity too find a feasible substitute for animal power. The alternate solution was a plentiful and economical source of kinetic energy: Maya manpower.

Development of Maya Transport Technology: Why Not Use the Wheel?

Along with being referred to as a Stone Age culture, archaeologists cast Maya technology in a negative light when they state that the civilization did not understand the concept of the wheel for transport. As the Maya culture progressed, hunter ,and gatherers turned into farmers, and the need for powered transport increased. The need for power supply then ramped up with the rise of villages, towns, and cities. Maya farmers and technicians developed methods of using manpower to supply the kinetic energy to lift, transport, and mobilize loads required for the implementation of agriculture, construction, and transportation.

So if the Maya technicians were so intelligent, say doubters, why did they not use a wheeled vehicle for transport? Examples of small toys with wheels with axels crafted by Maya are exhibited in museums. Then why was this important invention not used in the fabrication and use of wheeled vehicles for transport? First consider that, because of the lack of dray animals, the only source of kinetic energy available for the Maya was manpower supplied by their own workforce. To take advantage of the properties of the wheel, the construction of a wheeled wagon or cart would be required. The wagon would be constructed with a trace connected to the front of the vehicle to accommodate men rigged in harnesses. Applying the same energy to weight formula that was used on the large freight wagons pulled by horses or mules in the 19th century to calculate the number of animals required to pull a heavily loaded freight wagon, the number of animals was calculated using the loaded weight of the wagon and the weight of the animals. Each dray animal was considered capable of pulling a load equal to its own weight. The loaded wagon weight divided by the animal's weight calculated the number of animals needed to pull the wagon. This equation initiated the old expression "pulling their weight."

The Maya wagon would be fabricated of timber just as the European wagon. Assume, for this example, that the wagon weighted 1,000 pounds and could transport a payload equal to 1,000 pounds. The sum of the load and wagon would be equal to a total of weight 2,000 pounds. Using the standard "pulling their weight" criteria for calculating the number of pulling beasts for a wagon load. The weight of the wagon and load equaled 2,000 pounds and the weight of Maya workforce required were 20 men weighing in at 100 pounds each. Then a total of 20 haulers/pullers weighing a total weight of 2,000 pounds would be required. To equal the weight of the wagon and its load, simplistically it would require 10 men to pull the weight of the cart and 10 men to haul the load. That would be an average of 50 pounds of net payload carried by each 20-man team. Not a very good efficiency rating when Maya technology had developed manpowered transport devices that enabled a porter to transport a load of 125 pounds each. That is a 250-percent advantage over the use of a wheeled transport. It is easy to see the advantage of transport by porter over pulling a manpowered wheeled vehicle. For the Maya, the lack of work animals was the difference between the use of the wheel and the necessity to use manpower for transport.

The Maya developed a man-powered transport device known as the tumpline. This device enabled a single man to carry more than 125 pounds with relative ease. Using the heavy wagon, 20 men could only transport 50 pounds each, or a total of 1,000 pounds, of useful load. On the other hand, 20 porters could transport 2,500 pounds of useful load using a tumpline. In addition to the poor load-carrying capacity of wheeled transport, travel over the rough terrain and muddy jungle tracks made the wagon an overall poor alternate. The tumpline-equipped team could easily negotiate the rough terrain while transporting more than twice the load as a wheeled vehicle. It is apparent that the Maya logically recognized the disadvantage of a wheeled vehicle. The wheel without the use of a heavy, hoofed beast of burden was a negative factor in the economic game plan of the Maya civilization. Pulling the wagon loads required more than twice the kinetic energy per pound compared with a man with a tumpline load. Thus, Maya technology was built around manpower, and utilized its capabilities and advantages in a wide variety of applications. The wheel was not unknown in the Maya world. The circular motif of the wheel was depicted in art and architecture and used on toys, but in the evolution of Maya transportation technology it was a dead-end branch.

The Technology of the Tumpline: The Optimization of Manpower

The manpowered tumpline was the load-carrying mechanism that moved the Maya economy. The tumpline-equipped bearer transported trade goods, merchandise, and agriculture products, and carried construction material up and into the construction of the superstructure of monumental buildings without beasts of burden.

The tumpline consisted of a leather head strap that was positioned on the top of the head to direct loads from the skull and directly into the spinal column. The ends of the head strap were attached to a 3-foot-long tail or tension strap. The strap was connected to the frame or load container supporting the load. The tails were aligned with the center of the mass of the load to be transported. The head strap then carried the tension loads transmitted from the load to the top of the head.

The tumpline was a simplistic tension-based mechanism that distributed loading from the mass of the burden directly onto the load paths that frame the human body (Figure 11-1). The loads were vectored into the human skeletal structure from the skull, which supported the load, down the spinal column and directly into the pelvic arch, then into the bone systems of the legs and the support system of the feet. This interaction between loads and the human frame optimizes the natural resistance of the structural skeleton and reduces fatigue while minimizing the strain on muscles.

The advantage of the tumpline made the task of transporting material more efficient with the load aligned with the spine rather than being supported by muscles in the shoulders and back. Figure 11-1 details the pattern of load-bearing vectors of the tumpline and the load paths being transferred down through the skeletal system into the roadway surface. To position the tumpline, after placing the tumpline on top of the head, the bearer then leaned forward to balance and align the load, and started his march. The tumpline enabled the bearer with a heavy load to travel along level roadways at a pace of that could cover 15.5 miles (25 kilometers) per day. The pace in rough, rugged terrain would be slower, but a sure-footed porter would travel faster than a beast of burden.

The tumpline was used as a vertical lifter in construction operations, not unlike a modern material elevator. The bearer would place construction material such as stones, concrete, sascab, or soil in a container on his tumpline. The bearer would climb up ladders or scaffolding with the weight of construction material and his tumpline attached to his head, rendering his hands free to safely climb. These *cargadores* were the teamsters of the Maya culture.

The efficiency of the tumpline aided in moving large quantities of merchandise and materials at a low cost. Using a tumpline, the bearer could

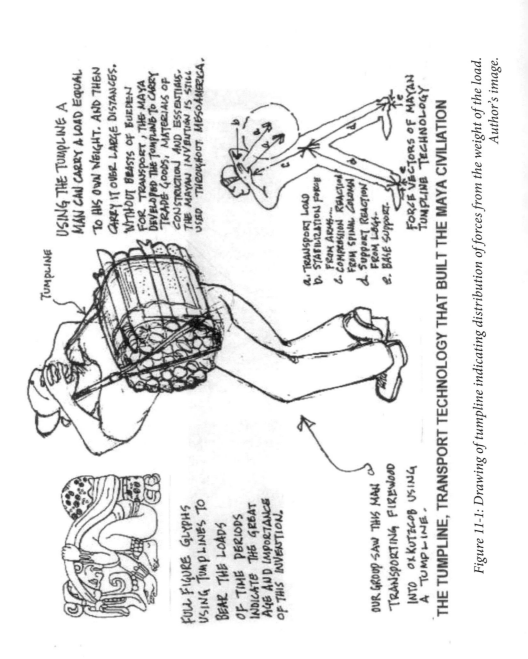

USING THE TUMPLINE A MAN CAN CARRY A LOAD EQUAL TO HIS OWN WEIGHT. AND THEN CARRY IT OVER LARGE DISTANCES. WITHOUT BEASTS OF BURDEN FOR TRANSPORT, THE MAYA DEVELOPED THE TUMPLINE TO CARRY TRADE GOODS, MATERIALS OF CONSTRUCTION AND ESSENTIALS. THE MAYAN INVENTION IS STILL USED THROUGHOUT MESOAMERICA.

TUMPLINE

a. TRANSPORT LOAD
b. STABILIZATION FORCE FROM ARMS...
c. COMPRESSION REACTION FROM SPINAL COLUMN
d. SUPPORT REACTION FROM LEGS.
e. BASE SUPPORT.

FORCE VECTORS OF MAYAN TUMPLINE TECHNOLOGY

FULL FIGURE GLYPHS USING TUMPLINES TO BEAR THE LOADS OF TIME PERIODS INDICATE THE GREAT AGE AND IMPORTANCE OF THIS INVENTION.

OUR GROUP SAW THIS MAN TRANSPORTING FIREWOOD INTO OXKUTZCAB USING A TUMPLINE.

THE TUMPLINE, TRANSPORT TECHNOLOGY THAT BUILT THE MAYA CIVILIATION

Figure 11-1: Drawing of tumpline indicating distribution of forces from the weight of the load. Author's image.

carry a load approximately equal to his weight. The ability to carry large loads relative to this small body size and the ability to pace himself was dependent on taking rest stops to regulate his heart rate and energy expenditure. He would rest by sitting his tumpline loads on load-resting platforms called *lab*. The bearers were multi-disciplined; in addition to being cargo carriers, the tumpline was a transportation device for passengers. A chair was attached to the tumpline of a single bearer. The occupant would sit in the chair facing backward. This type of manpowered transport continued to be used by the elite into the 18th and 19th centuries in Mexico and Central America.

Figure 11-2 illustrates a mural at Calakmul that shows a rare view of everyday activities in Maya life. The painting depicts a Maya bearer supporting a large pot filled with goods supported by a tumpline. Note the intricate web of rope placement securing the pot to the tumpline. It is a brilliant study in vectors.

Teams of bearers carried large loads over great distances. They were easier to maintain than beasts of burden. Working animals would require feeding, water, and currying. However, the self-sufficient bearer raised his own food, fed, watered, and curried himself. He was the horse, cart, and stable hand all combined into a single, dynamic package. The tumpline is still employed as a cargo carrier in contemporary Latin America. It is a common sight to observe men, women, and even children carrying loads with tumplines as they travel along rural roads and in markets. Their payloads range from fire wood to packs of merchandise and agriculture products.

The tumpline was an important symbol of load-carrying in Maya culture. It is part of an ancient hieroglyphic symbol representing the burden of each solar year or 365-day Haab year transported by the ancient Maya time lords. The burden of each year is carried on the back by one of the four bearers of time. The burden and responsibility of that year is carried on the back of a time lord and supported by a tumpline stretched across the forehead. The time lord gives that year its quality, or personality. The tumpline is a prime example of comparative analysis; it was developed by other cultures throughout the planet and can be found in Nepal, India, and Africa. The other cultures also had beasts of burden for transport, but the tumpline was superior to work animals in the economics of transport and on mountainous terrain. The word *tumpline* is another outlandish name given to a native device by archaeologists. The Maya word for the device is *mecapal*.

Figure 11-2: Ancient tumpline bearer from mural at Calakmul. Author's image.

Tumpline is the word for the same device used by the native Mohegans of Connecticut.

An overview of the variety of cargo transported by the tumpline will show the integral part that the tumpline played in agriculture, trade, construction, and other cargo transport. A review of the wide range of material indicates the influence that the foot freighters of the Maya had on the construction and wealth of the city-states. The following wide range of goods, materials, and agriculture products were transported by tumpline:

- Construction materials: cement, timber, worked stone, sascab, stone rubble, tools, rope, henequen, latex.

- Vegetable products: sweet potato, tomato, pumpkin, Jerusalem artichoke, chili pepper, cassava, melon, cacao, arrowroot, yucca, guava, strawberry, peanut, numerous squash varieties, maize and corn, honey, pineapple, cherry, prickly pear, tomatillo, manioc, jocote.

- Animal products: turkey, duck, deer, caiman, rabbit, turtle, fish, possum, quail, pheasant, dove, dog, iguana.

- Trade goods: chicle, rubber, copal.

Moving The Big Banana

Because the Maya depended on manpowered transport based on the tumpline, loads were sized to be transported by a single bearer. In construction, the size of building stone was limited to the size and weight that could be easily transported by porters with tumplines. The standard size of worked stone in Maya structures was based on a weight of approximately 125 pounds. The coordination between stone size and weight/carrying capacity simplified the type of transport used for the construction process. With few exceptions, Maya engineers did not utilize large-size or heavy building stones, as was done with other ancient civilizations. The other ancient civilizations applied work animals or mass human labor for transporting large stones. The Maya used transportable-sized building stones as part of the management, efficiency, and ease of their construction process.

In the course of constructing a monumental building, the use of large stones as part of the art and architecture was sometimes unavoidable and became an absolute requirement when erecting large components or art works. The transport of large stone sections was carried out by shaping the stone into the form of long cylinders (Figure 11-3 and Figure 11-4). The methodology of moving large stone elements from the quarry to the building site used a combination of henequen rope, timber rails, the sacbe system, and the kinetic energy of Maya manpower.

The circular stone transportation cylinders were shaped at the quarry. The diameter and length of the cylinder depended on the dimensions required for the art and architecture at the destination construction site. Timber rails were placed on the paved surface of the sacbe (Figure 11-3). The stone cylinder was then placed on the rails, and a pair of henequen ropes were wrapped around the cylinders at equal distances from the centroid. Two teams of manpower pulled on the ropes, and the rotation of the mass moved the cylinder forward. The rope-pulling team moved the cylinder forward when the ropes unwound and rotated the cylinder clockwise. When the ropes were pulled, a distance of 7 feet (2.3 meters) would be advanced by each turn of the stone cylinder. A pair of 100-foot-long ropes would rotate the cylinder 14 turns and 100 feet (30.3 meters) in distance. The rope would be rewound and the cycle repeated until the destination site was reached. The large stones were moved by the energy of Maya manpower.

Historical parallels to the transport of large stones include the movement of large stones by contractors during the Roman Empire. Roman contractors transported large stones in the shape of cylinders The Romans had the advantage of beasts of burden and metal in order to assemble their transport system. A hole was drilled at the horizontal centroid of the cylinder. Molten lead was placed in the hole to set an iron axel. A rectangular frame with a tongue was attached to the axels, and oxen were harnessed to the tongue. The oxen pulled the cylinder from the quarry to the construction site.

Examples of several Maya stone cylinders have been found and investigated. The cylinders are often positioned on or adjacent to ancient sacbes. Figure 11-4 illustrates a stone cylinder encountered at Santa Rosa Xtampak. The cylinder, which is in excellent condition, was resting adjacent to a sacbe. Archaeologists have opined that these cylinders are road rollers used to compact the road surface. This is not an accurate description of the purpose of the cylinder. The surface of sacbe was paved in cast-in-place concrete, and road rollers are not required for placing cast-in-place concrete pavement. The use of the cylinder as a device for transporting large sections of stone is more appropriate to Maya construction practices.

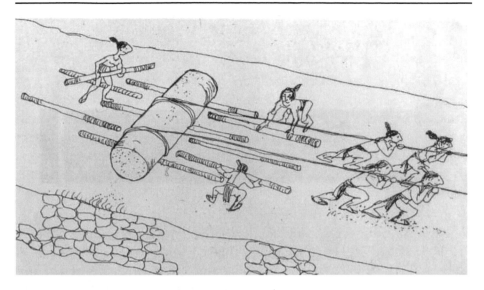

Figure 11-3: Moving large stones in the shape of cylinders. Author's image.

Figure 11-4: Stone cylinder investigated at Santa Rosa Xtampak in 1990.
Author's image.

The Unforseen Benefits of Living Without Dray Animals

In his book *Guns, Germs and Steel*, Jared Diamond discusses the lack of animal-derived contagious diseases in the New World prior to the conquest. After the arrival of Europeans, numerous major infectious diseases of Old World origins became established in the New World. There is a likelihood that not a single major infectious disease reached Europe from the Americas. The sole possibility is syphilis, whose area of origin is controversial.

New World cities were as large as or larger than European cities. Why were infectious diseases in the form of lethal crowd epidemics unknown in the New World? Studies indicate that crowd diseases evolved out of Eurasian herd animals that had become domesticated. Domesticated animals in the Maya world consisted of the turkey, the Muscovy duck, and the dog. The few domesticates in Mesoamerica were not exactly breeding pools for passing on infectious diseases. The Maya did not domesticate beasts of burden or cattle. The domesticated animals in Mesoamerica were unlikely sources of crowd diseases compared with cows, horses, and pigs in the Old World. Domesticated animals of the Maya did not sleep in houses as they had in Europe, and their numbers were low. As a result, the domesticated animals of the Maya were not a source of human pathogens.

Diamond points out that the lack of animal-derived diseases in Mesoamerica eliminated outbreaks of deadly diseases during the Classic Period. The animal-borne diseases and epidemics did not deter or interrupt the growth and success of the Maya economic culture as they did with the economic climate when European cities were devastated by epidemics. The story was different after the arrival of the conquistadors. Great numbers of Maya were killed by European diseases evolved from Europe's long intimacy with domestic animals. Without domesticated herd animals, the Maya path to success was not derailed by epidemic crowd diseases.

The Great Demand on Agriculture for Maintaining Work Animals

The natural environment of the Yucatán was a difficult place for producing high crop yields. The Maya relied on technology to increase their agriculture yields, considering the six-month dry season and poor soil. The Maya were successful with their agriculture systems and were able to produce a yield that fed the hinterlands and the non-producers in the city, as well as a surplus for export trading. They appeared to maintain a balance of supply and demand. However, the total of agriculture yield went for human consumption. What if the Maya actually had been able to domesticate beasts of burden and wished to optimize the usage of animal power for agriculture, travel, and transportation? A large portion of their agriculture yield would be required to feed their working animals, with a resulting shortage in the other sectors of the society.

What percentage of their maize might have been required for animal feed, we will never know. However, consider a modern parallel that involved accurate recordkeeping. To estimate the cost of feeding work animals, one can review the required amount of grain required for feeding working animals in the United States during the early 20th century. In 1931, the majority of grain grown in the United States went to feed domesticated animals: 80 percent of acreage that was used to grow grain was dedicated to feeding working animals. Only 20 percent of grain was for human consumption. As a comparison, if 80 percent of the Maya grain crop was diverted from human consumption and used to feed animals, it is apparent that a disaster would have taken place. It is known that grain was not being allocated by the Maya to feed domesticated animals.

Assets and effort were not required to feed and care for domesticated animals. The porters who supplied manpower for transporting the Maya economy only consumed 2 pounds of grain per day. The Maya porter grew his own food, secured his own water, and groomed himself. The mule or horse required 15 to 20 pounds of grain per day, plus a worker for attending the watering and care of the beasts. Application of the required care for domesticated animals would require time and food assets. It is apparent the Maya economy would suffer. Their science, technology, and the construction of monumental cities would react to the economic ripple effect and would suffer. To provide further examples of the impact of domesticated working animals on an economy, when the United States was converting from the use of draft animals to motorized vehicles (during the period of 1914 to 1939), the populations of horses and mules dropped by 13,500,000 head. The reduction in farmland dedicated to animal feed was reduced by 40,000,000 acres. The increase in farmland available for crops for human consumption successfully changed the course of American economic history. In the same manner, it can be seen that the presence of dray animals would have adversely affected the economic history of the Maya civilization.

Maya Nautical Transportation Technology

The successful economy of the Maya civilization depended on its active trading partners, not only on the land mass of Mesoamerica, but in long-range, seagoing voyages that searched for trading partners along the shores of the Caribbean Sea, the Gulf of Mexico, and the Pacific Ocean. Large Maya cargo vessels plied the open seas and ventured across the turquoise waters of the Caribbean to near offshore islands including Isla Mujeres, Cozumel, and the Belize Cays, but also sailed beyond the Yucatán, to the east across the Caribbean Sea to the 1,700-mile-long archipelago of the Caribbean Islands extending from Cuba to Antigua. Their seagoing cargo vessels traveled north to Mexico and south to Panama in Central America. Maya sea traders traveled afar and encountered trading partners with valuable resources that could be exchanged for the products of Maya industry, elite goods, and minerals that were unique to the Maya world. The long-range nautical trade in materials and ideas also had a great impact on the spread of Maya cultural influence.

The attraction of long-range trading partners available by sea routes influenced Maya engineering to expand their capabilities in nautical technology, and enabled the design and construction of large, stable, seaworthy cargo vessels. These large cargo vessels were swiftly propelled over the foamy waves by manpower in the form of paddlers. Maya shipbuilding technology combined their knowledge of seaworthy vessel stability, specialized tool design, and durable materials of construction. Maya woodworking skills produced hydraulically shaped, high-strength timber hulls that were compositely integrated with adhesive compounds, waterproof materials, and water-resistant caulking to construct stable seagoing vessels.

The wide-ranging and lucrative trading of the maritime commerce network promoted the founding of sea ports, riverine trading ports, and land-based navigation aids consisting of fixed, bearing landmarks, fire-illuminated lighthouses, and beacons. These were enhanced with a sophisticated system of celestial navigation enabled by their capabilities in mathematics and astronomy. Maya long-range trade continued well past the Classic Period and was an important part of Post-Classic Maya economy extending into the early 16th century, until the Spanish conquistadors banned their trading and took over the lucrative mercantile trade.

The Caribbean, the Gulf of Mexico, and the Pacific Ocean were the marine highways plied by the Maya sea traders. However, the Caribbean Sea was the principal seaway connecting the Maya to sea-based trading partners. Seaports were established along the seaboards of Honduras, Belize, Guatemala, and Costa Rica. The Maya traded unique minerals including jadeite, obsidian, and cinnabar; valued materials including colorful feathers, cotton cloth, clothing, and cocoa; and manufactured goods including ceramics, obsidian swords, and knives. In turn they traded for gold, copper, and metal axes.

The Maya sea-trading network and its trademark cargo vessels, powered by 30 or more paddlers and crewed by sailors and navigators, are not the fanciful stuff created from folk tales or notions from archaeological whimsy. Maya art has revealed clues to the design and construction of their seagoing vessels. Furthermore, artifacts of the large craft have been uncovered and investigated by experienced archaeologists.

Nautical engineering of seagoing vessels is an example of Maya technology that had a European eyewitness of outstanding character. Descriptions of Maya seagoing vessels were documented by the most famous of Spanish navigators and explorers. The first and most notable written account describing Maya sea traders involved the great navigator Christopher Columbus, during his fourth voyage in 1502. While traversing the Caribbean off the coast of Honduras, Columbus's fleet of galleys confronted a large Maya seagoing cargo vessel in the Bay of Honduras. Christopher Columbus's son Ferdinand described the encounter in his journal, as quoted from J.M. Cohen's *The Four Voyages of Christopher Columbus* (1969):

> ....by good fortune there arrived at that time a canoe long as a galley and eight feet wide, made of a single tree-trunk like the other Indian canoes; it was freighted with merchandise from the western regions around New Spain. Amidships it had a palm-leaf awning like that on Venetian gondolas; this gave complete protection against the rain and waves. Underneath were women and children, and all the baggage and merchandise. There were twenty-five paddlers aboard, but they offered no resistance when our boats drew up to them.

The large canoe was loaded with trade goods, the costliest and handsomest of which were cotton mantles and sleeveless shirts embroidered and painted in different designs and colors , long wooden swords edged with "flint knives that cut like steel" [perhaps obsidian]; copper hatchets and bells; and a crucible for melting copper. Notably, they also had "...*many of the almonds [cacao beans] which the Indians of New Spain use as currency; and these the Indians in the canoe valued greatly, for I noticed that when they were brought aboard with the other goods, and some fell to the floor, all the Indians stooped to pick them up as if they had lost something of great value.*" Impressed with "the great wealth, civilization, and industry of these people," Columbus nevertheless continued east in search of "a strait across the mainland that would open a way to the South Sea and the Lands of Spices." Columbus did retain from the canoe an older man and cacique named Yumbé, "who seemed to be the wisest man among them and of greatest authority, as an interpreter."

This historic description of the Maya cargo vessel included the critical essentials to re-create a basic design of the craft: the size of the craft, its composite nature, fabricated from a single log, the cabin/palm leaf shelter, the number of paddlers, crew, and passengers, and the trading merchandise. Columbus considered some of the merchandise to be valuable assets and seized selected items in the cargo. Limited images of Maya vessels have been encountered that provide illustrations of their configuration and design elements. A mural from the temple of the warriors at Chichen Itza, a frieze from a Maya structure, and a carving on a bone unearthed at the ancient city of Tikal indicate significant details of nautical engineering features that provided the craft with stability in open seas.

Descriptions carried out by marine archaeologist Dr. Paul Petennude and sculptor Philippe Klinefelter provided additional details. Petennude investigated a partially degraded seagoing canoe at Paalmul on the east coast of the Yucatán. Dr. Petennude, in a personal conversation with the author, described the canoe as constructed of *manilkara zapota* wood. The remnants of the canoe consisted of two-thirds of the original vessel. He estimated the craft to be 60 feet (18 meters) in length and 8 feet (2.5 meters) wide.

Klinefelter, an expert on Maya tools, encountered a large seagoing canoe on the shores of Lake Atitlán, Guatemala, in the 1970s. The lake is known for high waves and a rough, sea-like surface. Canoes on this lake would be built as seagoing vessels in order maintain stability in the rough water of the vast lake. Klinefelter stated that the canoe was 80 feet (24 meters) long and approximately 8 feet (2.5 meters) wide; the craft included the design elements of a Classic Period Maya canoe. The specimen was made of a single log from an avocado tree.

The Design Criteria for a Seaworthy Maya Vessel

The combination of eyewitness accounts, painted impressions by Maya artists, and *in situ* observation of artifacts of seaworthy vessels has presented forensic engineering with a wide range of clues for investigation of these craft. The various accounts agree on the size of the vessels, the nature of construction from a single log of high-strength timber, and configurations of the salient design features that were combined to construct a seaworthy cargo vessel. Studies of the design and construction of the fabled vessels of Maya sea traders could only extend to a certain point. The basic marine engineering configuration of the craft, proven materials of construction, specialized tools used to shape the hull, and methods of connection of the various component parts of the vessel were recognized by experts in marine architecture. The sum of the parts was the ability of the vessel to react in a seaworthy manner when traveling in heavy seas.

The capability to recognize the unique features of good boat-building practice was within the expertise of a professional experienced in marine architecture, Colonel Douglas T. Peck, U.S.A.F., retired. He is a historian of early seagoing vessels and navigation, experienced sailor, author, and investigator of the marine engineering of Maya cargo vessels. His identification of the principles of naval engineering in Maya cargo vessels, combined with the author's knowledge of structural engineering and computer reconstruction using virtual images, enabled the development of criteria for design features and methods of construction of seaworthy Maya cargo vessels.

Naval Architecture Design Features

The historical and contemporary observations and Maya renderings of vessels illustrate salient design features of a prototypical Maya seagoing vessel. Their feats of marine architecture were developed over 1,000 years. Figure 11-5 is a naval engineering drawing and specifications of the design features that shaped Maya seagoing vessels and developed the hydrodynamic factors that enabled sea voyages.

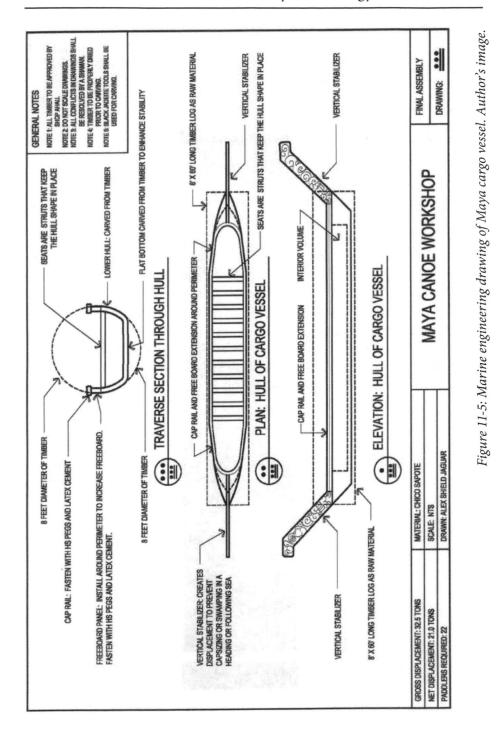

Figure 11-5: Marine engineering drawing of Maya cargo vessel. Author's image.

Construction of the Hull

The entire vessel was carved from the trunk of a single high-strength hardwood tree. Chico zapote (*manilkara zapota*) was the preferred choice of timber. The timber from this dense tree has a tensile strength of 20,000 psi. This is equal to the tensile strength of low-grade steel.

Composite Plank Elements of Bow and Stern

The profile of the bow and stern was shaped from the tree trunk. The high vertical elements of the bow and stern were assembled from timber planks shaped for that purpose and joined to the timber base structure at the bow and stern. Connections would be implemented using slotted joints interfaced along the base hull structure, connected by latex adhesive, caulking, and high-strength tensile pegs along the intersections of the planks and timber hull. The elevated vertical features at the bow and stern are vertical stabilizers and provide displacement or buoyancy to prevent swamping by allowing the vessel to rise vertically in the event of a head or following sea. Another feature of the high-mounted stabilizer is to provide resistance to complete capsizing; the displacement in the bow and stern structures would stabilize the vessel and prevent complete rollover by limiting capsizing to 90 degrees.

Composite Structural Elements to Extend Freeboard

The section through the hull in Figure 11-5 illustrates the vertical extension along the perimeter of the hull developed by the installation of a timber structural element. This vertical perimeter member is capped with a shaped wood cap rail. This vertical element increases the freeboard and depth of the hull, and significantly increases the displacement capabilities of the vessel. The vertical element installed along the longitude of the hull is constructed from a section of timber connected to the top edge of the hull structure. The composite shape is attached to the hull structure using high-strength wood pegs, latex adhesive, and caulk.

The same feature is found in modern vessels. The increased height of freeboard provides the hull with an added safety factor in providing righting displacement, preventing capsizing, or swamping in heavy seas. It must be noted that the vertical extension of the upper freeboard of the ancient vessels is common only to Maya vessels.

Hull Cross-Section Configuration: Athwart Stability

Figure 11-5 indicates the cross-section configuration of the hull of the vessel. The bottom of Maya vessels was flattened to provide athwart-ship stability about the longitudinal axis. The hard chime or flat-bottom hulls were common to early Greek and Roman vessels. Spanish chronicles report that flat-bottom canoes were used in the central Mexican Basin.

The completed cargo vessel was powered by paddlers kneeling or sitting amidships. This type of craft could accommodate 30 rowers. Some accounts describe 20–22 rowers. The specifications of the craft in the drawing had a gross displacement of 32.5 tons. Considering the size and weight of the construction and the paddlers, a net displacement of 21 tons was available for cargo. This was a lot of goods to be traded. The capacity offered the opportunity to ship a great quantity of goods using the ocean highway. A Maya cargo vessel could transport the equivalent load carried by 328 individual tumpline bearers.

The Maya Paddle Design and Steering Oar

Maya artists, including those who created the carved bone artifact found at Tikal, depict the rowers using an asymmetrical paddle. Recently an actual, intact Maya "paddle" was excavated by Dr. Heather McKillop. The dimension and configuration of the paddle provides a significant insight into its actual use. The asymmetrical paddle is 6 feet 1 inch (1.85 meters) in length. The length of the paddle would be excessive for the typical Maya paddler, who was of short height. The asymmetrical shape would create an imbalance of the hydraulic force generated by the movement of the paddle and would cause rotation in the hands of the paddlers. It appears to be a consensus of experienced marine architects that the asymmetrical paddle of more than 6 feet in length must be a steering oar for large Maya vessels. They are used as a rudder to keep the flat-bottom vessel on a straight course.

Other depictions by Maya artists indicate the use of pointed paddles of symmetrical shapes. This paddle configuration made entry and exiting the water easy. In the middle of the stroke, the wide part of the paddle would be fully immersed and would produce maximum forward force vectors. The pointed symmetrical paddle is hydrostatically superior to the blunt, rectangular paddle used in contemporary canoes. Maya paddlers on long sea voyages would kneel or sit amidships, and use a short paddle with a pointed symmetrical shape.

Construction of Vessels Using Jadeite Tools

Black jadeite or chloromelanite tools for the construction of Maya cargo vessels were used to hollow out the interior of the half-cylinder shaped tree trunk and to shape the exterior of the giant logs. Certain scholars have argued that the Maya used bronze tools to carry out the carving of the giant hull. They cite the account of Christopher Columbus and his encounter on the fourth voyage as evidence of metalworking by the Maya. The copper hatchets and crucibles for smelting ore were described in the journals of the great navigator. This was the 16th century, and the Maya may have learned the techniques of smelting copper and the fabrication of copper or bronze tools from South American trading partners. Columbus's encounter with the Maya vessel occurred more than 600 years after the collapse of the Classic Period; the design of Maya canoes was more than 1,500 years old at that time. (The prototypical design shown in this chapter was developed using typical design characteristics of Maya seagoing craft and technical capabilities in practice during the Classic Period.)

Chapter 5 presented the use of jadeite tools by Maya technicians. The appropriate tool for shaping logs has been the adze. The jadeite adze was mounted on a high-strength wood handle with a 45-degree contiguous element to connect the adze at the optimum angle for maximum cutting efficiency. The connection of the jadeite adze is made of latex adhesive and leather or henequen ties. The adze was the principal tool used in the hull-shaping operation of the vessel. Other critical tasks, including fine cutting of the composite components and drilling, were carried out using jadeite chisels and drills. The finished hull was completed by connecting the composite elements with wood pegs and latex adhesives.

The marine engineering drawing in Figure 11-5 illustrated the design for a basic vessel for seagoing trading. The drawing does not include the cabin structure as described by Columbus or other possible design features such as a sail. The use of a sail on this type of craft has been argued among maritime experts. It is highly possible that a civilization with sophisticated science and technology that independently conceived the number zero, calculated periodicities of the planets to minute accuracies, and created one of the five original written languages in the world could have conceived of a simple device as a sail for their seagoing vessels. In 2000, a French-Mexican team of sailors sailed a replica seagoing canoe with a square, rigged sail in the Caribbean near Belize. The team covered a distance of 30 miles per day under sail and determined that the sail was a logical progression of marine engineering.

The Long-Lived Service of Seagoing Vessels

The Maya seagoing cargo vessels traversed the tropical seas surrounding the Yucatán Peninsula. Their maritime trading network extended north along the Gulf of Mexico, south to Panama, and eastward to the islands of the Caribbean. Fleets of the trading vessels traveled up navigable rivers to trading posts that were connected to overland trading networks. Cities in Mesoamerica and south along the Caribbean were drawn into an "international," Pan-American trading network with lively commerce and ideas spreading over large distances. Evidence of Maya long-distance trading has been encountered on the far-flung islands of Antigua and Barbados. Jadeite axes found on these islands have been traced to sources in Guatemala. This trading product found its way on a 3,000-kilometer voyage to the east of its source, the Montagua Valley. These long-range voyages that were out of sight of land required sophisticated celestial navigation. This was a specialty of Maya navigators. Maya navigators did not rely on the North Star but viewed the entire sky as a charted map to steer the way to distant islands.

The Maya seagoing vessel served the culture for 2,000 years as viable trading vessels. Trade was terminated during the conquest when Spanish conquistadors took over the lucrative trade routes. During the conquest, during Spanish colonial rule, and later on, they served as seagoing passenger and cargo vessels. These working seagoing vessels were used by the Maya until the 19th century, when industrialized modifications were made to produce larger-sized craft, and plank hulls were substituted for the traditional carved tree hull. The spirit of these hardy craft can be seen today as their direct descendants, *cayucos*, transport agriculture goods, cattle, and passengers in the Bay of Terminus, over the mighty Usumacinta River and other rivers of the Yucatán. Today, however, the paddlers have been replaced by a 200-horsepower Mercury outboard engine.

12

The Collapse of
Maya Civilization

The achievements of the Maya civilization reached an apogee during their Classic Period. This golden age was marked by the sophistication of its urban life style, made possible by the success of Maya technology. The population growth was reflected by the continual expansion of the cities and their monumental architecture; the achievement of its arts, science, and technology; the bountiful harvest of agriculture; and high economic levels generated by industry and trade throughout the city-states and to markets far beyond the domain of the Maya.

The intellectual creativity of Maya engineering and technology had uncovered unique solutions to overcome the fragility of their natural environment, with its capricious rainfall, lack of surface water, poor soil conditions, and seasonal desert. Maya society optimized their disposable time for advancing science and expanding ideas. This disposable time was made possible by the bountiful harvests that enabled city dwellers freedom from farm labor. These food surpluses were a benefit of their triumph over the vagaries of their environment.

The Triumph of Maya Technology

Maya technology employed engineering solutions that kept pace with the expanding needs of their population of 15,000,000 inhabitants. Their engineered water-management systems satisfied the yearly demand for water, plus provided a factor of safety in the event of shortfalls in the annual rainfall. Sufficient rainfall meant life and survival to the Maya civilization.

Maya cities were masterpieces of artistic and technological creativity brought to realization by the invention of cast-in-place concrete, tall structures, efficient infrastructure, and city planning. The urban city-states were a tour de force of Maya intellectualism. The Maya transportation systems with all-weather roads and seagoing vessels brought wealth to the city-states by enabling successful trade throughout Mesoamerica and across the seas.

Maya-engineered water-management systems developed reservoirs, chultunes, and canal systems that provided water for the survival of cities and the enhancement of agricultural yield. The technological advancement of agronomy and engineered agriculture systems for irrigation, including raised fields and terraces for agriculture, enhanced the ability of Maya farmers to produce food to keep pace with the growing population plus a food surplus for trade. Maya farmers constituted 70 percent of the population, and they were able to produce 200 percent of the food requirement for their families, creating a sufficient food supply for the urban populations and a 40-percent surplus for trade.

The Balance of Need and Supply in Maya Society

Every sector of Maya culture was in balance due to the successful enhancements of the natural environment by Maya technological and engineering exploits. The balance between survival and disaster was in equilibrium as determined by the quantity of rainfall. For 600 years, the Maya had enjoyed a long string of good fortune, with 600 rainy seasons of sufficient rainfall to replenish the reservoirs of the cities and provide irrigation for the demands of their engineered agricultural systems. The average amount of precipitation was at a level that enabled the society to prosper by balancing the deficiencies of a year of low levels of rain with years of abundant rainfall by application of creative technologies. The chultunes and reservoirs of the cities were designed and constructed to collect and store an 18-month supply of water for the populace of urban places. The surplus would provide an adequate supply of water for the six-month desert of the dry season with a 12-month reserve in the event of an interrupted supply of rainfall. Agriculture, however, did not have the advantage of a safety factor due to insufficient rainfall.

The Maya urban zones had some of the densest population in history, with up to 2,400 people per square mile in populous cities. Their water supply and agriculture systems had maintained a delicate balance due to

600 years without a serious drought throughout the region. However, their streak of good fortune could not continue forever. A serious drought could change the equilibrium between technological improvements and Mother Nature's largess in precipitation. Without the generosity of natural rainfall, the safety factor in a period of drought would be insufficient. During a drought, the equation for predicting and determining the sufficiency of reserve in the water supply would fall out of balance; the reduction in the reserve would lead to disaster for the Maya population. Without regular rainfall, Maya cities dependent on a technologically enhanced water-supply system would be in a serious situation if 18 months passed without rain. Agriculture would be in serious trouble if a shorter period passed without rain; the success of the Maya agriculture systems required rain rather than a water-storage system. The lack of regular rainfall would lead to a disaster of unprecedented proportions for the Maya

The Balance of Survival Tilts Toward Disaster

The Maya had experienced droughts during their long history—with serious consequences. During the Pre-Classic Period between AD 125 and AD 250, Maya scientific advancements were set back during a serious drought that caused the Pre-Classic abandonment. At this time, Maya cities from the Northern Lowlands to the Pacific Cost were slammed by the severity of a 25-year period of drought that resulted in abandonment or impairment of the cities. The great city of El Mirador was abandoned during this period and was never reoccupied. However, once again the bountiful rainy season returned to the Yucatán, and for 300 years, Maya society prospered with predictable rainy seasons. The cities were reoccupied and unprecedented building programs were the result of the flowering and growth of cities; with population expansion, the power and wealth of the cities flourished as never before.

A period of slow growth occurred from AD 536 to AD 590. This period had a debatable effect on the Maya. Some experts argue that the hiatus was confined to Tikal and was not a widespread event. After the hiatus, the tropical rainy season returned, and, for 200 years, Maya society thrived and experienced a period of expansion of cities, intellectual enlightenment in art and science, economic growth, agricultural abundance, prosperity in trade and commerce, and additional technology-based projects that enhanced the factor of safety against environmental adversity. Then their lucky streak came to an end and Dame Fortune turned against the Maya: between the fateful period of AD 790 to AD 910 the greatest drought in 7,000 years engulfed the Yucatán, brought about demographic devastation on a scale unparalleled in world history, and destroyed their exquisite scientific civilization.

Richardson Gill, in his book *The Great Maya Droughts*, has developed an interdisciplinary scientific and historical analysis of data that provides a logical, chronological overview of world climatic events and their effect on historic weather conditions in the Yucatán. Mr. Gill's book reviews weather, droughts, and volcanic activity from 3500 BC through the collapse of the Maya civilization. Gill presents a scientific approach to assembling the history of climatic conditions and meteorology in the Yucatán Peninsula. He develops a logical analysis of historic weather patterns and climatic conditions using myriad scientific studies. His results were a mosaic of critical meteorological data indicating how worldwide weather patterns affected the tropical homeland of the Maya. Gill interprets paleoclimatic records; historical European, African, and Mesopotamia records of climate patterns; and anomalous weather records in Scandinavia and Peru. He presents a concise environmental milieu of data that integrates interdisciplinary sources to develop the history, nature, and causation of extreme weather conditions in the Yucatán.

The principal meteorological hypothesis of the book is that cold periods of weather somewhere in the world can be coincident with drought in the Yucatán. Cold weather in northern latitudes brought drought to the Maya. In addition, during the Classic Period drought, the Maya environment was affected by the negative effects of tropical volcanic eruptions. Gill identifies a number of tropical eruptions that occurred during the drought and compounded Mother Nature's disaster. The parched environment was attacked by the effects of volcanoes injecting sulfur-rich gases into the tropical stratosphere, reducing the amount of solar energy reaching the troposphere and affecting the weather.

He recounts how millions of Maya suffered and died in total isolation from other civilizations. This is the same isolated condition that prevailed when the Maya evolved their scientific civilization, and this isolation now affected their survival. No one came to their aid in relieving their suffering: no Red Cross, and no international relief organizations or assistance to offer relief. They created one of the world's greatest scientific civilizations in near isolation and died by the millions in the same geographic vacuum.

More than a century of severe drought quickly overcame the technological factor of safety constructed by Maya engineers. The intensity and length of the great drought was more powerful than Maya attempts at technological solutions to overcome the shortage of rainfall. The great drought overwhelmed the short-term efforts for survival created by Maya engineers. The totality of the overpowering effect of the great drought, volcanic eruptions, and environmental abuse by the Maya dashed man's feeble attempt to deter Mother Nature when her course was set on an environmental catastrophe. Technology created the overpopulation and it failed them; the Maya were left at mercy of Mother Nature's capricious disposition.

The Failure of Technology and the Collapse of Maya Civilization

Maya technology displayed its proud achievements in the construction of large cities and its triumph over the environment. Technology enabled the Maya to enjoy reliable water supplies and high agriculture yields that resulted in an artificially high population, one that could not be supported by the natural resources of the Yucatán Peninsula using traditional methods of farming. The support of this overpopulation could only be achieved with technological innovation. Maya technology contributed to the disaster by its continuous construction programs with its needs for cement and timber. The demands for fueling the kilns with timber when producing cement for construction, land for expansion of agriculture, and fuel for domestic use resulted in deforestation of the lush rainforest of the city-states. This loss of forest cover resulted in the erosion of agriculture areas. The demands of the dense population and environmental damage due to deforestation were leading Maya society toward disaster even before the great drought began its fatal stranglehold on the culture.

The advantage of technology combined with 600 years of lush rainy seasons had resulted in an over-confident society unaware that it was teetering on the edge of environmental disaster and unaware of the history of severe droughts in the Yucatán. Technology had been able to balance the basic needs of the over-populated Maya domain, as long as there were regular cycles of rainy seasons.

Archaeological research has linked the abandonment of Maya cities with the last dates recorded on stone structures in major cities. The collapse of the civilization can be traced to a distinct time period for each phase of abandonment. The initial phase occurred in the Petén from AD 760 to AD 810. The second phase was in the South Highlands between AD 811 and AD 860, and the cities failed in the third phase, occurring in the Northern lowlands, which had a more dependable water supply and was the last to collapse, between AD 860 and AD 910.

When the great drought increased during the mid-eighth century, the water reserves in the reservoirs quickly depleted, crops failed, and the Maya searched for a solution to aid in their survival. In a land without surface water and the lack of a viable aquifer, there was little that could be done without the return of rainfall. The choices were migration or taking action to alter the political power system that controlled the supply of water.

When Mother Nature finally released her grip on the Maya, the terrible drought had caused the classic collapse and destroyed the Maya civilization. The cities had been abandoned, and 98 percent of the population had died. Richardson Gill reports that he has catalogued more than 100 theories that have been advanced relative to the cause of the collapse. The root cause of the collapse of the Maya civilization was the drought and the failure of technology. However, each of the 100 theories probably had a hand in the death toll and collapse. The four horsemen of the apocalypse rode across the Yucatán: pestilence, famine, civil strife, and death.

The Maya were unaware when it actually started—just another year with less rain than usual. Next year it will be different, but it was not, and the worst was yet to come. It is probable that the massive death toll came first to the common Maya then worked upward in the class society. The elite prayed to Choc, the rain god, for intervention; the rains did not come. The people of the city-state became desperate and implored the elite to double their sacrifices and increase their pleas to the gods; still, the rains did not come. The people were weakened by thirst, they became desperate in their quest for water, they invaded the palace in search of water, and they massacred the elite. The people then controlled the city and its water resources. They emptied the reservoirs. Still the rains did not come. Desperation ruled, and people decided to migrate to other domains, to go to the adjacent city-state to seek water and food. As they slowly traveled toward the next city-state with their family and possessions, no rain came.

Midway in their journey they met other migrants traveling toward them from the adjacent city-state. These migrants were also traveling in search of water. The two groups of migrants were in complete confusion. How could it be? No water anywhere? They sat down on the white pavement and asked, Which way do we travel to our salvation? Some migrants lay on the pavement totally confused and depleted; others joined ranks and slowly continued on their futile journey in search of water. Still no rains came. The tropical sun arced across the cloudless azure sky, scorching the pitiful scene of the dead and dying. One by one, the travelers fell to the sacbe. Soon all had died a painful death, and rains never came for them.

Epilogue

The cataclysm that engulfed the Yucatán during the Maya Classic Period resulted in the collapse of the Maya civilization, but not the end of the Maya people and their ancient culture. The massive drought and the failure of Maya technology to resist nature's forces caused the demise of 98 percent of the population. The 15,000,000 Maya living during the Classic Period were decimated, but approximately 300,000 Maya survived the environmental catastrophe. The surviving Maya were scattered over the 125,000-square-mile domain, with the majority living in the northern Yucatán. When the rains returned, the survivors rebounded and started their lives again, living in small groups and villages, as returning to the abandoned cities was not an option.

Maya belief systems, culture, and traditions lived on within the surviving population. Their scientific books survived, protected and updated by Maya priests and passed down to their successors. As the population stabilized, a political model developed. The Maya political system evolved into independent states ruled by a chief or *cacique*. These political subdivisions arose in the Yucatán and the Guatemalan highlands. The Maya domain was divided into 20 independent states based on the languages, mores, and traditions of their subculture.

After its collapse in AD 900, Chichen Itza was repopulated in AD 1000; its resurgence was stimulated by the cultural contribution of the Toltec. This fusion caused a renaissance of the Maya civilization, along with its sciences and religion. Chichen Itza once again became the focal point of the

Yucatán. The city was the political and religious center of the area until it was sacked in 1212 by the forces of Mayapán.

In 1325, in a place 1,200 kilometers to the northwest of the Yucatán and 425 years after the Maya collapse, a wandering tribe of Chichimec founded their capital on an island in Lake Texcoco. They called themselves the Mexica, and would be known to the world as the Aztec Empire. They named their capital Tenochtitlan. In 1428, they grew into the Aztec triple alliance and led the Aztec Empire to dominate the Valley of Mexico, Oaxaca, the Gulf of Mexico, and the Maya states.

After the fall of Chichen Itza, Mayapán was founded in 1263 and became a major city. Mayapán grew into the political and cultural capital of the Yucatán. When the Aztecs came to power, Mayapán negotiated a tribute system with the Aztec. In 1441, Mayapán was sacked by revolt and collapsed. When it fell, the elite and priests fled with the scientific books and settled in separate polities.

Prior to the Spanish conquest, the Maya were living in independent city-states, warring constantly and paying tributes to the Aztec. This tribute ended with the defeat of the Aztecs by the Spanish conquistadors in 1519.

When the Spanish landed on the Yucatán coast in 1527, the population of the Maya was approximately 2,000,000 people. The first Spanish attempts at conquest were thwarted by the Maya, and in 1535, the Spanish were expelled from the Yucatán. The Spanish under Francisco de Montejo re-invaded in 1540, and the Yucatán finally succumbed in 1546. The northern area of the Yucatán was now in the control of the Spanish, but the Maya did not go easily: the remainder of the Maya population in the southern Yucatán and the Petén of Guatemala would not be defeated until 1697, a period of 150 years after the conquest of the Yucatán.

The Spanish conquerors attempted to change the culture of the Maya. They burned Maya books, banned the practice of their religion, and required that all Maya convert to Christianity. The Inquisition decimated the intellectual and literate Maya priests through torture and death. To better control the population, the conquistadors combined scattered Maya villages and transferred the population into European-style towns. In 1543 alone, 700 towns were founded, each based around a Catholic church. The new towns served the purpose of pooling the population and enabling the exploitation of Maya labor much more easily. The Spanish made all-out efforts to erase all things related to the Maya culture. The conquistadors and priests felt divinely inspired to civilize and evangelize the Maya. Attempts to Europeanize and Christianize the Maya led to the devolution of much of the Maya culture for the next 400 years. The Maya population was reduced to a relatively undifferentiated mass of peasants.

Spanish Bourbon reform allowed the Spanish to take ownership of Maya land and force the Maya into impressed labor by right of decree from the Crown. This was termed the *encomienda* system, and was developed as a means of securing land and an adequate supply of cheap labor. This system resulted in Maya land being expropriated by the colonial Spanish and, combined with the labor of the Maya peasants, created a wealthy system of trade between the Yucatán and Europe. The Maya were subjugated and enslaved, regarded as second-class citizens, and forced to endure barbaric practices. The Spanish hacienda owners made massive fortunes while the Maya were treated as slave labor.

In the late 18th century, worldwide demand for henequen rope, cordage, and fiber for burlap created enormous plantations in the Yucatán The demand for Maya lands by Spanish hacienda owners increased as the plantations grew in size and the number of labor drafts became more onerous.

The independence of Mexico from Spain in 1821 did not change this system. When Mexico threw off the yoke of colonial rule, conditions did not improve for the Maya. The hacienda system grew with the henequen markets, and the Maya were treated as slave labor even in the newly independent country of Mexico.

In 1840, the Yucatán seceded from Mexico and became the Republic of the Yucatán. The Republic of Texas Navy was retained to patrol their coast. The Yucatán rejoined Mexico in 1843, but conditions did not change.

In the early 19th century, the Maya rebelled against their treatment by the hacienda owners. A widespread rebellion known as the Caste War (1847–1901) had a mission of driving all of the European population out of the Yucatán. The Maya rebellion came close to realization, but it failed.

After the Caste War, the hacienda system greatly expanded in the Yucatán. The expansion was driven by foreign demand for henequen cordage products, once again trapping the Maya. The haciendas could not keep up with world market demand; prices rose and greatly enriched the hacienda owners. They called henequen "green gold."

Economic conditions changed in the mid-20th century, but they changed for the worse. With competition of exported henequen from other countries and the production of synthetic fibers, the henequen industry went into a short and terminal decline. The majority of hacienda plantations closed and were abandoned. The loss of revenue resulted in the Yucatán sliding into a poor and insignificant backwater. It was far distant from the nation's power base in Mexico City. However, reform in the form of a land-distribution program preventing the expropriation of village land was applied to rural populations. The Maya reclaimed their land.

Economic conditions in the Yucatán changed in 1974, when the Mexican government created the resort area of Cancun. The tourist business has boomed and turned the economy of the Yucatán around, and the yearly influx of millions of tourists have created a ripple effect and brought economic recovery to the Yucatán.

The Classic Maya civilization has faded into the dust of history, but the Maya people have not disappeared. The Maya people and their spirit live on today in Mexico and Central America. They are a homogeneous group of people who have occupied the same territory for thousands of years. They speak some 30 languages that are so similar that linguists believe that they all have the same origin, a proto-Mayan language that could be 7,000 years old. The *in situ* evolution of their language implies they were the original permanent inhabitants of the Maya area and suggests that today's 5,000,000 Maya probably share a very ancient, common, genetic origin.

The Maya cherish their heritage and are continually reminded of its past grandeur as archaeologists uncover the ruins of ancient cities constructed by their ancestors. Archaeological and archaeo-engineering studies are expanding the corpus of knowledge surrounding the Maya culture. Interpretation of the carved inscriptions has lifted the veil of mystery relating to the history of each city, and their towering structures reflect the unique feats of Maya engineering hidden by the rainforest.

Bibliography

Abbett, Robert W. *American Civil Engineering Practice.* New York: John Wiley & Sons, 1957.

Adams, Richard E.W. *Prehistoric Mesoamerica.* Boston: Little, Brown and Company, 1977.

American Concrete Institute. *ACI Manual of Concrete Practice.* Detroit: American Concrete Institute, 2011.

American Institute of Timber Construction. *Timber Construction Manual, 2nd Edition.* Englewood, Colo.: John Wiley & Sons, 1974.

Arguelles, Jose. *The Mayan Factor: Path Beyond Technology.* Rochester, Vt.: Bear & Company, 1987.

Ary, Donald, Lucy Jacobs, Asghar Razavieh. *Introduction to Research in Education.* Orlando, Fla.: Holt, Rinehard and Winston, Inc., 1990.

Aveni, Anthony F. *Skywatchers of Ancient Mexico.* Austin, Tex.: University of Texas Press, 1980.

Barnhart, Edwin. "Indicators of Urbanism at Palenque." In *Palenque: Recent Investigations at the Classic Maya Center*, edited by Damien B. Marken. Berkley, Calif.: Altamira Press, 2007.

———. *The Palenque Mapping Project: 2000 Field Season Final Report.* Crystal Waters, Fla.: The Foundation for the Advancement of Mesoamerican Studies, Inc. (FAMSI), 2000.

Baudez, Claude. *The Ancient Civilization of Central America.* Translated by James Hogarth. London: Barrie & Jenkins, 1970.

Baudez, Claude, and Sydney Picasso. *Lost Cities of the Maya.* Translated by Caroline Palmer. New York: Harry N. Abrams, Inc., 1992.

Berlow, Lawrence H. *The Reference Guide to Famous Engineering Landmarks of the World: Bridges, Tunnels, Dams, Roads and Other Structures.* Phoenix, Ariz.: The Oryx Press, 1998.

Bernal, Ignacio. *A History of Mexican Archaeology: The Vanished Civilizations of Middle America.* London: Thames and Hudson, 1980.

———. *The Olmec World.* Translated by Doris Heyden and Fernando Horcasitas. Los Angeles: University of California Press, 1969.

Bourbon, Fabio. *The Lost Cities of the Mayas: The Life, Art, and Discoveries of Frederick Catherwood.* New York: Abbeville Press, 2000.

Carper, Kenneth L. *Forensic Engineering.* New York: Elsevier Science Publishing Co., 1988.

Castello Yturbide, Teresa. *Presencia de la Comida Prehispanica.* Mexico City: Fomento Cultural Banamex, 1987.

Ceram, C.W. *Gods, Graves and Scholars: The Story of Archaeology.* New York: Alfred A. Knopf, 1975.

Chan, Roman P. *Cultura y Ciudades Mayas de Campeche.* Mexico City: Editora del Sureste, 1985.

Christie, Jessica J. *Maya Palaces and Elite Residences.* Austin, Tex.: University of Texas Press, 2003.

Coe, Michael. *Breaking the Maya Code.* New York: Thames and Hudson, 1999.

———. *The Maya. 4th Edition.* London and New York: Thames and Hudson, 1966.

Coe, Michael, and Mark Van Stone. *Reading the Maya Glyphs.* New York: Thames and Hudson, 2001.

Coggins, Clemency Chase, Orrin C. Shane III, ed. *Cenote of Sacrifice: Maya Treasures from the Sacred Well at Chichen Itza.* Austin, Tex.: University of Texas Press, 1984.

Craven, Roy C. *Ceremonial Centers of the Maya.* Tallahassee, Fla.: The University Press of Florida, 1974.

Davies, Nigel. *The Toltecs, Until the Fall of Tula.* Norman, Okla.: University of Oklahoma Press, 1987.

De la Vega El Inca, Garcilaso. *Royal Commentaries of the Incas and General History of Peru.* Translated by Harold V. Livermore. Austin, Tex.: University of Texas Press, 1987.

Del Rio, Antonio. *Descriptions of the Ruins of an Ancient City Discovered Near Palenque in the Kingdom of Guatemala in Spanish America.* Translated by Henry Berthoud. London: Henry Berthoud, 1822.

Demerest, Arthur. *Ancient Maya*. Cambridge: Cambridge University Press, 2004.

Diamond, Jared. *Collapse*. New York: Penguin Books, 2005.

———. *Guns, Germs, and Steel*. New York: W. W. Norton & Company, 2005.

Emkin, Leroy. *Computers in Structural Engineering Practice: The Issue of Quality*. Reston, Va.: ASCE Press, 1983.

———. *GTStudl User Guide*. Atlanta: Georgia Institute of Technology, 2002.

Evans, R. Tripp. *Romancing the Maya: Mexican Antiquity in the American Imagination 1820–1915*. Austin, Tex.: University of Texas Press, 2004.

Fagan, Brian. *The Seventy Great Inventions of the Ancient World*. New York: Thames and Hudson, 2004.

Feldman, Lawrence H. *A Tumpline Economy: Production and Distribution Systems in Sixteenth-Century Eastern Guatemala*. Culver City, Calif.: Labyrinthos, 1985.

Ferguson, William. *Maya Ruins of Mexico in Color*. Norman, Okla.: University of Oklahoma Press, 1977.

FitzSimons, Neal. *The Greatest Bridge Spans in the World*. Baltimore, Md.: Self-Published, 1995.

Folan, William J., et al. *Coba: A Classic Maya Metropolis*. New York: Academic Press, Inc., 1983.

Foster, Lynn V. *Handbook to Life in the Ancient Maya World*. New York: Oxford University Press, 2002.

Freidel, David, Linda Schele, and Joy Parker. *Maya Cosmos: Three Thousand Years on the Shaman's Path*. New York: Perennial, 2001.

French, Kirk D. "Creating Space through Water Management at the Classic Maya Site of Palenque." In *Palenque: Recent Investigations at the Classic Maya Center*, edited by Damien B. Marken. Berkley, Calif.: Altamira Press, 2007.

Gill, Richardson B. *The Great Maya Droughts: Water, Life, and Death*. Albuquerque, N. Mex.: University of New Mexico, 2000.

Glassman, Steve. *On the Trail of the Maya Explorer*. Tuscaloosa, Ala.: The University of Alabama Press, 2003.

Gordon, J.E. *Structures: Or Why Things Don't Fall Down*. London: Da Capo Press, 1981.

Graham, Ian. *Alfred Maudslay and the Maya*. Norman, Okla.: University of Oklahoma Press, 2002.

Guderjan, Thomas H. *The Nature of an Ancient Maya City: Resources, Interaction and Power at Blue Creek, Belize.* Tuscaloosa, Ala.: The University of Alabama Press, 2007.

Guillen, Michael. *Five Equations that Changed the World: The Power and Poetry in Mathematics.* New York: Hyperion, 1995.

Hammond, Norman. *Ancient Maya Civilization.* New Brunswick, N.J.: Rutgers University Press, 1988.

Harlow, George. "Hard Rock." *Natural History Magazine* (August 1991).

Hellmuth, Nicholas. *Monster und Menschen in der Maya-Kunst.* Graz: Akademische Druck-u. Verlagsanstalt, 1987.

Henderson, John S. *The World of the Ancient Maya.* Ithaca, N.Y.: Cornell University Press, 1981.

Hool, George A., and W. S. Kinne. *Reinforced Concrete and Masonry Structures.* New York: McGraw-Hill Book Company, Inc., 1924.

Hunter, C. Bruce. *A Guide to Ancient Maya Ruins.* Norman, Okla.: University of Oklahoma, 1986.

Hymans, Edward, and George Ordish. *The Last of the Incas.* New York: Dorset Press, 1963.

James, Peter, and Nick Thorpe. *Ancient Mysteries.* New York: Ballantine Books, 1999.

Ketchum, Milos. *Structural Engineers Handbook.* New York: McGraw-Hill Book Company, 1924.

Kirby, Richard, Sidney Withington, Arthur Darling, and Fred Rick Kilgour. *Engineering in History.* New York: Dover Publications, 1990.

Krupp, E.C. *Echos of the Ancient Skies.* New York: Harper & Row, 1983.

Lange, Frederick W. *Precolumbian Jade.* Salt Lake City, Utah: University of Utah Press, 1993.

Leon-Portilla, Miguel. *Bernardino de Sahagun: First Anthropologist.* Translated by Mauricio J. Mixco. Norman, Okla.: University of Okalahoma Press, 2002.

———. *Pre-columbian Literatures of Mexico.* Norman, Okla.: University of Oklahoma Press, 1975.

Mallan, Chicki. *Guide to the Yucatan Peninsula Including Belize.* Chico, Calif.: Moon Publications, 1989.

Mason, Gregory. *Columbus Came Late.* New York: The Century Co., 1931.

Maudslay, Alfred P. *Biologia Centrali-Americana.* Facsimile edition prepared by Dr. Francis Robicsek. 5 vols. New York: Milpatron Publishing Corp., 1974.

McKillop, Heather. *In Search of Maya Sea Traders*. College Station, Tex.: Texas A&M University Press, 2005.

Meyer, Carolyn, and Charles Gallenkamp. *The Mystery of the Ancient Maya*. New York: Atheneum, 1985.

Miller, Arthur G. *Maya Rulers of Time: A Study of Architectural Sculpture at Tikal, Guatemala*. Philadelphia: University of Pennsylvania, 1986.

Miller, Mary Ellen. *Maya Art and Architecture*. New York: Thames and Hudson, 1999.

Moll, Roberto Garcia. *Palenque 1926–1945*. Mexico City: Instituto National de Antropologia, 1985.

Morley, Sylvanus. *The Ancient Maya. 2nd Edition*. Stanford, Calif.: Stanford University Press, 1946.

Morley, Sylvanus, George W. Brainerd. *The Ancient Maya. 3rd Edition*. Stanford, Calif.: Stanford University Press, 1956.

Morley, Slyvanus, George W. Brainerd, and Robert J. Shearer. *The Ancient Maya. 4th Edition*. Stanford, Calif.: Stanford University Press, 1983.

Morris, Earl H., Jean Charlot, and Ann Axtell Morris. "The Temple of the Warriors at Chichen Itza, Yucatan." *Contributions to American Archaeology*, Volume I (Carnegie Institution of Washington, May 1931).

Murphy, Francis S. *Dragon Mask Temples in Central Yucatan*. Hong Kong: Scribe Ltd., 1988.

Nicholson, Irene. *Mexican and Central American Mythology*. Rushden, England: The Hamlyn Publishing Group Ltd., 1983.

O'Kon, James. "Bridge to the Past." *Civil Engineering Magazine* (January 1995).

———. "Computer Modeling of the 7th Century Maya Suspension Bridge at Yaxchilan." *Computing in Civil Engineering*. Reston, Va.: ASCE Press, 2005.

———. "Computer Simulation of 7th Century Maya Suspension Bridge." *Computer Applications and Quantitative Methods in Archaeology*. Berlin: Deutsches Archaologischens Institut, 2007.

———. "Forensic Engineering Research Uncovers Lost Maya Engineering Landmarks." *Structural Engineering Institute of the American Society of Civil Engineers*. Reston, Va.: ASCE Press, 2007.

———. "Journal and Sketches of the Puuc Region of the Yucatan." Atlanta: Self-published, 1990.

———. "Journal and Sketches of Travels on the Usumacinta River." Atlanta: Self-published, 1989.

———. "The Maya: America's First Water Resource Engineers." *Environmental and Water Resources: Milestones in Engineering History*. Reston, Va.: ASCE Press, 2007.

———. "Standard Methodologies for the Forensic Investigation of Pavements." *Materials: Performance and Prevention of Deficiencies and Failures*. Reston, Va.: ASCE Press, 1992.

O'Kon, James, et al. *Guidelines for Failure Investigation*. Washington, D.C.: American Society of Civil Engineers Press, 1989.

Osmanagich, Sam. *The World of the Maya*. Piscataway, N.J.: Eurphrates, 2005.

Pagden, A.R. *The Maya: Diego de Landa's Account of the Affairs of the Yucatan*. Chicago: J. Phillip O'Hara, Inc., 1975.

Parsons, Jeffrey R. *Prehistoric Settlement Patterns in the Texcoco Region, Mexico*. Ann Arbor, Mich.: University of Michigan, 1971.

Perera, Victor, and Robert D. Bruce. *The Last Lords of Palenque*. Berkley, Calif.: University of California Press, 1982.

Petroski, Henry. *To Engineer Is Human: The Role of Failure in Successful Design*. New York: St. Martin's Press, 1982.

Poirier, Rene. *Engineering Wonders of the World*. Paris: Barnes and Noble, Inc., 1957.

Pollock, H.E.D. *The Puuc*. Cambridge, Mass.: Harvard University, 1980.

Pool, Christopher. *Olmec Archaeology and Early Mesoamerica*. Cambridge: Cambridge University Press, 2007.

Portland Cement Association. *Building Code Requirements for Structural Concrete*. Chicago: Portland Cement Association, 2011.

Prescott, William H. *History of the Conquest of Mexico*. 3 vols. Boston: Phillips, Sampson and Company, 1859.

———. *History of the Conquest of Peru*. 2 vols. Boston: Phillips, Sampson and Company, 1859.

Proskouriakoff, Tatiana. *An Album of Maya Architecture*. Washington, D.C.: Carnegie Institution of Washington, 1946.

Ramirez de Alba, Horacio. "El Cemento y el Concreto de los Mayas." *CIENCIA Ergo Sum*, 1999.

———. *Estudio del Concreto Maya*. Toluca, Mexico: Universidad Autonoma del Estado de Mexico, 2000.

Renfrew, Colin, and Paul Bahn. *Archaeology: Theories, Methods and Practice*. New York: Thames and Hudson, Inc., 1991.

Rice, Prudence. *Maya Political Science, Time, Astronomy and the Cosmos*. Austin, Tex.: University of Texas Press, 2004.

Robicsek, Francis. *The Maya Book of the Dead: The Ceramic Codex.* Charlottesville, Va.: University of Virginia Art Museum, 1981.

———. *The Smoking Gods: Tabacco in Maya Art, History and Religion.* Norman, Okla.: University of Oklahoma Press, 1978.

Roys, Lawrence, and Edwin M. Shook. "Preliminary Report on the Ruins of Ake, Yucatan." *Memoirs of the Society for American Archaeology,* 1966.

Schele, Linda, and David Freidel. *A Forest of Kings: The Untold Story of the Ancient Maya.* New York: William Morrow and Co., 1990.

Schele, Linda, and Mary Ellen Miller. *The Blood of Kings.* New York: George Braziller, 1986.

Sharer, Robert J. *The Ancient Maya. 5th Edition.* Stanford, Calif.: Stanford University Press, 1994.

Sherratt, Andrew. *The Cambridge Encyclopedia of Archaeology.* New York: Crown Publishers, 1980.

Soustelle, Jacques. *The Olmecs: The Oldest Civilization in Mexico.* Norman, Okla.: University of Oklahoma Press, 1985.

Spinden, Herbert J. *A Study of Maya Art: Its Subject Matter & Historical Development.* New York: Dover Publications, Inc., 1975.

Stephens, John Lloyd. *Incidents of Travel in Central America, Chiaps and Yucatan.* 2 vols. New York: Haper and Brothers, 1841.

———. *Incidents of Travel in Egypt, Arabia, Petraea, and the Holy Land.* New York: Harper and Brothers, 1837.

———. *Incidents of Travel in Yucatan.* 2 vols. New York: Haper and Brothers, 1843.

Stirling, Matthew W. *Indians of the Americans.* Washington, D.C.: National Geographic Society, 1955.

Stuart, George E., and Gene S. Stuart. *The Mysterious Maya.* Washington, D.C.: National Geographic Society, 1977.

Tate, Carolyn. *Yaxchilan: The Design of a Mayan Ceremonial City.* Austin, Tex.: University of Texas Press, 1993.

Tedlock, Barbara. *Time and the Highland Maya.* Albuquerque, N. Mex.: University of New Mexico Press, 1982.

Thompson, J. Eric. *Maya Heiroglyphic Writing: An Introduction. 3rd Edition.* Norman, Okla.: University of Oklahoma Press, 1971.

Thompson, J. Eric, Harry Pollock, and Jean Charlot. *A Preliminary Study of the Ruins of Coba.* Washington, D.C.: Carnegie Institution of Washington, 1932.

Trautwine, John G. *The Civil Engineer's Reference Book.* Philadelphia: National Publishing Company, 1882.

Van Stone, Mark. *2012: Science & Propyesy of the Ancient Maya*. San Diego, Calif.: Tlacaelel Press, 2010.

Villa, Alfonso. "The Yaxuna-Coba Causeway." *Contributions to American Archaeology*, Volume II, no. 9 (Carnegie Institution of Washington, October 1934).

Waldeck, Jean-Frederic, and Charles-Etienne Brasseur de Bourbourg. *Monuments Ancients du Mexique*. Paris: Henry Berthoud, 1866.

Willard, T.A. *The City of the Sacred Well*. New York: Grosset & Dunlap, 1926.

Wright, Ronald. *Time Among the Maya: Travels in Belize, Guatemala and Mexico*. London: Futura Publications, 1989.

Index

About the Author

James A. O'Kon, PE, a graduate of Georgia Tech with graduate degrees from NYU, is a professional engineer with decades of experience designing award-winning engineering projects. In parallel, he has spent 40 years investigating Maya engineering feats and lost Maya technology. His interest in archaeological history began while playing in Civil War battlefields near his boyhood home in Atlanta, Georgia.

O'Kon's professional career has been devoted to bringing high-tech science to engineering. He is a registered professional engineer in more than 20 states, and has developed new techniques for engineering design and new methodologies for investigating distressed structures. This experience gave him the ability to "reverse engineer" complex distressed buildings and identify the cause of the distress, and to discover, dissect, analyze, and reconstruct lost Maya technology. He has led his multidisciplinary firm of engineers and architects for 30 years, carrying out state-of-the-art engineering designs and resolving problems of distressed structures. His leadership of an award-winning engineering firm with extraordinary talents enabled him to think outside the box and solve issues for complex projects.

O'Kon has pursued a lifelong passion for Maya archaeology and has combined his unique professional engineering experience with the search for lost Maya technology. He has applied his diverse engineering talents to explore and investigate nearly inaccessible Maya sites located deep in the dense rainforest. Traveling by dugout canoe, hacking his way through the tangled jungle, and sleeping in the open while fighting off millions of insects, his search went on. With the collected field data he was able to utilize digital tools, along with his creative engineering skills, to verify feats of Maya engineering and virtually reconstruct the mystery of lost Maya technology. He is also a gifted artist who has the ability to sketch examples of Maya technology in the field and begin unraveling the mysteries of Maya technology while investigating the site.

O'Kon's interest in Maya archaeology began more than 40 years ago when he took a year-long hiatus from his work as a professional engineer, packed up his Volkswagen camper, and headed south of the border to the Yucatán Peninsula. He explored numerous Maya sites, some of them recently discovered. Even then he felt a kinship with the ancient Maya engineers who had built these magnificent cities in the midst of tropical jungles. His initial encounter with Maya technology has been followed by four decades of deep jungle exploration of more than 50 Maya sites, gathering data combined with research, the use of forensic engineering skills, remote sensing, and other digital tools to develop virtual reconstructions of marvels of Maya engineering. This work has broken the code of lost Maya technology. He has collected scientific evidence that unveiled the innovative technology developed by the Maya engineers and utilized to build their great cities, tall buildings, roads, and bridges.

James O'Kon's discoveries in Maya technology have been recognized by *National Geographic Magazine* and a production on the History Channel. He has delivered scientific papers dealing with his discoveries in Maya technologies at international scientific and archaeological symposia. His discoveries in Maya technology led to his induction into the Explorers Club.

He has carried out the design of numerous award winning projects that have become landmarks. Following are representative examples of his projects:

- The Roosevelt Island Tramway: New York City, Sole example of tramway for mass transit in world.
- The Carter Presidential Library and Museum: Atlanta, Presidential human rights policy center.
- Walt Disney World: Various projects including Empress Lilly Steamboat and Walt Disney Village.
- United States Pavilion at World Expo: Tennessee, Special structure for pavilion at World Expo.

- Hangars for B-52 Aircraft: Barksdale AFB, Design of longest span hangar in U.S. Air Force inventory.

After 30 years of leading an award-winning, multidisciplinary engineering firm, O'Kon sold the ownership of his successful consulting firm in 2000. His current occupation is as a special consultant to large corporations for investigation of construction issues, problem solving, and investigation of distressed structures and development of remediation solutions.

He has written a book relating to forensic engineering, articles in magazines, and numerous papers for international symposia for engineering and archaeology. These papers were published in the proceedings of the symposia or in books relating to engineering history. The following is a summary of the works:

- *Guidelines for Failure Investigation: A Narrative of Methods and Techniques for the Investigation of Failures* (American Society for Consulting Engineers Press, 1989).

- *Milestones in Engineering History: Maya, America's First Water Resource Engineers* (American Society for Consulting Engineers Press).

- "The Riddle of the Rocks" in *National Geographic Magazine* (October 1995).

- "A Bridge Too Far" in *Civil Engineering Magazine* (April 1995).

- "A Turn Around for Hangar Design" in *Civil Engineering Magazine* (May 1997).

When he is not in the rainforest, O'Kon lives in Atlanta with his wife, Carol Ann.